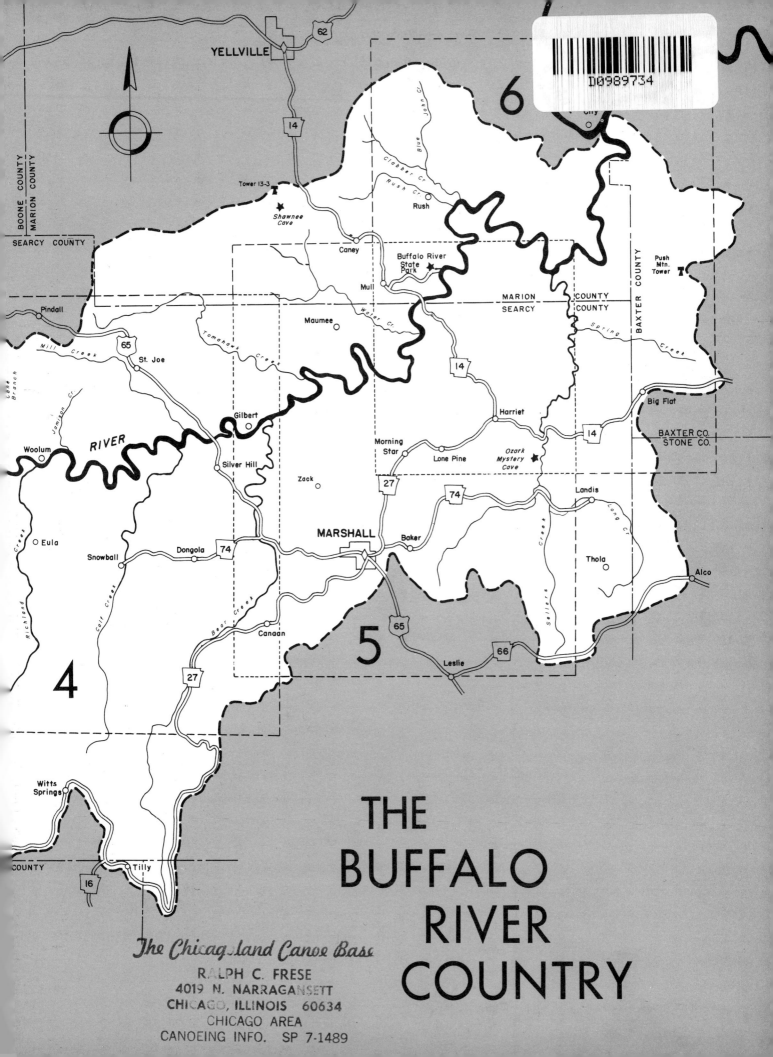

THE
BUFFALO
RIVER
COUNTRY

THE
BUFFALO
RIVER
COUNTRY

Devils Fork

THE
BUFFALO
RIVER
COUNTRY

. . . in the Ozarks
of Arkansas

by

KENNETH L. SMITH

THE OZARK SOCIETY
Fayetteville, Arkansas

The watershed and
section maps are by
DONALD B. WINFREY.

Photographs, unless
otherwise credited,
are by the author.

The book was designed
by the author.

Manufactured in the
United States of America

Litho preparation by
PEERLESS ENGRAVERS,
typography by
PUBLICATION TYPOGRAPHERS,
and printing by
THE PIONEER PRESS,
all of Little Rock.

Second printing
October, 1967

Thanks are due to
Oxford University Press,
Inc., for permission
to quote selections from
A Sand County Almanac
by Aldo Leopold,
copyright 1949 by
Oxford University Press.

Library of Congress
Catalog Card No. 67-18813

*Approaching
Peter Cave*

The Bat House

TO THE YOUNG

To the young in years
and the young at heart.
Let this be their adventure.

Acknowledgments

So many people have helped me put together this book that it is impossible to give them proper credit, but I should certainly mention the chief contributors.

Hugh Iltis and Kurt Stern, then of the University of Arkansas, first introduced me to the Buffalo River country in the years 1953-1956, and that's where it all started. Harold Alexander, Arkansas' conservation philosopher who has long preached for saving free-flowing streams, later supplied some basic ideas. Still later, Bruce Kilgore and others in the Sierra Club told me about book publishing. Neil Compton, ever helpful, then lent me not only his encouragement but also his canoe. Evangeline Archer was foremost among others in the Ozark Society who assisted in innumerable ways. Rabie Rhodes of Harrison proved a great help during my months of field work. Martha Johnson of Three Rivers, California, read the manuscript and suggested many improvements. Leonard Mizell at Peerless Engravers and Armitage and Lawrence Harper at the Pioneer Press have helped me on countless problems of producing the book.

Several friends have provided photographs: Joe and Maxine Clark, Neil Compton, Craig Rosborough and Jim Schermerhorn. Others have checked the manuscript and supplied information: Virginia Alexander, Arlis Coger, Oz Hawksley, Alice Kniskern, Orland Maxfield, H. R. McPherson and Margaret Ross. Moreover, each of the many persons introduced in the course of this book provided help—often important help. And I have relied on other authors, past and present, whose major contributions are mentioned elsewhere in the book.

And finally, two friends deserve special recognition. Don Winfrey spent many, many hours drawing the watershed and section maps, and patiently adding my afterthoughts during months of revision. Harry Pearson edited the entire manuscript, correcting and suggesting and otherwise immeasurably improving the written matter. Don and Harry, either separately or jointly, are due much of the credit for any virtue this book may have.

Kenneth L. Smith

Swinging bridge on the Little Buffalo

CONTENTS

Float fishing:
Near Rush Creek
and (opposite page)
at Red Bluff below Gilbert

The River

BEGINNINGS 1

So THIS is where it begins.

Just a spot, a tiny bit of a pool cupped in the fallen leaves. Small, unobtrusive. Limpid, liquid . . . in contrast to its matrix of brittle brown leaves. Water.

It comes silently, invisibly from under the leaf bed. It leaves quietly, glistening on a rock, sliding over and down . . . dripping . . .

Into, under the leaves.

Another pool caught among the leaves. Hidden inflow. Invisible outflow.

Several more puddles along the damp leafy trough. Then the drift goes a yard deep, choking the ditch, hiding all.

The stream emerges once again, audibly for the first time, trickling over a bed of gravel, pausing in a pool, sparkling in the sun. It stops, ducks for a moment under another mound of leaves, comes running over a boulder. The stream hurries along now, widening and breaking into a dozen streamlets sliding across a ledge and off—six feet down. The first waterfall.

From here on, there would be no more ducking and hiding under the leaves. In this quarter mile down the ravine, the Buffalo is born and begins its life.

I came alone on that winter afternoon to locate the highest source of the river. It seemed the right thing to do, finding the beginning of the Buffalo at the beginning of my project to explore the Buffalo River country.

And there at the beginning of the river, the final organization of this book began to be resolved.

Already I had marked off a map to divide the river and its watershed into six sections, each to include some twenty to thirty miles of the Buffalo plus a portion of its surrounding country. For each section, I intended to have an enlarged map and a chapter in the book. This would all fulfill my dual purpose, to show the reader not only the beauty of the river but also the fascination of the country which lies in its watershed.

But on seeing the Buffalo's modest beginning, it came to me that the young river for some miles below its source was more to be 'seen' than 'experienced'; the river adventure would not begin until I could set a canoe in the stream. And once I had done that, I discovered the floating experience was so rich, so all-pervading that it didn't seem proper to let anything interrupt the river's story.

When exploring the watershed, though, I found that experiences fell into a different pattern; they lacked the flow and continuity of those on the river. The scenic highlights of the countryside were separated in both time and locality. And unlike the sociable experiences in floating with my friends, my adventures in seeing the watershed often came when I traveled alone.

In the end these things demanded that river and watershed be treated separately, and to do this the book is divided into two parts. First there will be a continuous narrative of floating the Buffalo, a story of many successive human incidents in seeing and enjoying the river. Completing that, we move into the hinterland for a sort of once-over-lightly, a scenic inventory of the whole countryside. For both river and watershed in their turn, the overall plan of movement is from section to section down the course of the Buffalo, and the chapters are keyed to the section maps appearing at the end of the book.

Because the river at its headwaters *is* more to be seen than experienced, I am postponing further description of it for a chapter called Headwaters Country which will begin the second—or watershed—part of the book. That will now leave us free to travel to Ponca, to the 'head of navigation' of the Buffalo River float stream, and make ready to put in . . .

Big Bluff

(Map on page 165)

PONCA TO PRUITT 2

It was a bright Saturday morning in April, and it seemed that everybody was headed for the Buffalo.

Arriving in Ponca, I saw canoeists and canoes all the way down the village street. At Ponca's only cafe the canoeists had swarmed in for breakfast, overwhelming Deck and Juanita Curtis, the good-natured proprietors, until Deck, aside, complained to me "I wish they'd told us they wuz coming. We'd of had things better fixed . . ."

Through half the morning we made steady traffic to and from the river at the low-water bridge. We went to the bridge to unload, to put the canoes in the stream and pile in our gear. The cars were brought back to Ponca, for local folks to drive to our take-out at Pruitt.

Ponca is strung along a narrow creek valley which opens onto the Buffalo. The village's one thoroughfare is State Highway 43, yet unpaved. Nor have the highway engineers straightened out the kinks or shaved down the humps, so the winding, uneven road itself adds something to the local scenery—besides slowing down impatient motorists and thereby affording some protection to youngsters, oldsters, chickens, cows and sleepy dogs who use Ponca's dirt street as their own.

The village originated in a lead mining boom during World War I, when developers from Ponca City, Oklahoma, moved in and gave their name to the rising community. But since 1918 there have been only a few intermittent spurts of mining activity, and the diggings, scattered over the steep hillsides overlooking Ponca, are mostly long abandoned and caving in.

Many of our weekend canoeists were here for the first time; they knew nothing about mining but thought Ponca was picturesque. They had driven down Highway 43 from the top of the mountain, down the long, winding hill through the woods and past two or three of the ruined mines, down to the foot of the hill and—splash!—across the creek into Ponca. Past the miniature gorge with its cascading waterfall, past the tranquil little lake at the lodge, and on to the center of the village. 'Ponky' as we sometimes call it, still has some of the flavor of an Ozarks back-country settlement. That will largely disappear, I am afraid, with paved roads and development.

Enjoy it as we did, we hadn't come to spend the weekend in Ponca. It was springtime, the dogwood was in bloom, and the water looked right. Just downstream were the most spectacular sights of the Buffalo. These things had attracted the largest crowd of canoeists ever to float the river.

In our confusion nobody made an exact count, but we must have had nearly fifty canoes. Members of the Ozark Society, the official sponsor of the float, had come with fifteen or sixteen from different parts of Arkansas. These were outnumbered by some two dozen craft of the Ozark Wilderness Waterways Club from the Kansas City area. The Boys Club of Memphis had brought six more canoes, all neatly racked in a specially-built trailer. The Boys Club of Jackson, Mississippi, with two or three, had come farther than any of the rest of us.

For my Buffalo River explorations I had borrowed a 17-foot aluminum Grumman from Dr. Neil Compton, president of the Ozark Society. With it resting like a dead whale on my 13-foot Volkswagen, I crept in low gear through the milling traffic approaching the low-water bridge. The banks on both sides were lined with canoes being loaded. We would have to wait our turn to launch.

My canoeing partner was to be a friend whom I had met only weeks before, Harry Pearson from Pine Bluff, Arkansas. Harry, the investigative reporter for the *Pine Bluff Commercial*, had come with us on the middle Buffalo earlier in the month while researching a story about the Army Engineers' controversial proposal to dam the river. By this weekend of the Ponca-to-Pruitt float, his story had been published and he wanted to see more of the Buffalo.

That was fine, for Harry was a good companion, and I was anxious to have him see all of the river. However, there was going to be a problem in handling the canoe. Since Harry had floated only once before, he would have to take the bow (normally reserved for the person having

15

the less experience). But I had had only a little more experience myself, and that only as a bow man, where I'd fiddled with cameras while somebody else did the work. Now I was to be a stern man, and on the wildest part of the river!

Our ineptitude was on public display the moment we put in. I saw twelve or fifteen people still loading canoes as we swept into the long chute below the bridge. I dared not look back—just imagined their stares following us as I ruddered the canoe first to the left, then to the right, to avoid submerged rocks.

Wham! We were aground. I'd meant to go left as I'd seen the others do. Oh well, I told myself, this stretch always was a little shallow . . .

We stepped out and I guided the canoe over the two boulders that had stopped us. As I was getting back in, I noticed we weren't alone in our mishap. Our unpainted canoe left aluminum marks on the rocks. We also saw red and green and yellow ones.

We finished the first swift water and glided through a deep pool below a 50-foot bluff, past a pale waterfall streak on the dark gray sandstone. There a trickle of water splashed noisily into the blue-green depths at the base of the cliff.

Now we heard the roar of a rapids. This would be a good one, I told Harry. Steep, so that from the brink you could see the water sloping downhill.

As we slowly drifted toward the chute, I stood in the stern and picked the place we should go.

"Paddle, dammit!" I yelled. We had to get moving or I wouldn't be able to steer.

In we went and Harry let out a howl, mostly from sheer excitement. We plowed into a high white wave, but kept going—too deep to hit anything.

Suddenly we were through, and I steered to the left bank. On these trips we always hit the banks after a good rapids so we can take pictures of the others as they roar past. Neil Compton was already there with his movie camera, hoping someone would turn over.

We photographed the next three or four canoes coming through. Nobody had a wreck, and we knew we'd have to wait before the tail-enders would arrive, so we got underway again.

For several hundred yards we skimmed along a pool under trees arched across the water. Then I saw another picture. On the right bank a dogwood was in full bloom, and its snowy sprays reached down almost to the water. I climbed out on shore and photographed a passing canoe framed with white loveliness.

Around the bend to the left we floated past a smooth gray cliff looming two hundred feet above us, the first of the high bluffs below Ponca. This was the Bee Bluff, named for a colony of wild bees, and it reminded me to tell Harry a story from Walter Lackey's *History of Newton County*—

Through many years people watched the bees going to and from their home in a crevice high in the face of this cliff. Everyone believed the colony had been there for hundreds of years, and that meant just one thing—a huge store of honey. For decades, people talked about how to get it.

Eventually, in 1916, two local boys built a ladder (said to have been 80 feet high!) and set it up to the crevice in the bluff. About three hundred people gathered to watch and help collect the spoils.

But, on second thought, nobody wanted to go up that 80-foot ladder—not with those bees buzzing around up there. The crowd drifted back home.

That night the boys solved the problem. One of them climbed the ladder and thrust burning rags with sulfur into the cavity, killing all the bees.

When morning came the boys returned to the bluff, again with a mob of excited spectators. The boys had found the crevice too small to reach in and get the honey, but now they were prepared. Using a hand drill, one of them bored a hole in the obstructing rock and placed a stick of dynamite.

With a properly loud bang the rocks went flying. Streams of honey came pouring down the bluff.

Some four hundred pounds, though, remained intact. This the boys began scooping into buckets which they lowered by rope to the yelling crowd below. By the time the boys had finished their work and come down, the onlookers had eaten or taken home nearly all of the honey. That was that. The name Bee Bluff remains.

Not far below Bee Bluff we floated past a second great cliff, a long, south-facing wall known as Roark Bluff. Lackey's *History* mentions that Williamson Roark once owned a farm in this bend of the river. Roark wasn't the earliest settler, though; he bought his farm from one George W. Steele, who had first taken the land in 1847. Steele's name is affixed to Steele Creek, flowing into the Buffalo at the next turn below Roark Bluff.

Passing Steele Creek, we approached another towering cliff having a sheer face well over two hundred feet high. Now, simply by turning our heads, we could see three or four such bluffs up and down the river. The Buffalo was swinging from one side of its narrow, constricted valley to the other, carving an impressive bluff at the outside of each bend.

Within the bends we saw small clearings, fields and a few abandoned buildings, old farms that had become part of one large landholding. At each turn of the river

we passed a crossing of the wagon road that had connected those farms by repeatedly fording the Buffalo. This primitive road, once the farmers' main route of travel and exit from the valley, was itself a convincing reason why the farm folk had sold out and moved away. But those who left could not take with them the river, nor the beauty and peace of its valley. These things we had come seeking...

Another bend to the right, with its bluff on our left. Another bend to the left, with the cliff on our right. Then we moved into a long pool with a high bluff, higher than all the others, beyond the far end, straight ahead. Big Bluff.

Slowly we glided down the pool. Trees along the banks leaned out over the water. As the treetops gradually moved aside and behind us, the bluff ahead seemed to rise higher and higher, its broad face spreading wider... higher... towering above.

Paddling down a shallow riffle, we came alongside a gravel bar. Here, many of our floaters had already pulled ashore and spread lunch on the open expanse of gravel. Or, to take advantage of the warm sun, they had spread themselves.

We were supposed to eat lunch with Neil and Laurene Compton (since they had the food). They weren't anywhere among the crowd on the gravel bar, but finally we found them, downstream and across the river, sitting on top of a big rock. We landed and scrambled up to join them.

It turned out to be a delightful spot. A dogwood spread its open lacework of branches over us, even in front of us, crisscrossing the river and distant hills with a tracery of graceful boughs, new green leaves, and blossoms. And while we sat and lunched and talked we enjoyed a first-row view of the river, watching canoes coming down past us now as people left the gravel bar.

Close behind us loomed Big Bluff. I recalled the first time I had seen it from the river, early in March, just after several days of freezing weather. We'd had lunch here, too, on the gravel bar, and we had watched as the warming sun melted loose the gigantic icicles hanging on the face of Big Bluff. With thunderous crashes they had come pitching down on the talus slope—this place where, seven weeks later, we were basking under the dogwood blossoms.

That March weekend I was with the Ozark Wilderness Waterways Club, with canoeists who float the Ozark streams every month of the year, with people who've learned to live cheerfully with any kind of weather. Saturday night as we camped the clouds gathered and we found a skiff of snow on our tents in the morning. We floated on to Pruitt in a mist of snow and freezing rain.

Uncomfortable? Certainly. But not as much as you

Winter canoeing

might imagine. We had warm clothing, and tents, and hip waders for the river. And we kept moving. For me, it was an adventure, a gem in my collection of experiences in spite of the discomforts. I would never forget those icicles, crashing——

"How high is Big Bluff?" Harry interjected.

No one had ever made an exact measurement. I had found no less than seven different published estimates ranging from 500 to 1000 feet. Twice, then, I had measured it myself, and though my methods weren't precise, Big Bluff was evidently about 525 feet high.[1]

Even without exact measurements and comparisons, Big Bluff obviously is higher than any of the other cliffs along the Buffalo; also it is undoubtedly the highest cliff in the Ozarks. Further, it is likely the highest rock bluff

in the whole vast region stretching from the southern Appalachians to the peaks and canyons of West Texas, and to the buttes and pinnacles of western Nebraska and the Black Hills.

There is one qualifier: Big Bluff is not one unbroken rock face. Instead, Big Bluff is *two* cliffs, one above the other, separated by a steep grassy terrace.

From river level, the talus slope rises about 75 feet to the base of the lower cliff, a long, curving, water-streaked wall, sheer and smooth and around 150 feet high. Above that is the terrace for some 50 feet, and then the upper cliff, rough and irregular, sloping back in some areas and overhanging in others, reaching about 250 feet from the terrace to Big Bluff's highest point.

In our talk about Big Bluff we were overlooking one important feature, and now Neil asked me about it. "How high is the Goat Trail?"

"From the river, it's about 350 feet," I replied.

Harry was getting left out. The Goat Trail, we explained to him, followed a ledge all the way across upper Big Bluff.

From the wooded ridge at either end of the bluff, you could begin taking the trail. At first you walk along a broad shelf shaded by ancient, twisted junipers, then suddenly you come out from behind the trees onto the open ledge. You follow an ever-more-narrow path along the massive cliff wall. Finally, near midpoint of the bluff, your trail is a ledge of rock only two yards wide and 350 feet above the river.

From here you see the Buffalo coming down its mountain-rimmed valley, turning below other high cliffs and then moving directly toward you, under you, far down below. The river rapids send up a murmuring whisper . . .

You look downstream. The river is passing below the far end of the long, curved lower cliff, moving across the valley, turning to the left along the base of still another bluff, flowing on behind the hills and out of sight.[2]

While we talked about the Goat Trail, Laurene put away the leftovers. We all picked up our refuse and helped move the lunch baskets and icebox back down to the canoe. In a few minutes we were underway again.

[1]My first measurements employed a simple surveying device known as an abney level. With it I took sightings from both ends of a measured horizontal base line along the gravel bar across the river from the bluff. Calculations based on the abney sightings indicated an overall height of 497 feet.

As a check against error with the abney level, Jim Schermerhorn of Harrison and I took a second set of readings, using his Sears Roebuck farm transit. While the transit was not a precision instrument, we judged that it would be at least as accurate as the abney. Readings with the transit resulted in a calculated overall height, from the river to the highest point we could see on the cliff's rock face, of 552 feet.

The height of "about 525 feet" is an average between the heights found with the abney and the transit.

[2]The Buffalo within view of the Goat Trail on Big Bluff is a most spectacular example of an Ozark stream flowing in "entrenched meanders." In their *Description of the Harrison and Eureka Springs Quadrangles* (U. S .Geological Survey, 1916), Purdue and Miser offer the geologist's view of this scene and innumerable lesser ones throughout the Ozarks:

Most of the streams are swift and flow in deep, narrow, canyon-like valleys. Flood-plain deposits are rare and are narrow and short. Except along the bluffs due to escarpment-forming rocks, the surface on the inside of the bends slopes gradually from the highest points to the present stream beds. The descent to the streams on the outside of the bends is everywhere steep and at most places vertical.

Around the bend, opposite the lower end of Big Bluff, we pulled up on another gravel bar to take pictures. Then I realized we were standing on Center Point, this peninsula of land within the river's bend. Years ago, the first Center Point School had been here. Mrs. Harry Primrose of Ponca had told me there were more than thirty pupils crowded into a little log cabin.

"I used to take the path down past the end of the high bluff and wade the Buffalo to school," she had said. "The teacher had to let us out when it rained, so we could get back across before the creek got too high.

"I remember one time, when I was small, that I had to ride over on my brother's shoulders. The water came up to his waist."

Afloat again, we moved along a quiet pool. At its lower end was the place to beach for the hike up the hill to the Goat Trail. But we wouldn't have time for that steep, tiring climb on this trip.

This close to the river's headwaters, many of the rapids were shallow and we couldn't help but do some boulder-bumping. But I was getting more used to handling the stern, learning to steer with my paddle. Harry could provide needed momentum by paddling, and occasionally helped guide by using draw or pry strokes—pulling his paddle straight toward the canoe or pushing straight away to move the bow to one side or the other. In the rapids Harry had to draw (and did furiously) to keep us from smashing the banks.

Thus we blundered on, past Beech Creek, past Jim Bluff, then full speed down a couple of long, exciting chutes toward the mouth of Sneed Creek.

At Sneed Creek the river enters a short deep hole where the stream goes underground in times of drouth. Since the river is then literally "sucked out of sight", this place is locally called the Suck Hole. Evidently the stream short cuts for a fourth-mile across its horseshoe bend to reappear more than half a mile down the surface channel.

Not that we cared now. We had plenty of water and we swept over the shoal below the Suck Hole and kept going. After another fast run we pulled alongside several beached canoes at the mouth of Hemmed-in Hollow.

Several of our crowd soon appeared, coming down the trail. They had hiked up to see the waterfall at the head of the Hollow. We wouldn't have time for that today either—to Harry's irritation. Instead, as a pacifier, I told Harry a little history—

Hemmed-in Hollow is boxed in by a high horseshoe cliff and the river flowing past its mouth. Except for the old wagon road crossing the river and entering the Hollow there where we had beached our canoe, there isn't any way in but hiking and climbing. And yet, a family once lived in the Hollow.

Colonel William O'Neill and his wife were Pennsylvanians who settled in the Ozarks near Branson, Missouri, in the 1890's. Later, about 1917, they came with their several children and built a retreat in Hemmed-in Hollow.

The Colonel was an intellectual, and judging by his choice of homesites, a romantic. His daughter Rose was a poet, artist and sculptor who had become famous for creating, of all things, the kewpie doll.

With lumber carted in from the river, they put up a house. And in time they came to know, or be known by, a few of their neighbors. Mrs. Primrose, for example, remembered the O'Neills. "My brother worked for them, and I visited in their home, too," she told me. "They had a sort of summer cottage about half way between the river and the high waterfall. The house was on a steep bank above the creek. . . . They had a garden, too, sort of in steps up the hill."

Lex Burge, now the postmaster at Compton, as a boy delivered mail and groceries to the family in the Hollow. "Colonel O'Neill built a long, winding trail down the mountain—around the end of the bluff to their place. I'd walk down the trail with their groceries, but sometimes I took a shorter way back—up their ladder. They'd made it out of poles and set it in a crack in the bluff."

The O'Neills never became close to their neighbors. They were physically isolated of course, and they were Catholics in a region almost entirely Protestant. Religious differences seemed to cause no bad feelings, but the O'Neills remained apart.

Around 1920, three or four years after first building in the Hollow, the O'Neills moved away. The terraced garden soon went to weeds, and eventually the house disappeared and trees grew tall in the clearing.

Mrs. Primrose returned to Hemmed-in Hollow in 1955 to show her children the site of the cottage. "The only thing I found," she said, "was the wisteria vine that once bloomed in their yard. All the rest is gone."

"Paddle!"

Harry did. But we hadn't moved out quite far enough from our moorings at the Hollow, so we got caught in the bushes. Then the river raced through a chute and swirled around ledges. We misjudged depths and scraped the bedrock in the shallows.

Soon the river worked itself out and we passed the old Harper place with its 20-foot bluff to our right. Deck Curtis had told us to watch here for the exit of the cold underground stream coming from the Suck Hole. We saw nothing. Probably it isn't noticeable until the river is very low.

Some of this country was such that I was tempted to call it wilderness. But really it isn't. Not after more than a hundred years of settlement. It simply lacks the vast, untouched spaces of true wilderness, that "country in which the hand of man has not set foot."

Occasionally we did see some small part of the scenery that obviously had never been touched. Along the river below Hemmed-in Hollow, a chain of bluffs remained wild and primeval in appearance. Eroded and knobby, they called to mind ancient fortresses crumbling and returning to the earth. Pinnacles and walls were pocked and broken with holes and crevices, splotched with gray and orange lichens. Frequent random ledges supported gnarled shrubs and stunted pine trees. These bits of the original landscape, taken with much of the rest that is semi- or near-natural, constitute what I would call the Buffalo River wildlands. Not true wilderness, but something approaching it.

On the Goat Trail

Through the day Harry and I had floated in company with various members of the crowd, most often the Comptons or other friends in the Ozark Society. Now all the others had either moved ahead or taken an even slower pace than ours, and for the time being we were alone. We talked, and paddled, and daydreamed. Slowly we drifted down the long pool, listening to the rapids beyond the far end.

Gradually the sound grew louder . . . louder. We began a swing to the left—and I realized where we were. Well above where the water broke away, I steered for the bank. Several others had pulled in here as we did; they also were looking for the best routes. Some had gone down the bank, cameras in hand, anticipating, waiting for an upset.

This would be the longest and one of the roughest rapids on the upper Buffalo. For three hundred yards the river spilled over outcroppings and ledges, and raced down narrow twisting channels ending in hogbacks and

boulders. All this led into Gray Rock Shoals, where the river veered into a deep sluiceway along the left bank, running straight toward a rugged gray ledge jutting out to midstream. We'd really have to paddle hard to keep away from Gray Rock.

After some hesitation, we pushed out into the rapids. Zoom—we were swept down the first chute and aground, suspended on the first rocky ridge. We got out, and half-walking, half-sliding down the slippery rock, put the canoe in deep water.

We got in, went sweeping down the next chute—and again went aground. Again we got out and walked the canoe over the hogback into a deeper channel.

Two or three times more we got hung up in the shallows and had to pull loose. Then we moved into the sluice above Gray Rock, bearing on us, looming ahead. In seconds we had squeezed by, somehow.

We beached and walked back up the bank; the action at Gray Rock was too good to miss. We sat down right on top of the rock for the best view, and soon the others began coming downstream. Each pair of canoeists swept into the sluiceway, swiftly approaching, the lady wide-eyed with alarm and paddling wildly, the man in the stern straining to steer clear as the rock loomed ahead . . . then slipped alongside and behind. One couple missed only by inches.

Downstream from Gray Rock we passed a smooth-faced cliff that on another trip we had named the 'A' bluff. High on its face, three straight grooves in the rock form a prominent and perfect letter A. And soon we approached another unnamed bluff which I had heard some of our canoeists calling the Castle. Though the cliff is not large, it rises directly from the river, and its deformed, deeply weathered flanks are surmounted by several turrets and pinnacles of eroded stone.

If the 'A' Bluff and the Castle ever had other names, they are probably forever lost. The old-timers who first named many of these features along the river depended on a local, unwritten geography-by-tradition, and much of it has disappeared.

Downstream, the next cliff does have a local name, Buzzard Bluff. People say there was once a buzzards' roost in the oak woods on top.

We floated straight toward the cliff, a high dark pile of rock . . . very dark, almost black . . . gloomy. As we moved nearer, I was struck by its great height. I began to wonder whether Buzzard Bluff might be second only to Big Bluff . . .

Curving to the left along its base, we floated without paddling, now craning our necks and peering nearly straight up, viewing in detail the dark gray cliff. Scrubby junipers clung to the rock. Larger niches and ledges sup-

ported lusher growth. Water trickling down the face had left orange streaks of iron-rust.

At the bluff's lower end, a towering wall plunges into the river, and high against this precipice lies a long, heavy finger of rock. For a moment as we drifted past, I saw a needle's eye of sky between the finger and the main mass of cliff.

Then we went speeding through a shoal, and in seconds we had exchanged Buzzard Bluff for an entirely new aspect of the river—about the hundredth such complete shift of scenery since we'd set out in the morning. The basic elements such as water, bluffs and trees were forever changing in arrangement and detail.

Now we were approaching Camp Orr, the summer gathering place for Boy Scouts from all of northwestern Arkansas. But we would see very little of the camp from the river; its buildings were hidden in the woods up the hill.

One time I had hiked up into the camp area to see what thousands of friends of scouting in the 19-county Westark Area Council had patiently put together for the benefit of boys. I found a spacious dining hall, an equipment building, an office and other structures. Troop camp sites were scattered through the nearby woods. There was an outdoor council ring where scouts would assemble around the evening campfire. An old pasture along the Buffalo was available for field sports. Crossing the clearing, I had returned to the camp's tree-shaded swimming hole on the river.

Harry and I now floated past the scouts' simple boat landing, and past another Bee Bluff overlooking their swimming pool. This Bee Bluff is a long, yellowish cliff with splashes of pink and pale gray. Along its footings we saw masses of Virginia creeper which would turn bright red in the fall.

The young scouts who camp at Orr have what must be a boy's dream of the outdoors. We glimpsed several caves in the base of Bee Bluff just across their swimming hole, and I had heard they go hiking and exploring up the river as far as Hemmed-in Hollow.

The afternoon was nearly gone. Not far downstream from Orr we discovered a dozen members of our Ozark Society group already setting up camp on a sandy beach. We had planned a reunion with other friends farther downstream, so we kept on going.

After some minutes of steady paddling, we moved into a long, deep pool fronted by a low bluff. We had reached Goat Bluff, and knew that we should pull over to the broad gravel flat beyond its downstream end. Here we would camp for the night, and for the first time since Ponca, most of us would be together again.

Canoes and people and tents and piles of duffel and

newly-laid campfires were everywhere. The Ozark Wilderness Waterways canoeists had taken all of the gravel bar in sight. Downstream, they informed us, the Boys Club groups had put in to camp. Neil and Laurene looked around, and decided to pitch their tent on a plot of grass near the upstream end of the bar, where a shallow backwater provided a convenient landing for the canoes. Harry and I would share their campsite and (happily) Laurene's cooking. We began to unload.

All afternoon the clouds had been gathering, gradually becoming thicker and darker, and now they threatened rain. After carrying our baggage up from the canoes, we decided to bring the canoes up, too, as insurance against an overnight rise of the river. Besides, we could prop them bottoms-up for tables, one for Laurene's cooking supplies and the other for our supper.

Darkness had come when Laurene pulled the last cooking pot off the fire. And at that moment, as she began dishing it out, it began to rain. We hastily gathered our supper—food, plates, knives and forks and all—and retreated into the tent.

The four of us were soon sitting, cramped and cross-legged, inside the small tent, and Laurene again began to serve the meal. By now the rain was pouring down and—with Neil's tricky electric lantern frequently going out—it was pitch dark. Somehow despite these problems, Laurene gave us a delicious meal. And, just as we finished dessert, the rain stopped.

Neil reached up and drew aside the tent flap, letting in a rush of cool moist night air. Trees still dripped noisily on the canvas, but we could again venture outside.

We all walked down to the gravel bar to visit with our Waterways Club neighbors. Harold and Margaret Hedges invited us into their roomy tent, along with Joe and Puck Acuff, and Nancy Jack who writes for the *Kansas City Kansan*. We sat and visited, exchanging tales of the day's adventures until the hour grew late, time for bed.

Harold had re-kindled their fire. We gathered around it for a final few minutes, drying out the night's dampness. The rain clouds were on the move, breaking up, and we could see the stars . . .

When the rain had begun, Harry and I had folded a big tarpaulin over our pile of supplies outside the Comptons' tent. Now, with the sky clearing, we opened the tarp, pushed things aside, and spread our sleeping bags on the canvas for a night under the stars. Laurene had already retired into the tent, and Neil soon followed.

Sleep came easily. It had been a big day.

In the last dark hour before dawn the rain came again. Neil was up, putting supplies inside or under wraps, and urging us to come into the tent.

I'd had enough of that tent last night; I'd stay outside

under the tarpaulin. Harry seemed undecided, but when the first drops spattered on the tarp, I folded the other half over us. We could breathe, and see, out from under the lower end of our covering.

The only available ground space for our tarpaulin lay on a slight incline, and last night at bedtime Harry and I had loudly debated one question: Which end of us should point downhill? I had asserted that our heads should be downhill. Harry asserted otherwise, but I won the point, though without having particular reason, except that I didn't want my blood to run downhill out of my head. Out of my feet, all right. But not out of my head.

The morning rain drummed steadily on the stiff canvas. Now I sensed that something was wrong, up there at our feet. But I couldn't get up to adjust the cover. There wasn't room to wiggle around under the tarp, and outside it was pouring——

The rain drummed on, and a chilly wetness soaked through the foot of my sleeping bag. If only we'd slept uphill! I could then have pulled the tarp . . . Except for a loud groan now and then, Harry wasn't saying much, except to remind me whose idea it was to sleep downhill.

After daylight, the downpour finally slackened and I crawled out of my half-soaked sleeping bag. I laid the tarp back, looked at Harry's . . . dry! Taking the outer edge of the cover had been my undoing.

Down on the gravel bar the OWWC people were stirring around, having breakfast and getting ready to shove off. They would have to make Pruitt by noon for the long drive home to Kansas City.

No one at our campsite had thought to save dry firewood. Making fire with wet wood proved slow business, until at last we scrounged some dry newspaper (Harry's *Pine Bluff Commercial*) and shaved an ample pile of kindling for our reluctant hearth-logs. By our breakfast time the Kansas City canoeists were leaving.

We would wait for the rest of the Ozark Society members, the ones who had stayed on the sand bar below Camp Orr, and others who had camped even farther upstream. After breaking camp, we put out into the pool along Goat Bluff and paddled about, killing time.

Before long our people began to arrive. They, too, had suffered a damp night in camp.

Finally our two fiberglas canoes came into sight; we'd left them behind yesterday near Hemmed-in Hollow. I'd had my doubts about those fiberglas canoes. On the OWWC winter trip I'd seen a homemade one crack up in the shoals above Gray Rock. But here were these in seemingly good shape, one belonging to the Joe Marsh Clarks from Fayetteville, and the other piloted by Dave McDonald of Rogers.

The Castle

They did have trouble. Dave had bumped into Gray Rock, puncturing his canoe below the water line. Luckily the Clarks had a fiberglas repair kit, and with that Dave made his canoe whole again in less than an hour. It put them late, though, and they'd stopped to camp at the next site downstream.

We moved along together, past our now-deserted gravel bar and around a bend. Ahead of us was a swinging bridge across the river. On the left bank the bridge cables were tied to a large tree. On the right they were anchored at a ledge halfway up a 40-foot bluff. We glided under, and I glanced up. Floor boards were hanging loose, and several were missing.

Then we reached Erbie Ford, where a concrete road slab forms a broad shallow spillway. We got out, walked the canoes across, let them down in deep water below . . .

From Camp Orr to Erbie Ford we had emerged from the river's narrow, deeply entrenched valley in the Boston Mountains into the milder country of the Springfield Plateau. It was a notable change in scenery; today's bluffs and ridges would be much lower and less spectacular than those of yesterday. Now off to our right and left I could see Mutton Point and the rock-rimmed promontories of Gaither Mountain, the last landmarks of the Bostons, gradually moving farther behind us.

The river itself remained just about as lively as that upstream. The quiet stretches were becoming longer, but often they ended in long, narrow, swift chutes where we could go racing down for a hundred yards or more—the speedaway kind of ride that I'd found to be one of the greatest joys in canoeing.

Mrs. Joe Clark (whom we all know as Maxine) is a botanist, and on our river trips she proved a trove of information about the plants and about nature in general. Not to be outdone, Mr. Clark, a geologist, filled me in on the rock formations.

Harry and I drew alongside the Clarks' canoe, and Maxine and I were soon comparing notes on the flowers we had seen. Mine included the black haw (she'd told me where to look) and *Silene virginica* or fire pink on Castle Bluff above the Scout Camp. And dogwood of course.

Maxine rattled off a list of common and scientific names that made me wish I knew a tenth of what she did. She had seen three kinds of phlox. And a yellow honeysuckle. "And all kinds of violets—there really are a good many kinds. . . . I saw wild iris; they have beautiful delicate blooms. It's the wood iris or crested iris, *Iris cristata*."

At that moment we were floating past a bluff, and she showed me shooting stars, pink dart-shaped flowers of the primrose family, growing in a crevice of the rock.

Maxine had seen a redstart, a tiny orange-and-black bird, fluttering and diving among the bushes along the river bank. I reminded her that in just a few days the spring migration of birds through the Ozarks would be at its peak; her redstart was returning from a winter in the tropics.[3]

About the middle of the morning the low-hanging clouds began to dissipate and we floated in sunshine. Droplets of rain glistened on every leaf. Little rivulets poured into the river everywhere; bluffs dripped and perspired and trickled. Foliage looked fresh-green, healthy and lush.

Yesterday the river had been clear, and we had glided as if suspended above bottoms several feet below us. Today the water was cloudy from the rain, with a pale green cast in its deeper parts. We had expected a more noticeable rise in the river, but perhaps it hadn't rained so much in the parts upstream . . . .

We traveled together, a half dozen canoes strung out in procession, all in sight of one another through the lengthy pools, lost from sight when rounding the bends and sweeping down the chutes.

Moving into faster water, Harry and I turned a short blind corner—and were immediately dragged over to the left bank by the current. We worked free, went racing down toward a rock, missed it but scraped bottom, then dodged limbs, paddled desperately to miss another reef . . . and hit clear water again.

"Hey," called Harry, "we did fine——"

Scrunch! We were hung, swinging sidewise, tipping, about to dump—Harry dived overboard.

He was a good swimmer and bobbed up immediately. His abandoning ship had freed the bow; the canoe swung around crazily and I was going downstream backwards, my aplomb shaken.

Neil had been standing on the bank watching us, I suppose taking movies of the whole disaster. Harry came dragging out, soaked but unhurt, as I landed farther downstream.

The others were coming—now the Clarks were plunging

[3]At flood-tide of the spring migration, around May 1, warblers like the redstart come flitting through the woods by the hundreds, waves of varicolored butterflies: The chestnut-sided warbler. The golden-winged. The yellow-throat. The black and white, the worm-eating, the prairie, the parula . . .

While many of the warblers keep moving north, other birds become summer residents: The summer tanager, red as the cardinal but without the crest. The yellow-breasted chat. Indigo buntings and blue grosbeaks. Orchard and baltimore orioles. Whip-poor-wills and chuck-will's-widows to enliven the nights. Swallows and kingbirds and ruby-throated hummingbirds and the lark sparrow . . .

Spring migration is the best time of year to observe many of these species along the Buffalo. A good spotter moving on the river and through farm lands and woods can see or hear as many as a hundred different kinds of birds in a day.

into the chute. Heeding our shouted warnings, everyone else avoided the underwater rock we had hit.

The river here was lovely, but anyone floating as we did from Ponca would feel a sort of scenic letdown after passing Camp Orr. Some of the wilderness feeling, too, was now dispelled by the occasional distant drone of a truck, or, worse still, by power lines crossing overhead. The joys here were in running the chutes, in noticing the bits of nature that the spectacle upstream had made us overlook.

A kingfisher went rattling down the pool ahead of us . . . swept around and came back toward us, swooping past, close to the water.

We approached the lower end of the hole and two blue-winged teal sprung from the backwater and buzzed away down the river.[4]

Then we floated past the gravel bar, close enough to see the cluster of zebra swallowtail butterflies by the water's edge . . . .

[4]When floating this stretch of the river two weeks earlier, we had seen teal by the hundreds. That rainy morning there were water birds at every pool and bay—coots and shoveler ducks, green herons, a few great blue herons, many bobbing sandpipers. An osprey, or fish hawk, had risen from its perch on a dead tree and flown directly overhead. Most surprising, we floated to within 50 feet of three Canada geese standing on a gravel bar.

Paddling and talking, Harry and I had moved ahead of the others when we passed two boys in a homemade boat. They were twelve or thirteen years old, shirtless and suntanned. Their boat was a dark, unpainted, heavy-looking thing, though built on the traditional lines of the Ozark johnboat: long and narrow and tapering to high, squared-off ends.

Both boys were sitting in the stern. One paddled with a crude oar whittled from a rough one-by-six board. The other boy had dropped his oar to wield a turquoise-colored plastic wastebasket, dipping it between his feet and then pouring overboard . . . dipping . . . pouring. Dipping . . . pouring. Dipping . . . pouring.

Harry and I paddled around the pool for several minutes, waiting, but our crowd didn't appear. We then moved into the channel leading off to the right. The boys were putting in to the bank to empty their leaky boat. We paddled past, down the shallow chute, moving a little hesitantly now, for there might be trouble . . .

The channel swung to the right against a high bank—and abruptly back to the left. Now we were caught by the current, fighting to keep clear, swinging against a big tree jutting from the right bank . . . shoved sidewise against the roots, water piling against the gunwale——

"Get free—we'll capsize!"

Suddenly we began sliding ahead and loose, out to

midstream—and in seconds the fickle river slammed us into the other bank.

At last, feeling much beaten, we pulled alongside the gravel bar downstream. Then I spied Neil and Laurene, just about to enter the chute above the rapids.

They must have seen us rushing for position with our cameras; certainly they sensed something was wrong, for they pulled over to the bank and got out. We saw Neil looking intently at the sharp turn downstream, and talking with Laurene. They took the bow and stern lines in hand and began walking the canoe down the channel.

They came wading along the shallows, guiding the canoe by the lines. Then at the corner the swift cross current caught the canoe, pulling it hard toward midstream, dragging them both after it . . . and Laurene lost her footing and sat down in the water. Still doggedly hanging on to the bow line, she scrambled to her feet and they kept working the canoe downstream. In a moment it was beyond danger and Neil moved it down to a safe anchorage with ours.

The johnboat boys had been watching all this from their landing up the river. Now they pushed off and came floating down. Again we hurried to the corner with cameras—but the boys' performance so astonished me I forgot to take a picture. In seconds they paddled their clumsy-looking boat through the tricky twisting channel with precision near perfection. *They* knew how.

We stayed around hoping someone else would try to shoot the channel. No luck. Everybody hand-lined through, and after the Compton's near-disaster they kept their canoes on shorter leashes, close by the bank.[5]

Again we moved downstream, almost immediately passing the boys in their boat. One of them was busy with the wastebasket.

I'd forgotten about the next hazard—a chute ahead with two trees across it. They'd been lying there for months, one trunk about three feet above the water and the other directly underneath, just below the surface, with two or three inches of water skimming over.

[5]Appropriately enough, the Ozark Wilderness Waterways Club had been calling this rapids Crisis Curve.
On Memorial Day weekend, 1965, extremist advocates of a dam on the Buffalo cut 18 large trees along the banks at Crisis Curve and dropped them across the channel, principally to stop the OWWC from completing their float to Pruitt that weekend. Most of the club canoeists were forced to take out upstream. A few days later a group of boy scouts sawed and chopped through the downed trees, reopening the channel.

We had all beached and were checking out the obstacle when the boys again came paddling down the river. I watched, expecting them to land and join us.

But they didn't. They deliberately headed into the chute, coming toward us, straight toward the trees——

The following happened much more quickly than can be told: Just as the bow of their boat touched the submerged tree trunk, the boy in the bow leaped onto the upper tree, lightening the bow which went sliding forward across the lower log. Then the boy amidships also leaped onto the upper tree, further lightening the boat which went sliding rapidly across . . .

Then the stunt backfired. The boat slipped past before either one could leap back in and grab a paddle. Even worse, the boat went swinging sidewise into a fallen treetop, capsizing and wedging beneath the limbs.

For fifteen minutes five of us struggled to get the boat loose, fighting its sodden weight with the swift water surging and pressing it under the tangle of branches. After much grunting and heaving, we pulled it free, turned it over and emptied it. With the paddles, wastebasket and one of their shirts which we'd also retrieved, we gave it back to the boys. They were a bit crestfallen.

Most of our people then hand-lined their canoes between the fallen trees. Harry and I walked ours among the willows down a shallow overflow channel.

A short distance downstream we passed the boys for the last time. One was paddling with the one-by-six. The other was using the turquoise wastebasket, dipping and pouring. Dipping . . . pouring. Dipping . . . pouring.

We shot one more rapids, another chute having a rib of bedrock across its bottom, where Harry and I left one more bright streak of aluminum scrapings. Then we were moving down the last quiet pool, and around the last bend, with the bluff at Pruitt now ahead of us . . . beside us . . . now behind us as we swung in to the sandbar.

Canoeists had been unloading here for hours as our long string of floaters had come down the river. The Kansas City people were gone. The Boys Club members from Memphis and Jackson had also left for home. We of the Arkansas group were the last wave to hit the beach.

For an hour or so we were engaged in unloading from the river, putting canoes and baggage onto and into our cars, and talking and reminiscing about the float.

Finally we too were saying our goodbyes, pulling out toward the highway, beginning our long drives homeward.

(Map on page 166)

PRUITT TO MOUNT HERSEY 3

WE DRIFTED, waiting for the last of our people to catch up.

Ahead, the dark gray cliff appeared to slowly expand, to grow higher as we floated down the pool.

This was the first bluff below Pruitt. From the head of the pool it had seemed to be one unbroken wall of rock. Closer now, we saw its truer complexion, the ledges, shelves, offsets, the balconies and overhangs with flat surfaces underneath.

Our last floaters had come into sight. Good. We just might stay together, at least for a while—though it had never been so for very long.

This weekend we had gathered a smallish group of Ozark Society members for a trip down the relatively short stretch of river from Pruitt to Mount Hersey. We planned to explore along the riverside as much as possible, take pictures, and take our own sweet time.

Our number was uneven, and I was odd man, lounging between the thwarts amidships while Harry handled the bow paddle and Neil the stern. The Imhoffs from Fayetteville had paired off two and two: John and their son Carl, eight, in their red canoe, Lois and their daughter Karen, fourteen, in a stubby green fishing boat they had borrowed. Maxine and Joe Clark were in their brown fiberglas canoe. Behind them, in a green square-stern canoe, were John and Lee Heuston from Little Rock.

It was the middle of May, and spring had advanced considerably since the dogwood float from Ponca to Pruitt three weeks before. Now the trees were solid walls of foliage along the banks. From the willows with their roots in the river to the scrub oaks on the dry ridges along the skyline, the country was green with living things.

While I daydreamed we floated down to a second bluff, the Welch Bluff, standing on the north side of the river. We glided along its base through a pool known as the Crow Hole.

Though neither very high nor very long, Welch Bluff is one of the most curiously formed cliffs on the entire Buffalo. Along its face are balconies, towers, pinnacles and setbacks adorned with a latticework of dark green junipers and shrubbery. Its pale rock is splashed with pastel shades of blue-gray, yellow, and pink. I took another long look at Welch Bluff. In my imagination I could see it becoming a row of multicolored and gingerbreaded old Victorian houses.

Joe Clark pulled in to the gravel bar where we were standing opposite the bluff and told me about his observations. The big crack from top to bottom of Welch Bluff near its upstream end was a geological fault.

From the Crow Hole we entered a chute bending right, then sharply left; I grabbed the spare paddle to help draw clear of the right bank.

Seconds behind us, John Imhoff and Carl were floating into the rapids. Suddenly the strong current caught them, banged their canoe into a tree leaning from the bank, began to turn them sidewise. I looked back just as John jumped overboard and grabbed the canoe. The water was chest deep.

In a moment he pulled the canoe free and started moving it (with Carl still aboard) into shallow water. Then all at once he gave out a loud groan. He'd just realized his Leica was still hanging around his neck.

The camera had gone clear under; we'd have to stop and let him try to dry it. We landed on the next gravel bar, and while we ate an impromptu lunch, John dabbed and polished his camera with a handkerchief, hoping for the best.

Later, as we moved along, I mentally compared this portion of the river with the parts upstream. At Pruitt the Buffalo seems to begin another distinct phase of its growth, becoming a little larger, a little less rambunctious. The chutes aren't often as long or as swift as the ones above the Highway 7 bridge.

In one of the lengthy pools below Welch Bluff we approached a guided fishing party, the first I'd seen this far upstream.

The two guides had moved their boats close to the bank on the deep side of the hole. Their guests, two

27

Welch Bluff

to a boat, were seated comfortably in camp chairs at the bow and amidships. All were fishing, so they drifted in silence. Occasionally one of the guides would dip a paddle to straighten his boat with the slow-moving current. The fishermen were casting toward the bank.

We moved over to the other side of the river and passed them. One of the fishing boats had its name painted in big white letters: *Buffalo Gal.*

Soon we approached the mouth of the Little Buffalo, easily recognized because it is the only place on the Buffalo where bluffs stand close on both sides of the river. The left-hand cliff is a 35-foot rock, split into several thick pillars standing at water's edge. To the right, a higher bluff rises beyond the narrow flood plain, on the neck of land between the Buffalo and Little Buffalo.

We landed on a gravel bar at the mouth of the Little Buffalo and got out for a stretch. Neil opened the icebox and handed out Cokes. Several of us were idly picking up pretty stones. Carl Imhoff was trying to skip the flat ones across the river.

Maxine and Karen Imhoff had gone wading across one channel of the Little Buffalo to examine a plant growing on the gravelly overflow area. I decided to follow them.

Their shrubby plant had rows of tiny purple blossoms. It was lead plant, Maxine called back to me. It was a legume, kin to peas and beans. Maxine and her pupil Karen were already striking out for new territory, wading the other channel of the Little Buffalo to reach the base of the bluff we had seen on the right when coming down the river.

I waded across and climbed onto the lowest ledge. Small things were growing here in the crevices and pockets of soil. Maxine was showing Karen the leaf pattern of a fern, showing her how to identify it. Next they turned to examine the flowering plants.

"Why was this one called 'bearded-tongue'?" I asked. Holding one of the little purple-veined blooms for me to see, Maxine pointed to one of the flower's stamens. It had a beard of tiny hairs.

We sloshed back across to the overflow area and stood looking at the bluff. Maxine, who translated scenery in terms of its vegetation, began identifying the plants we saw on a shelf halfway up the cliff. Yucca was in bloom there, green pincushions with tall stalks of cream-colored flowers. Then she spied the larkspur, slender flower stems poking up from the grass on the ledge. Oh, if she could only have *Delphinium carolinianum* for her plant press——

That triggered Harry to action; he would get one for her. Off he went.

Somewhere upstream he was able to climb to the ledge, for soon he appeared, picking his way along the sloping

Buffalo Gal

shelf, calling to Maxine to ask if he were near the flower she wanted.

The best blooms were those nearest the edge of the cliff, but Harry unhesitatingly edged down among them. He dug out a good specimen—leaves, roots and all, as Maxine instructed—and climbed back along the ledge.

Harry appeared with the *Delphinium* and Maxine was happy—but look, he was covered with scratches! Yes, he had suffered for his gallantry. He'd found the only route to the ledge was through a dense patch of greenbrier.

Presently we pushed off, moving down a pool past a rock wall where we could float below a long overhang. Reflected ripples played across the shadowed ceiling, and in sheltered crevices the ferns were wearing their new green.

Then on the right bank we discovered a great mass of ferns, the first 'fern fall' that I had ever seen on the Buffalo. Layer on layer of lush green maidenhair fronds spilled over a low wall at the water's edge. Streams from a hidden spring trickled down among the fronds and dripped and splashed into the river. For several minutes we back-paddled against the current, hovering around the cascade of ferns and taking pictures.

Not far downstream we passed Wells Creek, and then a line of low bluffs with heavy slabs of rock projecting over deep water—the old swimming hole with ready-made diving platforms. The swimmers had hung a length of

At the Little Buffalo

woven wire fencing up the bluff for climbing out of the water.

Now a flight of swallows came racing past the cliff and downriver . . . . They returned, making sudden rippling rushing noises in the air as they went dashing upstream. What were they doing—feeding on insects? Perhaps, but as they went chittering on their way, it looked as if they had no purpose but to have an exhilarating time, holding speed trials among themselves, or maybe competition for most graceful flight.

Summery white cumulus clouds had been piling up in the blue expanse of sky. All the rest of our world at the moment was green—dark for the distant hill in cloud shadow, bright for the willows on the gravel bar ahead. Light and dark greens together in the nearer trees.

And, except for a patch of reflected sky, the river was green . . . a liquid sort of green in shades from jade through blue-green, depending on countless combinations of depth of the water and reflections from above. The subtle greens of the Buffalo are better seen than described.

Midway down this pool of green we caught up with *Buffalo Gal* and her sister craft drifting along the right

bank. Save for their momentary greeting and an occasional clunk of paddle or whir of reel, the fishermen were silent, tending to business . . .

Suddenly I saw one of the fishing rods bend in a deep arc; the reel sang as taut line swung across the water. There was a brief explosion of fighting bass beyond *Buffalo Gal*. As we moved past, the luckless fish was being swung aboard.

Neil was looking at the cottonwoods lining the low bank to our left. "That's where the beavers will be . . . where the cottonwoods are . . ." He was right. We soon saw the chisel-pointed stumps of saplings the beaver had cut and dragged away. And within the next mile we came upon a 12-inch sycamore that a beaver had felled straight across the river. We all had to get out and hand-pull our boats under its trunk and between the limbs.[1]

[1]The original beavers on the Buffalo were exterminated before 1900 by fur trapping. Today's animals result from a restocking program in which a few beavers were brought in from elsewhere and released along the stream. They have multiplied so well that we saw beaver-cut and -peeled limbs and saplings on every float.

At times the beavers make futile efforts to dam the river—

Before long we saw another high bluff looming ahead. It was my cue to motion everybody over to the left for a landing. Upstream from the bluff we pulled alongside the bank in deep water at the foot of a steep hill. It was a poor anchorage but I insisted. I had something to show them.

We all tied fast and climbed ashore. I led the way up the ravine, dodging poison ivy and hoping there would be no snakes, assuring doubters that this was worth the effort.

Two hundred feet up through the dense woods, we approached a bluff with a deep, shadowy overhang. In a moment we could see the patch of sunlight at the rear of the cavity . . . then the hole through the roof. We all scrambled up to the opening, under the natural bridge.

Several of us climbed the ledges up through the hole and around to stand on top of the massive rock span. Fully ten feet thick, it supported a covering of topsoil and small trees.

Did this feature have a name? I answered that it did. Local people called it the Chimley Hole. I added that it illustrated an advantage of floating the Buffalo in the wintertime. We had first seen it in February, when the trees were bare and it was within plain view from the river.

Floating again, we moved down the pool past the high cliff, locally known as Riggs Bluff, and approached the mouth of a narrow side valley named Stillhouse Hollow. A neighborhood distiller once operated a whisky works there at the Hollow's big spring.

A county road comes down Stillhouse Hollow and crosses the Buffalo on a makeshift low-water bridge, a concrete causeway ending with a ramshackle deck of timbers thrown across the main channel. Avoiding the swift current racing under the wooden span, we paddled over to the causeway for a portage.

I had thought we'd have to unload and reload our canoes for just this 20-foot haul across the roadway, but it wasn't to be so. In one area the river was overflowing across the road, and we partly floated, partly carried each loaded canoe along the shallow channel. At the downriver side of the slab our stream spilled several feet over large rocks into the backwater. With a little more effort, we carried each canoe forward from the causeway until

their work usually disappears with the next rise. Normally they know better and attend to homemaking in burrows under the banks.

Unlike their pond-dwelling cousins in the North who have to live through long winters on foodstuffs stored in deep water under the ice, the Buffalo River beavers can get out on shore to feed the year round. Not that they're often seen; they venture forth mostly at night. Occasionally a camper or fisherman does glimpse or hear them swimming and at work.

we could lower its bow to be buoyed up in the pool below. Then we carried the stern forward, off the slab and beyond the rocks, and lowered it into the water. Within ten or twelve minutes we had all our canoes and the Imhoffs' boat moved across the causeway. We walked our craft out of the backwater into the main channel again, climbed in and went on our way.

We'd gotten well on into the afternoon, but we were not well on our way down the river. With our frequent stops along the way, we'd floated hardly six miles from Pruitt. Still, the run to Mount Hersey totaled only eighteen miles. Neil wanted to put in early to set up camp. He and Harry dug in with the paddles to move ahead of the others, and the three of us searched for campsites.

How about that bar on the left? We agreed that it looked too low. A rain tonight above Pruitt could flood us out before breakfast.

The next bar, on the right, wasn't what we wanted either. Nobody would enjoy camping on a field of cobblestones—look out!

First dodging boulders and then scudding through high white waves, we raced down a long straightaway. Now in the clear, all three of us joyfully paddled full speed.

Fern-ology

At the end of the ride we pulled ashore, as usual, to watch the others.

Neil set up his movie camera on the spot, but Harry and I wanted to be closer to the rough water upstream. We went racing up the bank, hoping to see the others coming through the first rapids.

The closest viewpoint was in a willow thicket, too much a tangle for taking pictures. I waded into the river to get beyond the branches—and nearly got swept off my feet, cameras and all. I grabbed a limb for support and climbed back ashore.

Now John and Lee Heuston came barreling through the waves, and the Clarks, and both the Imhoffs' boats. Harry and I stood among the bushes and watched. I was disappointed not to be putting it on film.

We were all together again, and looking for a camping spot. The next gravel bar was high enough, several feet above the river, but the landing was nothing but a steep bank lined with young willows. However, we did see a couple of openings where we could tie up . . . .

We strolled around the bar, picking places for our tents. It would work out all right after all.

Tonight we had time. There was no need to hurry. While the sun sank lower and out of sight, we unloaded, carried baggage to the tent sites, set up tents, spread tarpaulins and then went about getting supper. When we were finished it was deep dusk, and John Heuston had built the evening fire.

John and Lee were certainly camping in style. They had brought two comfortable folding chairs, and light-weight folding cots of aluminum. And mosquito netting; John had already stretched it above their cots. The rest of us questioned the need for mosquito netting. We had encountered few mosquitoes on these gravel bars, presumably because the flowing water keeps the air in motion. And we'd seen few snakes or crawling insects on the gravel; for them it must be a barren wasteland.

But John would keep using his mosquito netting; he believed in total safety from crawling and flying critters of the night. We all did agree, though, that the gravel bars are the best summer campsites on the Buffalo, far better than the tick- and chigger-infested fields and woods.

For a while we sat around the fire and continued talking. As it grew darker we heard the intermittent chirping of cricket frogs, and the long drawn out trills of tree frogs. And before long, other noises of the night: A cowbell, tinkling in the distance. Dogs, with something treed over on the hill. Background music of crickets, with bass notes from a bullfrog down the river. Now and then the tremulous wailing of a screech owl in the woods behind our camp. At half a dozen points out in the blackness, whip-poor-wills began calling, repeating their three

syllables endlessly. Their southern relations, the chuck-will's-widows, soon chimed in, and their chorus was to continue far into the night.[2]

Evening sounds on the river had a lulling effect. Long before our normal bedtimes, we turned in.

During the night, the afternoon's clouds assembled, moving around and thundering for a while after we went to bed. I still refused to go into the tent as Neil and Harry had done. In an hour or two the clouds moved on, and later a full moon rose.

Next morning, our first side trip was a visit to John Eddings Cave. After tying up along the bank, we picked our way across a driftwood-choked stream gully, climbed the embankment and followed a footpath leading up the hollow. That was all. Barely two hundred feet from the river we stood in the cave's entrance.

It opened into the base of a gray limestone bluff, and was nearly 50 feet wide. A spacious front hallway extended back into the twilight to a bend which blocked the deeper reaches from view. A stream trickled along the hallway floor, turned toward one wall and flowed outside.

We ventured no farther than the daylit zone at the entrance. On an earlier trip I had seen a pool of water, too deep to wade, spreading from wall to wall just beyond the bend of the hallway. Two of us had then detoured into a dry passage to the left, but after two hundred feet it had become a crawlway, and it had no decorative formations.

Someone now asked what lay beyond the pool in the main passage. I answered that Jim Schermerhorn, the cave explorer from Harrison, and companions had once paddled a rubber boat about four hundred feet along the lake to several mud-floored rooms. The cave then appeared to extend much deeper, but Jim's group had run out of time and they turned back.

Today we discovered a bed of ferns growing on the moist slope within the entrance, luxuriantly green ferns in the shadow under the cave roof. Maxine believed they were wood ferns. Whatever their kind, they lent a touch of eerie loveliness to the sunless, rainless floor of John Eddings Cave.

A mile downriver we floated under the Highway 123 bridge, a high, narrow, one-lane, rusty old iron span, the

[2]These two related species of birds have somewhat different calls which are often confused. The whip-poor-will's is *WHIP-poor-WEEL, WHIP-poor-WEEL* . . . which he may utter more than a thousand times in rapid succession.

The chuck-will's-widow gives a less-vigorous four-syllabled call: *chuck-WILL-WIDow.* The chuck's first syllable is faint and the others are slurred; a better suggestion of the sound is *chips, butter, and white oak,* said very fast.

kind with plank flooring that rattles as you drive across. It will be replaced when the road is paved. Neighborhood boys used to walk the top beams of its trusses, fifty feet above the river, to collect bets.

Big Creek flows into the lower end of the long pool below the bridge. For diversion we paddled up the creek for about two hundred yards, until we reached the first rapids. At times when there is enough water, lower Big Creek can be floated for several miles.

Past Big Creek the hills drew in closer to the river. Well up on one of the slopes, Maxine spied a clump of azaleas, masses of pink blossoms in the woods.

"*Rhododendron roseum,*" Neil remarked. I knew the azalea's sweet pervading odor better than its name.[3]

The opposite shore appeared quite different from the dry hillside of the azaleas. Usually the banks of the Buffalo are that way—one high and the other low, one shaded and moist while the other is sunny and dry.

Here the low shore was thicketed, and from the bushes a catbird gave its plaintive mewing call. An American elm leaned over us, limbs drooping into the water. Maxine then saw Dutchman's-pipe, vines with heart-shaped leaves, spreading along the bank. At that moment the catbird broke into snatches of song.

From downriver came a murmur, the ever louder rushing sound of rapids. The Heustons had moved ahead out of sight and we were next in line. In a minute or so we swept through the shoals, a short run with white waves down the best channel. We pulled in and waited for the others.

The Imhoffs were coming. First John and Carl paddled down the rapids in the canoe. Then we saw the girls approaching, frantically trying to keep the flat-bottomed boat straight as it began to accelerate into the shoal. It hit a bush and stuck. More frantic pulling and pushing. They had the boat loose . . .

Here it came, bow first, turning sideways, finally backwards, swinging around in an eddy. Not until it floated into quiet water downstream did the girls get the bow forwards again.

The Clarks swept through easily enough, but they missed the big waves down the deepest chute. Since these were wide, shallow rapids, a lot of the excitement came from steering into that one best route. Joe and Maxine had shot the biggest waves on an earlier float, and now

Fern fall

(for old times' sake?) they wanted to do it again.

Slowly they walked and pulled their canoe up through the swift water along the near shore. About fifty yards upstream they climbed in. Young Carl Imhoff was going with them for the ride.

Down into the chute they came, plowing through the highest waves at top speed, skimming down into the less turbulent water and the eddy. With a grand flourish, Joe stood up in the stern and clasped his hands overhead in victory.

The hole below the rapids was an especially long one,

[3] Why *Rhododendron roseum* when simply 'azalea' would seem to do? Neil explained to me the great confusion of common names of plants. This azalea, for example, was called early azalea, mountain azalea, honeysuckle, or election pink. Furthermore, it has a similar though odorless relative, *Rhododendron nudiflorum* or pinxter-flower, which also grows here and may mistakenly be called by any of those names. The scientific name is exact and universal, one name for one species of plant.

extending straight ahead for nearly half a mile. And it was broad, maybe a hundred feet wide. And shallow, so that at times we nearly touched the pebbly bottom. And clear, so that in deeper water we seemed to float in suspension. Small green sunfish swam about, coming alongside and even beneath our boats. Another catbird in its thicket gave its plaintive cry . . . but no song this time.

We were approaching a bluff, a wet, dripping wall fronting the bend. A catalpa tree, white with blossoms, stood in the ravine at the near end. We'd stopped paddling to look when we heard someone calling us. Farther around the turn, John and Lee had landed on a beautiful sand beach and were unloading their chairs and the makings of lunch.

After we carried food chests and ice boxes to the shade along the upper edge of the sand, we sat and snacked and talked. Mostly we compared our impressions of this part of the river, for none of us had floated this section as much as portions farther upstream and down.

Obviously the stretch from Ponca to Camp Orr had the most spectacular bluffs of any on the Buffalo. But here we had found a hundred things just as fascinating. We remembered, too, that this section could be floated through much of the summer and fall when the river upstream was too low for boating.

We were reaching a consensus that no one part of the Buffalo was (to us) much superior to other parts. We had found *all* the river filled with beauty, alive with interesting sights and experiences. Maxine summed up our feelings when she made the remark "We happen to like best whichever part we're floating at the moment."

Before long we got underway again.

Soon to stop. We'd discovered another fern fall on a bluff above the right bank.

From the river it seemed to be little more than a patch of greenery where water dripped down the bluff. But on climbing the talus slope to its base, we beheld a lush, thick bed of maidenhair fronds reaching from underfoot to well overhead, a hanging, dripping cascade-garden of exquisite beauty. We were viewing a creation that no mortal could hope to imitate.

In the wet tangle of growth at the foot of the fall, golden ragwort was in bloom, and among the boulders at the river Maxine had discovered a new plant for me—nine-

bark, a low bush with little snowballs of white flowerlets. Above us at the head of the fern fall, shooting stars were darts of white on a background of mottled green shadows.

We approached a higher cliff on the north bank, with a splashing waterfall up among the trees. We landed once more, and across the river boulders and up the steepening hill we climbed to the foot of the fall. A heavy shower of spray fell from a ledge twenty feet above us.

Harry and I had noticed that the stream did not come over the top of the cliff, but from a hole just above the ledge. Harry was already working around to the left, looking for a way to climb. I followed.

Well, we'd have made it but for one thing—poison ivy. We found a thick patch of poison ivy spreading all over the hand and footholds. That was enough for us.[4]

We floated again, past a series of massive block-cliffs separated by narrow ravines, past a gravel bar on the left and another high bluff on our right. Rubbery little sedum plants with pink flowers grew on the cliff's lower abutments. A basswood tree, decked with white blooms, stood on a high ledge.

We swung to the left and floated past a hollow where we heard the bubbling and gushing of a stream hidden beyond the steep river bank. There was a big spring, I recalled, only about a hundred feet back in the woods. I scanned the shoreline—where did the spring branch come into the river? No sign. Had I not looked soon enough?

Below the hollow we glided alongside still another bluff on the north bank, then into a chute to the right where we went scooting down a deep rapids, nosing through a set of bucking waves that slapped loudly into the bows of our canoes. Here for a brief moment was some of the best water of the weekend.

Those were the last rapids. For another mile we drifted along a tranquil river, continuing our relaxed bank-watching. It was only mid-afternoon.

We rounded one more curve, and there ahead was the landing at Mount Hersey. On this trip, for once, we'd come in with time to spare.

[4]Ward Phillips, a local float operator, later assured me that the cave was a crawlway, man-sized for only a few yards beyond the mouth.

(Map on page 167)

MOUNT HERSEY TO GILBERT 4

Mount Hersey (or Hershey) has known better days. In years nearer 1900 the community boasted a school, a store and post office, a boarding house, and a water powered grist mill and cotton gin. Now there are only a few aged houses along the roads near the boat landing. Three rural mailboxes stand and wait at what was once the village center.

The landing is at the mouth of Davis Creek. In dry weather you can drive to the river's edge. When it rains, you'd better not—the last eighth-mile is all mud.

We worried about that mud, among other things, the Saturday in April when we put in at Mount Hersey.

The day had begun brightly enough. But, by mid-morning, just as the Ozark Society floaters finished unloading at the landing, it began to rain. On the chance it would stop, we started the car shuttle to the takeout point at Gilbert.

We drove down Highway 65 through the rain. What we'd thought might be a fifteen-minute thundershower had instead become a slow, steady downpour. When Neil Compton, who was leading our caravan in his red Scout, pulled off the pavement and stopped, we knew why.

The clouds were low and leaden in all directions. Obviously it was upon us for the day. Nobody wanted to canoe in an all day rain. There was nothing to do but go back and load up—quickly, because soon the mud would be impassable.

In less than an hour we had picked up our gear and gotten off the river bank. We moved the cars up the road beyond the muddy stretch and waited. Neil was taking the Scout back to get one of our number who was stuck, unstuck.

Minutes passed. The rain had stopped, but the overcast remained. Somebody opened his car door and stepped out. Then, one by one, we all got out. We stood around waiting, talking about our bad luck with the weather. The ladies went and looked into a decaying old house just above the road.

In those moments, the clouds overhead began to dissolve. Suddenly the sun came out, full force.

Neil returned. There was a babble of talk.

"Let's float, Neil——"

"Look, it's clearing off."

Neil looked, first at the sky, and then at us. "Well, I believe it'll clear up and stay that way . . . . I don't think we even need to take a vote on that. We'll just put in."

Back to the landing, across the already drying mud. Unload again. Send the cars to Gilbert.

After an hour and a half, Neil returned with the drivers. Then everyone helped himself to a lunch the ladies had spread on a tarpaulin by the canoes, and we loaded the remaining loose gear. At last, at one-thirty in the afternoon, we shoved off and were afloat.

The Buffalo makes a fast getaway from Mount Hersey. White water begins only yards below the landing, and we swung down a fine chute around to the right, past Mill Branch, on past the red-stained bluff we had seen from the landing, around the bend and out of sight.

That first quarter-mile was deceiving, though. Below the rapids we found ourseles in a long, windblown pool. Ahead, I knew, were some of the lengthiest placid stretches of the middle Buffalo. There would be only a few fast runs in the nine miles to Woolum.

We all made slow progress against the headwind. My stern man, Larry Burns from Bentonville, was a seasoned paddler, so we dug in and soon caught up with Joe and Maxine Clark. After we'd drawn alongside, Maxine began naming the flowers along the banks.

"Now there, the box elder is in bloom. You've seen the redbud—it's just coming into full blossom. I've seen phlox . . . Over there's some more . . ."

The lavender-pink phlox appeared in patches and bunches on the hillside. Then, along the margin of an old field above the river bank, under the trees now breaking into hazy yellow-green with new spring leaves, I spied the May-apple plants, dozens of them, hundreds of

'Crossbar' Cave

flowers, they revealed beauty in their simplicity. And their color was a yellow so rich, so intense that it alone made the little blossoms strikingly lovely.

"It's the celandine-poppy. It's rare; I've never seen it before on the Buffalo. This cliff shades it here, so there's more moisture . . . Marsh, will you bring the camera?"

Joe Clark gets to know his wild flowers looking through an Exakta. In a minute he was bent down over a poppy to take a close-up photograph. Maxine, leafing through her Gray's *Manual of Botany,* found a description of our celandine or wood poppy, scientifically named *Stylophorum diphyllum.*

We saw no more of the celandine-poppy, but as we paddled downstream, almost without effort now that the wind was to our backs, new sights and scenery seemed just to roll backward past us. All we had to do was look. Conversation turned on whatever happened to be interesting along either bank.

Cave Creek flowed in hardly noticed from behind a gravel bar to our right. Straight ahead, rising beyond the far end of a long hole of water, there was a large bluff topped by a dark green mass of cedars. Jack McCutcheon of the Cave Creek community had told me it was the John Reddell Bluff. John Reddell (Jack had pronounced it 'Riddle') still lived on the hill above the mouth of Cane Branch, down by the lower end of his bluff.

Reddell Bluff looks south and gets more sunshine than the cliffs facing north (such as the one shading the poppies). As my gaze wandered across the red-streaked rock, I began to realize the subtle differences in appearance between bluffs having different exposures.

I could recall several north-facing cliffs having a distinctly gray and somber look about them. Buzzard Bluff above Camp Orr and the first bluff below Pruitt had been this way.

On the other hand, I remembered several bluffs that faced south or west as being notably pale, maybe bleached by the sun, but often with gay streaks and patches of orange or yellow or pink, as on Bee Bluff at the scout camp and Welch Bluff below Pruitt.[1]

To me the bluffs are endlessly fascinating, for their

them—a parade of glistening green umbrellas on stems a foot high.

"There, up on the ledge—see the yellow? It's gooseberry in bloom."

Again, with spring coming to the Buffalo, I was happy to be traveling with a botanist.

Then my turn came: "There's a cave up there on the left, about a hundred feet up the hill—we climbed up there last month. It's not a deep cave, but it has a funny sort of crossbar in the entrance, a ledge of stone right across the opening." Young leaves were already veiling the cave from view. We paddled on.

Presently the river began bending to the left, deflected by a high dark bluff. Larry and I moved ahead of the Clarks. Then we heard Maxine talking excitedly.

"Marsh, I want to stop here—pull over! Stop this thing, Marsh! I see something——"

We turned back and followed the Clarks to the south bank. By the time we'd scrambled up the slope below the bluff, Maxine was already examining some bunchy low-lying plants and their blossoms.

The little four-petaled blooms weren't at all 'showy' as fancy garden hybrids are. But like so many of the wild

---

[1] Joe Clark had a geologist's explanation for all this. Rusty orange or yellow streaks on the bluffs most likely came from divided clay particles stained with iron oxides. The clay had washed down from the hillsides above, where the reddish clay soil was usually the residue of dissolved Boone limestone.

Gray streaks could come from gray clays; black from an oxide of manganese or from carbon in clay. Black could also be algae, Maxine suggested.

Joe believed the coloring was more noticeable on south-facing bluffs because water oozing down the rock evaporated more readily and deposited its colorful clay particles. On north-facing cliffs getting less sun, the water simply ran off and carried the clay away. Also, any color remaining on the north-facing bluffs could be hidden by the heavier vegetation there.

color, for the shape and form of their curious architecture, for the geological histories they reveal, for the collection of plants that each displays. Each new bluff is different from all the others; it has its own individual character, something unique to say.

A huge slab of rock is split off the Reddell Bluff near its lower end, and for a few minutes some of us climbed up and into the 30-foot grotto between the slab and the main cliff. Then we pushed off again, down past Reddell's spring on the left bank, past Cane Branch arriving from the left, and into another extended quiet stretch of river.

Local people who have known the Buffalo all their lives have their own names for these long pools. Between Cane Branch and Woolum, a friend had told me, we would float through Akins Hole, Leafy Hole, Bat House Hole, Roughedge Hole and the Blue Hole. 'Outsiders' floating the river usually move on before they hear these local names used by generations of bank fishermen and johnboat floaters from the surrounding hills.

Now we were being swept past another bluff towering over the right bank, a cliff with eroded pinnacles, and dark cave openings . . . the current coursed swiftly along its base and carried us beyond.

Little hollows above the south bank sheltered ledges splashed with gray and green lichens, boulders covered with cushiony dark green moss and tiny sprouting ferns. As Maxine had already suggested, in the shade there was moisture, and here in the shade a special community of moisture-loving plants lived and thrived.

On the north bank a drier condition prevailed, and along a sunlit slope two miles below Cane Branch I saw my first shortleaf pines that grew down to the river's edge. I had often seen pine trees along the Buffalo, but until now they had always been up high, on the cliffs and up the ridges.

White-trunked sycamores, always tolerant of water, braced themselves with sinuous roots clutching the south bank and leaned out over the water. A spring gushed from the ground a few yards above them. Another crowd of May-apples lined the embankment.

The long hole ended in a millrace cut through the gravel bar, angling to the right into white water . . . and at this moment the Narrows came into view.

Rising from the river ahead was a ridge of bare rock, pale in the late afternoon sunlight, standing in relief against the blue of distant hills. This rock was the Narrows—'Nar's' in the dialect of the Ozarks—perhaps the most talked-about natural feature of all the middle Buffalo.

In a few minutes Larry and I joined the others who had pulled in to the gravel bar opposite the Narrows. Neil squinted at the sun and decided we'd better remain here to camp. The gravel sloped up to a wide, long grassy area lined with some large old trees. The ten of us were soon carrying duffel to four scattered sites. We began to put up tents.

Laurene Compton is an accomplished cook, and Larry Burns has earned local renown as the camp chef extraordinaire. We left them preparing supper at our campsite; Neil, Harry Pearson and I wanted to paddle across the river and climb the Narrows. (The present trip was Harry's first on the Buffalo. He was on assignment for the *Pine Bluff Commercial*.)

We discovered we could tie up along the bank at the upstream end of the bluff, then easily scale the slope and the stair-step ledges up to the ridge. We walked out on the Narrows.

Now we stood on the knife edge of a sliver of solid rock, rising from sixty to eighty vertical feet above the river bank. On the landward side the drop was nearly as abrupt, down to a country road skirting a wide plowed field that spread across lower Richland valley. The view was spectacular. And the walk across, once the path narrowed to about three feet and climbed a portion of the crest overhanging the river, was something of a test of nerves.

I urged Harry to climb high up on the ridge and stand for photographs. He tried—reluctantly. But he had to stay so close to the edge that he got a bad case of the jitters. I took my pictures with Harry standing farther down.

Ages ago, Richland Creek had swept against this ridge, and with the Buffalo chewing at the other side, had eroded it to the mere sliver that now lay beneath our feet. Richland has long since changed course; today it flows nearly half a mile away, beyond the broad field.

Neil remembered a story. "Ken, you know Jack McCutcheon . . . Well, he told me about 'Pink' Daniels, who used to live up near Cane Branch.

"'Pink' came down here fox hunting one night, and about midnight his dogs chased a fox right across the Narrows here. But they were scared to follow it. 'Pink' just picked them up, one under each arm, and carried them across.

"Can you imagine that—walking across here at midnight, without a light, and carrying two foxhounds?"

Back in camp, Laurene and Larry had put together a splendid meal—steaks, baked potatoes, green beans, salad with our choice of dressing . . . plus coffee, milk or tea, eventually topped off with cake, cookies or fruit.

After the dishes were done we sat and talked, mostly about the Richland country over beyond the Narrows.

Richland's history seemed tied to its soil, to the rich earth for which the valley was named. Some of the first settlers to come up the Buffalo had put down stakes there, about in the 1820's. Those flat, fertile bottomlands helped men make an easy living.

Even before the Civil War, farming in Richland was more like that on the plantations in the Mississippi valley than on the little one-family clearings through most of the Ozarks. In the broad fields of this isolated valley, slaves cultivated the crops. Cotton was important.

The Civil War made Richland a no-man's land. Gangs of outlaws or bushwackers, attracted by the harvests, plundered and terrorized the countryside. Columns of Confederate and Union troops occasionally passed through, and they too raided the crops. But neither side had the manpower to occupy or protect this country.

Through early 1864, northern and southern forces did move around in the area, skirmishing, finally colliding in brief, desperate battle near the mouth of Richland. Twenty-one men died before the Confederates were forced into retreat. Both sides had to leave wounded in the care of neighborhood families. For years afterward, farmers plowed up corroded relics of war in their fields.

Bedtime. The Comptons moved into their tent. Larry Burns and Harry and I crawled into sleeping bags spread on a tarpaulin outside. I lay for a few minutes watching the stars, then rolled over and dropped into deep sleep.

Neil's insistent voice awakened me. "Come on, get up and put your stuff in our tent. It's about to pour down rain!"

Uh . . . yes! Now I head the thunder in the west, saw the black clouds rolling in. To the east, the first streak of dawn made the sky look even more ominous. Lightning began to play overhead.

Within minutes, the five of us were in the Comptons' tent, waiting and listening for the first drops of rain. After a long silence, they came, big drops splattering on the canvas for a moment. Then another long silence. The storm was passing over.

We crawled out. Joe Clark poked his head from the next tent. "Hey, I was listening to my transistor radio . . . They said a while ago there's a tornado warning across where we are right now."

"Yeah! There it goes!" Larry retorted. We were now watching the cloud bank breaking overhead, moving eastward.

We hurried through breakfast and broke camp. Then, for those who hadn't yet walked the Narrows, we all crossed the river, tied up, and scaled the ridge.

Harry was still much shaken by the height, so I talked Boyd Evison, the national park naturalist who had come up from Hot Springs, into standing on the crest for another series of photographs. Boyd admitted he was nervous but stayed put.

I turned to find Maxine on all fours at the brink of the bluff, urging Harry to hold her by the waist. She had scissors and she wanted to reach something——

Maxine edged forward. Harry, alarmed, quickly knelt and grabbed her, and she lay down, wiggling farther forward until she could reach far out and down at arm's length.

Snip, and she wiggled back onto the trail, now intently studying a sprig of gooseberry in her hand. She thought she might have a new species. . . .

Our late start yesterday hadn't helped today's schedule; we now faced a 20-mile float to Gilbert. And on the way, there were bound to be delays. Ozark Society floating was very, very leisurely—though that itself enhanced the experience.

We'd hardly gotten away from the Narrows when we stopped at another attraction, the Bat House, a bluff reputed to contain a large subterranean chamber reached by an underwater passage from the river. Here the cliff plunged into the Buffalo to green depths that might indeed have been hiding the cave's entrance. At water line were two strange holes in the rock, like the eyes of a skull. We moved downstream into the larger eye, even two canoes at once floating into the stony socket.

The next quiet mile ended in another fast chute; we maneuvered to the right to avoid a big rock jutting out into the current and swept on, into the pool above Woolum Ford.

Woolum is another vanished village on the Buffalo. Today there is little but the wide gravel bar where a county road tracks down to the left bank and across the shoal to lower Richland valley. In the past, though, on the flat beyond the gravel bar, storekeepers and a ginner served a large farm population up and down-river, across in Richland, and back up the ridges toward St. Joe. Isolation, depletion of soil and timber and a longing for better things in life led many of the farm people to leave, and Woolum faded away. From the river we could glimpse all that remained of Woolum— one small store building, long abandoned, empty windows gaping, standing at the site.

Down the riffle below Woolum Ford we floated, past the broad outpouring of Richland Creek and around the bend through the Robinson Hole.

The river was bank-full from recent rains, flattening out many rough spots that make exciting canoeing when the Buffalo is lower. Above Jamison Creek, the river at

The Nar's

a lower stage spills over the edge of a flat ledge almost as a waterfall, and floaters have to quickly find a sluiceway wide and deep enough to shoot down into the pool below. Now we scarcely noticed as we swept over the spot.

Ahead we faced a sheer wall of rock over a hundred feet high. The brink of this bluff, easily accessible from a county road along the ridge, is locally known as the Lookoff. From among the twisted junipers lining the edge of the Lookoff, I had gazed down on the river and up the open valley to Woolum and beyond.

Here, in a pool below the Lookoff, the Buffalo River disappears.

That is, it does after prolonged summer drouth, when the much-diminished stream sinks into its bed of gravel and takes an underground short cut across three miles of river bend to White Springs. Now, with the river running full, we were unable to detect any loss of water to the underground channel.

After floating around the bend we looked for the White Springs, the exit of the river's subterranean passage. But the springs were lost from sight, somewhere beneath us as we glided along in the fast-moving current.

In times of drouth, though, the springs are readily seen. Dozens of streams of crystal clear cold water come welling up, mostly from fissures in the rocky bottom of the river itself. Some of the springs are under such pressure that they make little bubbling 'boils' on the river's surface. Charlie McRaven of St. Joe, who had taken me on several floats down this portion of the river, had described the springs in late summer. "It's sure strange to watch the river there," he had said, "and to walk through that hole of water barefoot, with those cold springs coming up right under you."

We floated along below the high palisade of White Bluff, towering above us for more than three hundred yards downstream. Now the river was getting lively. Larry and I found the channel swinging to the right, then left—and we paddled furiously, barely avoiding an overhanging tree.

Still we were missing some of the thrills. Below White Bluff, summer floaters encounter a foot-high ledge and have to choose among several narrow channels spilling through gaps in the rock. With the water up, we simply floated over.

Suddenly we heard a splash and a flapping noise, and ahead of us a great blue heron was rising, moving downriver with slow, majestic beat of its three-foot wings . . . moving round out of sight.

We paddled around the bend, and there was the same big gray bird taking off again.

Soon we met a smaller wading bird that seemed much less alarmed at our presence. It flew, but only a short distance, setting down in plain sight by the right bank. First the canoe ahead and then ours floated to within 15 yards of the bird; it may have been curious about us, too, as we glided nearer and nearer. Before it finally took wing, I had a close look with binoculars.

He (she?) was a strange fellow, gray, nearly two feet tall, with bold black streaks across his face and a light-colored topknot combed straight back. After he had wheeled and flown directly overhead and upriver, I pulled out Peterson's *Field Guide,* and discovered we'd seen a yellow-crowned night heron.

We had fallen behind, Larry and I and the Clarks, but on rounding the next bend we found everyone else pulled in to a gravel bar, having lunch. Soon, by common invitation, I was making the rounds, sampling what was left to eat: Three Vienna sausages. A peanut butter and jelly sandwich. The last of the orange-coconut ambrosia. Two carrot sticks. Three sugar cookies and a canned Coke.

Just as we'd not all arrived at once, the first to finish lunch began packing up to leave. Neil wanted to get moving to show Harry the river. Boyd and Barbara Evison had a deadline for relieving their baby sitter.

Before long Larry and I and the Clarks were the only ones left on the bar. Joe Mills from Wisconsin, floating the middle Buffalo for the first time in his lightweight aluminum canoe, had Laurene Compton as bow paddler, and they were shoving off.

Our gravel bar fronted a quiet bay behind a row of willows where the overflow raced through into the next rapids. The others had walked their canoes down the shallow spillage at the lower end of the bay and into the main channel. Joe decided to paddle back upstream along the near bank, then sweep out around the partly submerged willows and into the head of the rapids. We were involved with our packing.

"They're in trouble!"

Joe and Laurene hadn't gone far enough upstream to cross clear of the willows. Now they were paddling, paddling desperately . . . and were being swept down, pulled down—into the trees.

They hit the first willow, lodged a moment, struggling— and suddenly the canoe wrenched sidewise and tipped over. Laurene plunged in waist deep, nearly off her feet; then she managed to grab a willow. The canoe turned bottom against a tree and torrents of water poured into it, against it, collapsing and folding it around a tree trunk.

As we watched helplessly, Laurene climbed over into the next, larger tree, climbed higher onto a limb, almost out of the water. There seemed no way to reach her.

Joe was taller, able to stand against the rushing water.

Still in the river, he started wrestling with his packs, trying to tie them to limbs. Now Joe and Laurene both appeared safe for the time being. Larry and I raced down through the overflow and downstream to pick up things floating away. The Clarks were unloading their canoe for a rescue.

We beached, hurried back across the bar. How could we get to Joe and Laurene, out there in the rapids?

Larry went plunging into the overflow fifty yards below the wreck and started wading up the long line of willows toward them. I followed, into water that became much swifter, and waist deep. Then chest deep. We could grab holds hand-over-hand along willow limbs, though, to avoid being swept away.

Joe had climbed into a tree and was hacking at a limb pinning his battered canoe, which blocked the way to Laurene. She was still perched in her tree, calmly waiting for help.

Larry and Joe pulled mightily at the canoe and I snubbed the bow line on a tree to hold its position. It began to come un-wedged.

In ten minutes more we had it free, upright and nearly emptied of water. But its back was broken, bent so that the bow and stern pointed downward while the midsection stood high out of the water. Larry and I steadied the canoe and Joe climbed in, grabbed overhead limbs for balance, and put his weight on the bend. The canoe partly unfolded.

Now they could get it out of the way. While I remained with Laurene, Joe and Larry slowly pulled the wrecked canoe down the row of willows and onto the gravel bar.

Joe Clark had their unloaded canoe waiting at the lower end of the willows. He, Joe and Larry pulled it into the current and started walking it out the row of willows toward us.

Looking off the Lookoff

The Lookoff Bluff

loudly pounding it back into shape. It began to resume its original form—except for a six-split down each side. Even so, Joe believed he could take it downstream, by paddling alone without baggage and being careful. Larry and I, then, would carry most of the waterlogged gear to our canoe and set it aboard. Laurene would ride with us, too.

Joe was feeling pretty low. "I've never had such a serious wreck in five years of canoeing," he told us. "I want to apologize; you've been caused all this trouble by my mistake. And Mrs. Compton, especially——

"I knew better," he admitted. "I never should have tried to paddle across that current."

We were floating again—slowly. Joe went ahead. He had seated himself in the stern to make the bow and midships ride high, and the cracks just about cleared the water. The Clarks followed Joe. Larry and Laurene and I came last, wallowing along, riding low in the stream. Laurene sat behind me in the bow.

Our slow pace at least meant more time to look at the sights. I began my usual commentary (probably unheard) on the points of interest.

First, there was the Tie Slide—

Crosstie cutters used to have a cable that began high on the bluff to our right, and crossed over the river down to the sand bar on our left. To move a log from the ridge down to the river, they'd staple it to the cable, up there on the bluff, and give it a shove. It'd come whizzing down the cable, sliding on the staples, and whump!—it'd hit the sand bar, usually knocking the staples loose. The crew rolled the logs into the river, then, for rafting down to the mill.

Beyond the Tie Slide a cliff rising from the river contained a large scooped-out cavity in its face. Charlie McRaven and I had once climbed up to the center of the depression, fifteen feet above the water, to test it as a natural reflector of sound. I had breathed deep and let out a mighty yell, and the echoes seemed to go booming all the way to Woolum. However, folks then approaching in another boat don't look so impressed.

"Larry, let's keep away from those rocks . . ."

Two monstrous boulders half blocked the river. Swift water broke against the first and veered back into a whirlpool. We moved well away, toward the left bank. McRaven had heard two men drowned here in boat upsets.

Above us on the right, the bluff formed a broken line of fins, turrets and towers protruding from the steep hill. I pointed toward the top of the ridge. "Up there's Peter Cave," I remarked.

"Where, Ken?" Laurene asked. "I don't see it."

"No, I guess we can't see it now—only in the winter.

We all pushed the canoe into position beneath Laurene's perch in the tree, steadied it and Laurene stepped it. Joe untied his waterlogged packs and we hoisted them aboard. Finally we were returning down the line of willows, Laurene in the canoe, the rest of us wading and stabilizing it, and ourselves, as best we could. Now we had to catch up with the others—they'd been gone fully an hour. Somewhere downstream they must be waiting, worrying. . . .

We'd lost only one small pack of groceries, plus Joe's axe which had slipped out of his hand as he'd finished cutting the limb. How could we carry everything? The Clarks' canoe was amply loaded already, but they could take one of Joe's packs. Larry and I weren't carrying as much.

Joe was jumping up and down in his beached canoe,

Bucking Shoals

But see that spire of rock, that one about 40 feet high—up there on the hill between the two parts of the bluff sticking out? The cave's in the bottom of the cliff just beyond that spire."

Peter Cave had an entrance room, maybe 15 feet wide and 10 feet high, that the Indians had occupied. Its dusty floor must have preserved perishable remains of some importance, but pothunters had gotten in there during the past year or two. In grubbing for arrowheads they had torn up and destroyed the entire site. Among their pits and piles of dirt we had seen broken mortars and river-rounded stones used for grinding corn, and many age-whitened periwinkle shells.

A few yards inside the cave, its ceiling sloped down to crawlway height. I had heard the passage continued for some hundreds of feet into two or three small rooms.

I was still talking when we turned into faster water. I heard the roar of rapids and looked ahead – Bucking Shoals! The wildest of the whole trip, and it was too late——

The first high bucking wave slapped into our bow, dumping several gallons of chilly water over my feet. Then another wave . . . another . . . and another as we careered down the long chute. We were too low in front!

Gallon on gallon of river came splashing in.

Now we were racing over many yards of mossy bedrock, the old Slick Rock Ford, smoother water but no place to land. We plunged into another series of waves, higher ones breaking over the bow with spray flying. I tried to duck——

"Don't lean!" Larry screamed. "We'll turn over!"

Larry worked desperately now, trying to to hold our half-swamped craft straight with the current. "Keep paddling! We gotta keep with it!"

Still another set of waves—and I could sense our precarious balance. If any one of us happened to lean, we'd all be dumped into fast, deep water.

Larry proved himself a good steersman. In a few more long seconds we were out, through the whole quarter-mile course, being carried into a quiet eddy. Now we were able to ease the canoe over the bank where Neil and Harry and the others were waiting.

I was in water to my ankles. Laurene, seated low between the thwarts, had gotten soaked again. The water-tight ammo boxes holding my cameras floated under my seat. Gingerly, we stepped out.

The Clarks had come through all right, and surprisingly, Joe's split canoe had taken only a little bit of water.

Everyone else wanted to know why we were so late, and of course we had plenty to tell them about the wreck and rescue.

Everybody helped us unload gear and then we flipped the canoe bottoms-up to empty it. As we began reloading, we took care to put the center of weight—and Laurene—farther astern.

Soon we got underway again, paddling down a tranquil pool under an archway of trees, moving toward a cliff that lay straight ahead, beyond the end of the hole. We were approaching Blue Bluff.

The cliff was named for the blue-gray cast of its sheer 70-foot face. Blue Bluff is set in the river itself; as we drifted through the deepest part of the pool along its base we looked up at solid massive stone bulging out almost directly over us.

In a moment we went speeding through a chute and into the wider channel below Red Bluff. Its hundred-foot cliff stood high above us on our left, a wall of deep rusty orange nearly cresting the ridge.

Red Bluff's color makes it a notable landmark of the middle Buffalo. Just as striking are two eroded stone knobs, like massive heads with misshapen noses, perched on the brink of its painted cliff. From their high vantage point the two stone heads seem to gaze impassively across the valley, past the river and Blue Bluff to the fields and woods and hills beyond.

It was now after four o'clock, and Gilbert was still about nine miles downstream, so we kept at our paddling.

Rounding the bend below the mouth of Mill Creek, for a minute we floated past the projected Gilbert Damsite. A fine sand beach lay opposite a high cliff, rising on our left. The Army Engineers had proposed that this bluff should be the northern anchorage for their dam, a structure which would obliterate all the miles of river we had seen these two days, and more besides.

Below the damsite, the hills seemed to move perceptibly closer, and I realized that from Woolum we had floated past the widest, most open portions of the Buffalo's bottom lands (a fact the Corps of Engineers had undoubtedly translated into acre-feet of reservoir storage). We had passed broad fields in crops and pasture laying within the river's bends, rich farm lands occasionally in view but usually hidden from us by trees and undergrowth along the banks. This had been a pastoral country, quite unlike the narrower valley both upstream and down.

We had seen few houses. Not many people live along the Buffalo, or even close enough to be within sight of the river. But nearly every landowner has cattle, and we often passed cows standing on the banks or even knee deep in the water. Always they would lift their heads and stare at us with placid curiosity.

A mile downstream from the damsite, cars speeded high above us, crossing the Buffalo on U. S. Highway 65. Several teen age boys leaned over the bridge railing, dropping rocks into the water.

"Where'd y'uns put in?"

Mount Hersey, we told them, and paddled on.

We still had four miles of paddling to Gilbert, around a sweeping horseshoe bend that doubled the straight line distance. And beginning the bend, we faced a short, steep rapids — white water, with waves like Bucking Shoals'. Would we make it, as heavily loaded as we were?

In a moment we plunged into the chute, racing past a picturesque bluff topped by pines . . . then hitting some of the highest waves. And in seconds we were through. With our load farther back, we'd stayed dry.

On around the horseshoe, I remembered that a bluff along the left bank had four or five good-sized cave openings begging to be investigated when Charlie McRaven and I had floated past a month before. There wasn't time then to take a look.

Now, as we approached the bluff again and I saw the caves, I thought again about exploring—but this time, alas, there was even less chance. The sun was nearly gone.

We paddled through the last rippling shoal, down the last stretch of quieter water to the long gravel bar at Gilbert. Then I was out, pulling the canoe ashore. Some of the others were already walking up to the village to get the cars.

The rest was anticlimax.

Soon we were going our separate ways home.

(opposite page)
The view downriver
from Red Bluff,
five miles upstream
from Highway 65

5 GILBERT TO STATE PARK

"CATCHIN' ANY FISH?"

"No, we're just floating."

We must have been asked that question a hundred times. Always by fishermen; they simply assumed that we were fishing, too. If we didn't happen to be fishing at the moment, then we must have been, or were going to.

While I'm convinced that canoes are stable enough to be good fishing craft, I've seldom seen canoeists fishing. Most of the canoe people float for other reasons, maybe to enjoy the scenery. Or to delve, here and there along the banks, into the river's botany and geology. Or maybe to go hell bent, thrilling in top speed and the wildest rapids.

Fishing, though, is as much a part of the Buffalo River story as anything else. Canoe floating 'arrived' just a few years ago, but float fishing by johnboat has been around—well, as long as johnboats has been around.

Much of the johnboat traffic on the Buffalo is now generated by the guided float business. Several guide services headquarter along the river, and most of the White River operators in the Bull Shoals-Cotter-Norfork area also run floats on the Buffalo.

The guide outfits can set you up on the river in a variety of ways. Some operators, for example, offer economy-class travel—you just rent the boat and paddles and have the man come pick you up at the end of your float. You provide everything else—fishing tackle, food, camping equipment and what not.

Next up the list is the one-day guided float, a 'package tour' including boat, motor, cushioned deck chairs, thermos jugs, ice boxes and soft drinks, also lunch if you want that furnished. Plus delivery to the put-in and from the take-out points. Plus the guide—and there you have an expert boatman and fisherman. If it's at all possible, he'll put you at the right places to catch 'em.

From that you graduate to overnight camping floats. For these the operator provides the usual boats and guides, plus camping equipment for the entire party.

All you need is your personal gear, and of course your fishing tackle.

Overnight outfitting also includes an experienced camp cook who runs the commissary, a johnboat almost barge-like in its capacity for carrying the party's food, duffel and camping equipment. The cook motors the commissary downriver ahead of the party, landing at some predetermined gravel bar to get lunch ready, or to have camp set up and the evening meal prepared when you arrive.

Weather and the river permitting, you can take a guided float trip any time of the year. The big 'season', though, begins in April, reaches its peak in May and June, and tapers off as the river gets low in the summer. If early fall rains come, floating may resume in September and October.

Jack Coursey of St. Joe is a float operator, a genial ex-Oklahoman who moved to the Buffalo and "became a hillbilly", as he puts it, after military service in World War II. One day in May I went floating with Jack, not to fish for fish, but to fish for information. I wanted to hear an expert.

Jack, his good natured red-headed guide Bennie Stills and I put in at Gilbert for a day's run down to Maumee. While Jack and Bennie and another guide unloaded the boat from an old army carryall, I stowed away notebooks and adjusted cameras.

Our johnboat was new and of lightweight fiberglas, but built in the time-tested style—narrow, flat-bottomed, square-ended. 'Narrow' meant only in relation to its length, which was a full 20 feet. Actually the boat was amply wide for the two canvas deck chairs Bennie set aboard. One chair went in the bow for Jack, the other amidships for me. I could fire cameras either at Jack or at Bennie in the stern, as they fished.

In a few minutes we had put all our gear aboard. Jack's driver promised to meet us at Maumee late in the afternoon. Jack and I took our seats and Bennie pushed us out into the river.

Bennie started the five-horse outboard and we bubbled downstream through the first shoal and beyond the village. Then, after cutting off the motor, he moved us toward the left bank with his paddle.

Both Jack and Bennie started fishing. Occasionally Bennie would lay down his rod and take a turn with the paddle to keep the boat straight. Then back to fishing. I checked camera settings, hoping to be ready when the big one hit the surface.

Jack was casting with a Hellbender, and before long he hooked one—which turned out to be a small rock bass, or goggle-eye as he called it. I thought Jack was going to throw it back. But he motioned for me to lift the cover of the live box, built into the bottom of the boat in front of my seat. He dropped the fish into the box.

"I'm keeping him because of an old superstition about throwing the first fish away," Jack told me. "We'll throw him back when we catch the next one——"

At that instant, Jack motioned for me to look over to the right shore. Along the low gravel bank overhung with willows, a muskrat was swimming. The animal disappeared under a willow stump.

"There's no way of predictin' what the fish want," Jack went on. "That's really what makes fishin' fun. It's kinda like gambling, you know."

"Oh, oh!"

Bennie's exclamation swung me around, camera raised. In a moment he hauled in another 8-inch goggle-eye, all so quickly I missed the picture.

Soon I noticed the right bank had become a 10-foot cliff of sandy earth, with tree sprouts on top tipping toward the river. The Buffalo was washing into an old field.

Jack had seen the river take away more than a hundred feet of that bank in the past fifteen years. The original channel curved along the base of the hill to our left. A low gravelly flat spread most of the way over to the eroding earth cliff on our right.

In the length of the Buffalo I knew of a dozen such places as this where the stream was cutting away deep topsoil. And now I remembered: Every one of them was along the edge of a cleared field.

Now from upstream came the low-pitched drone of outboard motors. I looked around. A heavily loaded johnboat with one man in the stern came into sight around the bend. Then a second boat. And a third. Three commissaries. We could expect a large party of fishermen to follow.

We'd fallen into a sort of routine . . . Jack casting, idly reeling in his lure, casting again as we slowly drifted down the pools, following the bank on the deep side . . . Bennie casting, reeling in, putting down the rod, paddling a moment . . .

Camera in hand, I watched first one man and then the other. At intervals Bennie started the motor to carry us through a shoal or shallows. Most of the time we just drifted, guided by Bennie's paddle.

The best fishing areas lay close by the banks which were lined with overhanging growth. Both Jack and Bennie skillfully worked the gaps and holes in the bushes, trying to set their lures within inches of shore. Occasionally one of them would misfire and tangle his plug in the shrubbery; then we would all paddle the boat around for position while he coaxed or jerked it loose. Perfect casting was impossible.

We floated into the Sand Hole, alongside a sheer 40-foot cliff with its footings in the pool. From the Sand Hole we drifted into the Red Bluff Hole, straight toward the high, irregular wall of Red Bluff. I saw that its largest face was only pale orange, much lighter than the rusty hue of the other Red Bluff above Highway 65. Here to the left were weathered towers of rock, gray except for sheltered areas which were a buff color. Along the top of the bluff was a scattering of pines.

Below the salmon-tinted cliff the river swung to the right, directly away from the bluff and through a rapids into a long, curving pool. I happened to look down over the gunwale. The river bottom here was solid rock.

Bennie cut off the motor. We drifted. They resumed casting.

Suddenly Bennie's rod twitched, bent toward the water; the reel whirred as line whipped out and upstream. "I got a smallmouth!"

Bennie reeled in nimbly. The brownie surfaced in a momentary fury of splashing, then headed for the bottom. A worried frown crossed Bennie's face; the fish might have gone under submerged brush.

No, the line was free. Bennie kept reeling it in, and then there was another furious splashing, closer to the boat. It was all over in a moment—three or four explosions as the bass jumped, fighting to get free from the thing pulling him, inexorably, out of his home.

Bennie grabbed the line close to the lure and hauled in the exhausted brownie. It wasn't large; maybe it weighed a pound. Bennie removed the hook.

I opened the live box. Bennie dropped the bass into the box—and the waterworks exploded again as I hastily dropped the cover. Then the brownie settled down, except once in awhile I heard an angry flop from inside the box.

Pound for pound, the smallmouth black bass—bronze bass or brownie as he's called—is one of the fightingest game fishes to be found anywhere.

The smallmouth bass favors clear, fast, cool water, and some say that water flowing over limestone is the best. Having big rocks on the bottom for the bass to hide under also helps. The Buffalo wins on all counts; sportsmen consider it a 'classic' smallmouth stream.[1]

We pulled in for lunch at the mouth of Tomahawk Creek, running crystal clear past the little gravel flat where we set up the grill and laid a fire.

The morning's catch made the main couse. Bennie cleaned the fish while Jack heated the skillet and fried potatoes. Then the potatoes came out, the fish went in, and in a few minutes the tantalizing aroma of browning fillets told us they were about ready.

Who can imagine anything better than a fillet of Buffalo River bass, a piece of fish so hot it's too hot to hold a bite in the mouth, too hot even to hold in the fingers . . . then cooling just enough . . . so tender inside and crunchy around the edges, so tasty with that finest delicate flavor of being freshly caught. Jack and Bennie both ate their fill, and there were a couple of pieces left. I finished them.

Through our entire lunch hour the guide boats kept passing. The country-boy guides and fishermen from the city all waved greetings.

[1]While the smallmouth is the most prized game fish in the Buffalo, anglers can also do battle with the largemouth black bass, locally called 'lineside' for the dark stripe down his flank. And the river has several other kinds of game fish: Spotted black or Kentucky bass. The courageous little rock bass (or goggle-eye or warmouth bass), Jack's and Bennie's first catches that morning. Green sunfish, which I learned were also called black perch, green perch, shade perch or bream. Bluegill sunfish (or bream or sun perch). And walleye, and channel catfish.

On the water again, we drifted into a still pool at the point of a sharp bend to the right. Along the base of the bluff, the river became dark green, very deep.

Here was one of the first 'step' or 'terrace' bluffs so often seen along the lower Buffalo. Instead of having one sheer face, this bluff was set up in layers. A vertical wall extended for the first twenty feet above the pool. On top of that rested fifteen feet of etched rock showing its horizontal strata. Above that was a ledge on which trees had taken a foothold. Above the ledge lay another band of rock.

The first terrace bluffs also signal the beginning of a rougher, more isolated country than that upstream . . . and so it would be from here to the mouth of the river.

We left the bluff behind. Now much of the river bank was a jungle, with sycamore and willow at water's edge, and river birch, silver maple and ash, all with a tangle of underbrush and vines. Willow fuzz floated in slow circles in the eddies. A kingfisher sat on a bare limb near the water. He flew off, turning to beeline across the river.

We drifted into a chute. Bennie started the motor to move clear of tree branches which dipped into the rushing water.

"Jack, why do trees always overhang these chutes?"

"That fast current washes the roots out."

I should have known.

At the next gravel bar the guided fishermen were having a late lunch. Beyond the row of boats, fishermen were lounging beneath awnings thrown up for protection from the sun. The cooks were just now bringing on the food, probably all that their guests could pack away and

Guided floating: Commissary

Roark Bluff below Ponca, Newton County

THE RIVER

At Gilbert damsite

50

*What's so unusual
  about the Buffalo?*

Why, it's a People river,
  often exciting
  but seldom dangerous
  for anyone, old or young.
And always fascinating.

Near Ponca

Fishing camp

Siesta

First bluff below Pruitt

It's a river
for all seasons.
Through the Spring
as pale-green leaves
unfold to become
the lush foliage
of Summer . . .

Waitin'

The Buffalo near Terrapin Branch, ten miles above Boxley

. . . and as the leaves turn gold in the days of Autumn,
   finally to be swept away, opening the vistas of Winter,
   the Buffalo always beckons . . . fascinating always.

The river has that feeling of wilderness—
   not real wilderness, but a sort of near-wilderness
   in its miles of woods, lonely farms, jungles along its banks,
   high bluffs atop the hills or rising from the stream itself.
No city spreads its blight,
   no industry pours its wastes into this river.

And the Buffalo is so strangely green, liquid green . . .
Oh, at times it's on a rampage, tearing at its banks,
   carrying a burden of silt, and then it is brown.
But the floods go quickly and the river turns green again.
Olive. Emerald. Jade. Crystal in the shallows,
   in the deeper places subtly shading into that lovely green.
Here is living water, ever changing in color and mood,
   carrying us swiftly, carrying us suspended . . .

At journey's end, we sprawl on a flood-washed sand bar.
A rhyme comes: The water's green, the sand is clean.
Silly, but good summary.

Craig Rosborough

October at Ponca

Red Bluff, between Woolum and Highway 65.   Blue Bluff is in view along the river upstream.

*Winter's
decorations*

The Narrows

Guided floating: Chicken in the skillet

then some. These float operators usually believed in feeding very well.

Bennie steered toward the right bank and eased the boat to a stop to let the current carry it down. And they fished.

As time passed, with little but the soft whip of line and whir of reel to punctuate the silence, my thoughts, and then my gaze, drifted. Two catalpas over on the left bank were clothed in white blossoms. On the river bottom, six feet under our boat, a turtle glided away . . . .

From a high dead snag there came a wheezing sound. Repeated. Again.

"Sounds like a flying squirrel," Jack said.

But, as we drifted a little farther downstream, a pileated woodpecker swooped down to the snag and popped into a hole. We now supposed the wheezing had come from young woodpeckers.

The woodpecker reappeared, large as a crow in silhouette against the snag. Then it flew away, giving its wild cackling *kuk-kuk-kuk-kuk-kuk-kuk-kuk* as it disappeared over the trees.

About this time we saw a snake ahead of us, swimming across the river. But it wasn't swimming in smooth, easy flow, trailing a silvery ripple like the other water snakes we had seen. No. This was a snake—but what odd, pitching, movements as it arched out of the water, almost turning pinwheels . . .

Or was it two snakes?

We drifted closer. It seemed to make no attempt to get away. Then we saw what had happened. A cottonmouth moccasin had caught a banded water snake nearly as large as itself. The moccasin had a bite-hold behind the victim's head and was hanging on, at the same time trying to swim to shore.

We floated to within six feet of the two snakes in the water. I was taking pictures——

Whap! Jack cut down on the moccasin with a paddle. The moccasin broke loose, writhing.

Whap!

The moccasin went limp, began to drift in the current. The water snake, still alive, went swimming cripple-fashion toward the bank, no doubt with a considerable pain in its neck.

For a while we followed, or were followed by, the dead moccasin floating down in the current. Fishing had been forgotten.

I asked Jack to tell me what he thought were the main attractions of float fishing. Perhaps the fisherman thought differently from, say the canoeist. But no . . .

In fact Jack's answers surprised me, for he played down the fishing angle. First, he said, the floater enjoys the beauty of the river, and the bluffs—the scenery in all its variety. This can really be more important than the fishing.

And the experience of camping is important. "The last two parties we had were business and professional men," Jack said. "Six of them, from St. Louis, spent four days camping at one spot—they didn't want to move on. And we had three more from Kansas City, two lawyers and a tax expert . . ." For these men, or anyone else from a city, camp life on a gravel bar is a different world.

"As for the fishing, I'd say it's important, but the least of the three lures of floating. Maybe it depends on a man's ability to catch fish . . . on his dedication."

I had heard a saying that ten percent of the fishermen catch ninety percent of the fish. And here were Jack and Bennie—I counted them among that top ten percent, but their catch today wasn't anything spectacular. I suspected a lot depended on how hungry the fish were. In other words, success all depended on the chance meeting of a good fisherman and hungry fish.

Jack had been trying everything in his tackle box. Now he was using an old wooden plug, a Lucky Thirteen. He said it was one of his favorites.

"Got a lineside!"

Bennie had the largemouth, and was playing it in. It swam alongside, and I could see the stripe along its flank. It surfaced for an instant, swam forward under the boat. Relentlessly, Bennie pulled it back. It splashed again, then hung on a taut line, seemingly exhausted. Bennie slackened—and the fish headed out again.

The tussle ended shortly as Bennie hauled back in, and the bass went into the live box. The largemouth was game, but that smallmouth was a far better scrapper.

Guided floating: Noon recess

Approaching Maumee

We rounded the last left-hand bend toward the point at Maumee and Jack's Lucky Thirteen began to produce. By this time the afternoon sun was low and bankside trees were throwing shadows across the river. I guessed the fishes were thinking about supper.

On our right the long terraced bluffs of the ridge toward Maumee reared up in the sunlight. Along the left bank, we floated in the shade.

We drifted into the Ezell Hole, as Jack called the pool rounding the point at Maumee. On reaching the point we saw Jack's man on the high left bank, waiting with the carryall to pull us up the boat slide.

Jack made one more cast, reeled in, and put the rod down. That would be all for today.

From the same Maumee boat slide where Jack and Bennie and I pulled out, I began another day's float down to Buffalo River State Park.

For that trip, Joe Mitchell—a Paducah, Kentucky, news-paperman—and I were outfitted by the park's boat con-

cessioner, Leon Dodd. I had asked Leon for a guide who knew local place names along the river, and he gave us one of the best men available. Troy Webb had lived around Maumee nearly all his life; he knew this part of the Buffalo 'by heart.'

After easing the big new wooden johnboat off the trailer and down the 30-foot incline into the river, we scrambled down with the rest of our gear—cameras, lunches, Joe's bucket of fresh shiners. Troy clamped the motor in place; then we were in and assuring Leon we'd reach the Park's landing about five o'clock.

Troy pulled the starter cord and we moved off, leaving Leon on the bank. "If we're not there, you come hunt for us," Troy called back.

Joe and Troy promptly started fishing. They shared the minnow bucket, which I periodically passed back and forth between them. I was also in their cross fire of shop-talk, mostly from Troy. Joe was quieter, tending to his fishing.

Troy, about his minnow: "I'm gonna hafta put me a

shot on him. He ain't goin' down too good."

Troy crimped a shot on his line and made his cast. Something still wasn't right. He reeled in, changed the minnow, moved the shot farther away from the hook. He made another cast. He seemed satisfied.

Joe Mitchell had come out in the cool morning wearing an old sport coat. Now the sun came out. Off came the coat.

Joe had fished mostly on the Tennessee River reservoirs near Paducah, and had only recently discovered and fallen in love with the Buffalo. Now he was experiencing the tanglesome problems of casting into its brushy banks. Before long, though, he was setting a few into the little breaks of the shoreline brush like an expert. Slowly he reeled in, twitching the minnow.

I watched a water snake come swimming out from the other shore toward the boat. It saw us and turned away. Downriver a bullfrog began to croak.

"Listen——" said Troy. "When them begins to holler, the fish begin to bite. Now, if we can only see some snakes . . ."

In spite of the good omens, fishing was a little slow at first. Again my eyes and thoughts turned to the ever-changing, ever-fascinating variety of things to see along the river, and on the terraced bluffs above . . . .

"Oh, what a beautiful place," Joe murmured to himself.

"And we're a-hurtin' when we go through here and don't catch one," Troy added, misinterpreting Joe's reference to the scenery.

Leaving the first long hole below Maumee, we motored through a shallow riffle to the right, then a sharp, swift sweep to the left . . . and into calm water again.

All at once Troy's rod bent and the reel went spinning; and Troy abruptly began reeling in. The fish appeared in an explosion of splashing and I knew that he had a smallmouth.

Several quick explosions later, Troy swung the brownie into full view. I was astonished to see how small it was, less than a pound.

Encouraged, Troy paddled a few yards farther down the Stepp Hole, as he called it, and dropped anchor. Now he and Joe went to work in earnest. Troy hooked another smallmouth, bigger splashing and a bigger fish than the first one. Then Joe connected, and his was larger still, about a pound and a half. Minutes passed.

"Hey, I've got somethin' a little different——"

Just by the 'feel' of this one taking the minnow, Troy knew that he didn't have a smallmouth. After a few

Putting in at Maumee

Playing 'im

minutes playing the reel against the struggling fish, he hauled in a largemouth, nearly two pounds.

For some minutes neither of them got a nibble. Troy pulled anchor, saying we'd run out of luck at that place.

And so the morning passed. We moved down the deep sides of the pools, occasionally anchoring at some promising spot. After they worked all the deep water within casting distance, Troy pulled anchor, started the motor to guide the boat down the next shoals, then cut off the motor as we entered the next pool . . . .

Midday was approaching and the fishing slowed down. We looked for a place to have lunch.

Reaching the mouth of Spring Creek, we found a shady little gravel bar bordering the creek, with a rapids just downstream and Spring Creek Bluff just beyond that for a scenic backdrop. We pulled in, carried the chairs into the shade and opened our sack lunches.

After a half hour at lunch we prepared to move on. Troy pushed us off toward midstream, started the motor and we moved into the fast water. This was a wonderfully long rapids, and with the outboard going wide open the banks went racing past. Even in this square-ended john-boat, I felt some of the thrill of speed.

But it wasn't canoeing. In this heavy boat we just couldn't be as much a part of the river itself. And in a rapids like this I could fully understand the canoeists' dislike of motors. Besides being so noisy, the outboard subtracted a lot from the intensely personal experience of running fast water. However, we had come not to paddle through rapids, but to fish . . . .

A mile below Spring Creek we settled down in a quiet stretch called Sutton Eddy. While Joe and Troy resumed casting, I walked the lengthy gravel bar to photograph them drifting below the terraced bluffs lining the far shore.

Joe had hooked something small; from a distance I couldn't tell what he had. "What is it?" I called.

"It's a warmouth perch."

"A what?"

"A warmouth perch—a shade perch," Joe answered.

That set me to thinking. Jack Coursey had called a rock bass a warmouth bass. And shade perch had been green sunfish, not warmouth anything. These popular names for fishes seemed to vary a lot from place to place, just as with the common names for plants.

There wasn't time to think any more—Joe had already

caught another perch, or whatever, and they had drifted downstream. I ran to catch up with them at the lower end of the bar.

From the shoals below Sutton Eddy we floated into the Jackpot Hole. 'Why the name 'Jackpot'?" I asked.

Troy replied it had come from the Jackpot Mine, old diggings for zinc on the hill at the lower end of the Jackpot Bluff. The bluff, on our left, was a series of isolated blocks and pinnacles projecting above the woods high on the hill. Past the bluff, Troy showed us the site of the Jackpot ore mill on the steep river bank. Save for a crumbling pier or two half-hidden in the bushes, every trace of the building had disappeared.

Soon we floated and fished into the Stairstep Hole, along beneath Stairstep Bluff, and past a small field on the other shore where Troy told us he had grown cotton in the early 1930's. Cattle, which we were often seeing along the river, had replaced cotton and the field was in pasture.

In rapid sequence we passed through Water Creek Shoal by the mouth of Water Creek coming down its narrow valley; then Kimbrell Hollow on the right and through Kimbrell Shoals. Beyond the Hollow we saw Kimbrell Bluff, first a 40-foot wall rising from the creek bank, then a series of terraces and bands of stone to the top of the ridge several hunded feet above the river.

Next was the Tie Chute Hole. The chute for crosstie logs had come off the ridge above the left bank. Now we found a steady current along that side, cool water in the shadow of the hill, and we drifted . . .

"Look out!"

I swung around—and saw Troy's rod bent down so it almost touched water. The fish headed upstream and we were rapidly drifting down. Troy played out line. With one hand he yanked the starter cord. Nothing happened.

He yanked again. The engine started—and stopped.

"Here," he muttered, thrusting the rod into my hand, "hold 'im while I crank——"

I grabbed at the wrong place; for two or three seconds my thumb stopped the reel from unwinding and the line stretched, tightened—and went slack. The fish was gone.

Troy forgave my clumsiness, but we both knew he'd lost the biggest smallmouth of the day, maybe of many days. I was still feeling regrets—and no doubt Troy was too— when we reached the Highway 14 bridge. We floated between great concrete pylons over 50 feet high, tall enough to let the biggest flood of record pass beneath the roadway. The bridge was built in the late 1950's to replace a ramshackle but picturesque wooden ferry.

Below the bridge were rapids turning left into a long chute with big waves, some of the most exciting water we'd seen today. Then we leveled off in an extended straight pool. Once more, Joe and Troy started casting.

"Have you got ary live minner?"

Joe looked in his bucket and saw three or four. I handed the bucket to Troy. They wouldn't go to waste.

For nearly half a mile we drifted, gradually moving toward a bluff in view beyond the far end of the pool. Eventually I realized where we were. Along the top of the ridge was the State Park's picnic ground.

Before long we were rounding the bend at Skull Rock, swinging into the gravel bar at the upper end of the park swimming hole. Leon Dodd was there waiting for us.

Troy's young son had come down to clean our fish. We stood around talking, finally comparing our respective plans for tomorrow. Joe was going to try the fishing on Crooked Creek. I had errands in Harrison.

"Troy, what about you?"

"I'm goin' back up to Tie Chute and try to catch that big 'un."

(Map on page 169)

STATE PARK TO WHITE RIVER 6

THE BOTTOM of their green canoe was dented and scarred, battered by many a scrape over the rocks. But what intrigued me was the name, painted on the bow in a strange alphabet. It looked Greek.

Tricia Otto, the college girl who owned the canoe, now approached. I asked her about its name.

"Yes, it's Greek," she replied. "It's pronounced *Atarexia.*"

"What does it mean?"

"Tranquillity."

Tricia and her partner Jo Rosenberg were among twenty-five canoeists who had just arrived at Buffalo River State Park from Wisconsin. Now we were making ready to embark on a float to Buffalo City on the White River.

I circulated among the people on the gravel bar, getting better acquainted. Harold and Joan Sipperly from Milwaukee had brought their children. Robin was ten years old and Bill was eight. Bill would be our youngest.

The next canoe had its name in large capital letters: DIGBY. I soon learned that it belonged to Jim and Margaret March, who were floating with their friends Harry and Win Kunze. This was the first real trip by canoe for any of them, and the ladies especially were professing great ignorance. Harry Kunze and Jim March, both well into their sixties, seemed to be relishing the new adventure.

The Kingsburys, Alan and Leilani, were the typical young couple on a budget, with a second-hand canoe, the only 15-foot one among our 17-footers. Leilani was teaching school while Al finished his master's degree at the University of Wisconsin.

Farther up the beach, slightly-built Werner Kappes was boarding his kayak, the first I'd ever seen on the Buffalo. I watched as Werner stepped into the cockpit, seated himself with legs straight forward inside the thin shell, adjusted the spray cover around his waist. He re-set his lighted pipe between his teeth, picked up his double-bladed paddle—and moved off at terrific speed, skimming across the pool like a big red water bug.

For all their diversity, these people now had a single topic for comment—the change in weather. Two mornings ago they had left Wisconsin in wet snow and chilling rain. But here this morning it was springtime, mid-April with trees coming into leaf, a pleasant sunny world with overtones of pale green.

Joe Mills, the fellow from Wisconsin who wrecked on the willows during our Mount Hersey-to-Gilbert float, had conceived the idea of this group trip. A year ago he had floated the Buffalo for the first time, for two days, but that wasn't enough . . . .

Later on, a mutual friend had given me Joe's address in Ripon, and in January he'd written me that he wanted

> . . . to get to know the river intimately . . . to live with it, learn its moods, and if possible develop a feeling for it. You can't accomplish this by canoeing a segment now, another portion later. The place to begin is up at the headwaters.

His hobby, he told me, was canoeing on scenic free-flowing streams—and helping to save the few that were left. Joe and I made arrangements to see the entire Buffalo.

Joe had given me no inkling of his age, and when he arrived I was surprised to find that he was white-haired and retired. He had recently sold his sizeable bees'-honey business, and at an age when many men settle in front of their television sets, Joe planned to get out and do more river-running than ever before.

Through the past week Joe and I had had—except for the wreck—a beautiful trip, all the way from Ponca to this gravel bar at the State Park. Now, in the canoe I borrowed from Neil Compton (Joe's was still laid up from the disaster), we would finish the river.

But Joe had wanted to share some of his experience. He had alerted his fellow canoeists in the John Muir

Departure

Chapter of the Sierra Club to the delights of the Buffalo. He and Don Scribner of Milwaukee, the Chapter's river touring chairman, had laid plans for this outing during the spring vacation from Wisconsin schools and colleges.[1]

Many of our people had already launched and were paddling around and waiting for the rest of us. I helped Joe finish loading. Then we tucked young Bill Sipperly among the baggage and climbed in ourselves. Joe pushed off and we were afloat.

Joe had made one other arrangement. On the river above Gilbert we had met Ben and Marion Ferrier, canoeists and outdoor writers from Minnesota, and Joe had invited them to join us on this float. Because the Ferriers were the only ones of us who had ever floated to the White River, they moved into the lead position. Joe and I would man the 'sweep' canoe, keeping to the rear.

How well everyone stayed together! Compared to our hang-back, run-ahead, scattered-out canoeists on the upper and middle Buffalo, this float was a marvel of organization. Where had I ever seen twelve canoes and a kayak on the river all at one time?

[1]The Sierra Club, founded in California by the Wisconsin-reared naturalist and writer John Muir, now has some 40,000 members in chapters from coast to coast. Since 1901 this famed conservation organization has been conducting club outings. The Muir Chapter's Buffalo River float was to be the first Sierra Club trip ever made in Arkansas.

It wasn't just organization, of course. Even the most adventurous were reluctant to dash past the Ferriers into an unknown river. And here, too, the Buffalo was wide enough to take us all without crowding . . . .

Soon we approached white water, a swift, deep channel to the left with foaming 'haystack' waves. Ben and Marion pulled over to a gravel bar upstream, and we all beached for instructions. We would run the rapids one canoe at a time while everyone else watched. The Kunzes and Marches would go last.

After two or three boats had swept through unscathed, Tricia and Jo approached the lip of the rapids, floated over—and with a wild whoop of delight plunged through the highest waves. Waaaahoo! Rapids are for joy——

Then we heard a loud bump, sounds of scraping as the girls' canoe momentarily stopped, shook loose, dragged over the rock and swept on. *Atarexia* now had another dent in its bottom.

Finally the Marches and the Kunzes came through, paddling with vigor if not precision, and clearing all the obstacles. Each of them appeared to be happy that it was over, successfully done.

Regrouping, we moved down the next long pool. Tricia and Jo had now become thoroughly indolent, paddling no harder than necessary, planting feet on the thwarts and the bow, one lying back to rest while the other propelled the canoe.

We passed the sun-bleached, rotting deck of the old Highway 14 ferry tilted against the left bank. A flood had brought it down here after the bridge was built.

Joe and I lagged some yards behind the crowd, observing bits of nature the others may have missed: A gray squirrel scampering from behind a log and into the bushes. A school of 10- and 12-inch bass swimming through the shallows near our canoe. A green heron which flew from the backwater to light on a willow root opposite us.

We had come about three miles now, and were gliding past a square fortress of rock a hundred feet high, rising above the trees to our left. Three hundred feet still higher, a series of battlements lay along the skyline, a chain of red-stained bluffs fifty to eighty feet in height, with pines along the top.

In another mile we were floating beneath a much more elaborate terraced cliff set back and stepped up to the crest of the ridge on our right. Four distinct walls of gray and buff streaked stone alternated with tree- and grass-covered slopes to form one of the most impressive of all the 'step' bluffs of the lower Buffalo.[2]

Tricia was now paddling sidesaddle, with her feet touching the water on one side of the canoe. Jo, with one foot on the bow and the other on the gunwale, was

reclining against a pillow and taking it easy.

Rush Creek flowed in at a shaded landing and picnic spot. I showed Joe the black opening of the abandoned Lonnie Boy Mine on the opposite bank of the river. We moved on, though, without stopping to explore. Gliding down the broad pool below Rush Creek, we heard another rapids. This would be Clabber Creek Shoals.

Well above the Shoals we moved close together for a conference. Ben and Marion thought we could all make it through the rapids; we'd just have to go one at a time and keep to the left. We would pull in to the beach downstream to wait for everyone to come through.

The mouth of Clabber Creek was a quiet estuary to our left. To the right, the Buffalo dropped away into

the shoals. Joe and I were next behind *Ataraxia*. The girls were approaching the top of the rapids . . . "Waaaa-hoo!"

Joe and I pulled ahead, toward the easier left-hand side. At that moment we glimpsed Tricia and Joe plunging into the highest waves, shouting again in glee. Waaaahoo!

—and we were on our way, racing down the shallow channel, suddenly turning left into a narrow deep chute —paddling furiously to avoid being pulled to the rocky right bank. The chute straightened out and we skimmed easily through the rest. In a minute we landed with the others.

Everyone, including the Kunzes and the Marches, came through without any upset. Clabber Creek Shoals would have been more exciting with less water; the narrow channel would have been constricted toward that rock-studded right shore.

From this point on the country would be noticeably lonely, deserted. We would not see much more of man's

²This bluff lies along the west side of a high narrow ridge which is at both beginning and end of a long, meandering bend of the river. From here the Buffalo would take a course roughly describing a duck's head, passing Rush and Clabber Creeks at the top of the skull, then Cedar and Boat Creeks at the tip of the bill, then flowing back to the far side of this ridge, only half a mile away from the beginning point but seven miles downstream.

Morning break

doings this side of the White River, twenty miles ahead. Hardly a soul lived on this reach of the Buffalo.

People did come down to the river to visit. We passed fishermen in homemade johnboats; inevitably they would ask "Havin' any luck?" A few of the float guides were out, too, taking their early-season guests fishing and sightseeing.

This was country with long ridges looking down on the river; rough, wooded hollows; occasionally an old clearing nearly concealed behind the trees and brush lining the banks. Like that country along the river below Ponca, it had the atmosphere of near-wilderness, though here at intervals we saw cattle, solitary cows or a few together, foraging for their living in the woods and abandoned fields.

We stopped at an expansive bar of gravel for a late lunch. After a half hour or so, we moved on again.

We paddled down a wide river with our backs to the warm afternoon sun, bathed in its bright flat light. I could see every one of our craft, dispersed from bank to bank and for an eighth mile ahead. In each boat, each person dreamed his own dreams under the spring sun.

Two turkey vultures lazily circled across the sky. Ahead, the paddlers kept a rhythmic, almost monotonous pace. Slowly the scenery glided past and behind us. There was little other movement.

The Buffalo began to turn due south, and we floated into the shadow of the high ridge on our right. The sun was moving farther west.

I thought it still early, though, when we saw the Ferriers drawn up on a gravel bar at the next bend, beginning to unload duffel, beckoning all to join them.

Joe and I pulled in and Ben called over to us. "We're

nearly half way, in easy reach of the White River tomorrow. This is a fine place for all of us to camp. One of the best down this way, in fact."

Ben was right. The bar was high and clean and of ample size, with a scenic view of a hill and bluffs across the river. We carried our things to campsites scattered for two hundred yards along the gravel. In five minutes I had put up my simple shelter, a plastic 'tube tent' just big enough for my sleeping bag, strung between two sycamore saplings. Most of the others were putting up tents of more elaborate sorts: pup tents, pyramid tents, igloo-like tents with outside frames. One fellow, though, dispensed with tents by hanging his hammock between the trees.

While we were talking about preferences in camping equipment, Tricia and Jo came along. They had quietly set up their camp at the upper end of the bar.

"You've gotta come and see our tent!" Tricia exclaimed. "It's seventeen feet long and aluminum."

They had spread their sleeping bags on the open ground and overturned *Atarexia* for shelter to keep the morning dew off their faces.

Happily for me, I had received several invitations to supper. Now while others began preparations for the meal, I was free to go a-wandering. First, I wanted to photograph dogwood in bloom. Along the edge of an overgrown field above camp, several sprays were hanging low enough for close-ups.

That accomplished, I strolled across the clearing and discovered a wagon track up through the woods. Following it, in two hundred yards I came to another, larger field. The road circled to the higher end, overlooking the river bend and hills on the far shore.

Here was another abandoned farm. A decrepit gate stood open to a barnyard full of weeds. The barn door stood open to a barn full of shadows, nothing more. Near the barn, tall persimmon sprouts grew among the teeth of a rusty hay rake.

I walked around the house, a nondescript place, tin-roofed, with a porch along the front. It was empty, slowly going to pieces. Where was the road out to civilization?

Beyond the house I found it . . . only a wagon track up the hill over the ledgerock.

Supper wasn't yet ready when I returned to camp, and across the river, members of our younger set had gone exploring, climbing up the hillside and out on the rocky abutments at treetop level. Already, fourteen-year-old David Royal had appeared atop one, standing with arms folded, commanding all with his glance. Jo and Tricia were heading up another.

Somebody gave the first call to supper. I ate mine on the run, making the rounds of the campsites to take pictures of the others having theirs.

The Kunzes and Marches had set their two canoes on the flat ground, one overturned for a table and the other right side up beside the first for a seat. I wondered what twists and strains their canoe-bench might be suffering—

Rapids are for joy!

Ben Ferrier telling his adventures

but seemingly none, and the four ocupants were certainly enjoying themselves.

As the twilight deepened, some of us gathered round one of the campfires where Ben Ferrier was relating his past adventures in canoeing. Only then did I begin to learn what extraordinary things he and Marion had done.

The Ferriers, I knew, had been floating the Buffalo each spring for the past several years. Now I discovered they were perpetual travelers, living most of the time in a trailer while Ben lectured and showed his movies on the far north and on survival in the wilderness, principally to audiences in high schools all over the United States.

In his younger days Ben had been an athletic coach, and a canoe guide in the Minnesota north woods. Later he struck out on canoeing expeditions into the wilds, helping pay for his adventures by writing about them.

Ben had floated on rivers whose very names inspired visions of the north: the Athabaska, the Saskatchewan, the Mackenzie flowing into the Arctic Ocean. He had run Gods River in northern Manitoba eleven times in heavy freight canoes carrying trade goods and furs. All over western Canada he had voyaged by canoe, on dozens of rivers, too many to even repeat their names.

And he had floated on rivers all across the United States, from the Eel in California to the White in Vermont, from the Rogue in Oregon to the Suwanee in Florida. In Iowa, where he had grown up and had once coached, he had run 22 rivers. In Missouri he had done the Current, the Meramec, the Big Piney. In Arkansas, the Mulberry, and of course the Buffalo.

"How did you get started canoeing?" Several of us wanted to know.

"When I was seven years old," Ben answered, "my mother and dad brought me down to Fayetteville, here in Arkansas, to see some relatives. During that visit we went for a float on the White River. That was fifty-five years ago, and I've been running rivers just about ever since."

Someone now asked Ben how the Buffalo compared with other rivers he had seen.

"Well, you know I've been on a lot of rivers in the United States, and Canada too. At least in the central United States, I'd say the Buffalo is the Number One river. From the Gulf to Canada, and from the Rockies to the Appalachians, the Buffalo is unique.

"These gravel bars are out of this world for camping. The bluffs are outstanding . . . This river's got more adventure to it than most of 'em—it's got shoals, and it's

Breakfast

wild, even yet. The country looks wild.

"And the water has beautiful color . . . that indescribable green color."

Marion, who had finished her supper dishes and joined us, wanted to speak. "Yes, the camping is ideal. No mosquitoes, no poisonous plants, no snakes on these gravel bars. And they're *clean* places to camp."

"How many rivers do we have in this country," Ben asked, "where we can float for days without having to go through towns? Or have to look around cultivated farms for campsites? *That* is unique about the Buffalo. You feel as if you're in the wilds."

Almost at that moment we were reminded that man could easily change the Buffalo's unspoiled setting. One of our group pointed into the darkness, across the river. "What's that light over there?" he asked. I turned to look.

It was a woods fire. It had been set, I knew, by some cattle owner who thought that burning off the leaves would let more grass grow for his cows. I'd been told such fires would be set all through these hills early in the spring.

The fire illuminated a break in the dark silhouette of the hills; it was coming down a ravine which opened on the river. Its light grew brighter. I was sure the fire was spreading only on the ground, but maybe a dead snag had caught . . . .

Probably it had been burning for hours before spreading this far. We had no tools for fighting fire; there seemed nothing we could do but watch. Several of our group did decide to paddle across for a closer view.

Before long we heard the chugging of an engine. Someone was bringing a piece of equipment down the ravine —a bulldozer, probably, for building a firebreak. I guessed it would be a crew from the Arkansas Forestry Commission. They bore most of the burden of keeping these woods fires in check.

Above the ravine the halo widened, became much redder. Now, at the mouth of the hollow, spots of fire appeared up the black bulk of the hill on the far side . . . a row of blazes being extended, one by one. Backfire.

As we watched, blaze joined blaze to form a line of fire creeping along the side of the hollow—fire to stalemate fire. The river approaches would be burned off before any night wind could carry sparks to the other shore.

Weird, lurid reflections played across the rippling black water in front of us. From the opposite bank came the thump of a paddle, a splash in the darkness. Our river-

crossers were coming back.

With them we gathered again around our own campfire. Several of us had asked Marion Ferrier to tell of her
experiences in canoeing with Ben. She drew a camp stool
into our circle and began her story.

Marion was teaching at the University of Wisconsin
when she married Ben. He took her off to the north
country their first summer, and she, a complete greenhorn
in the wilderness, had stuck it out. Their first trip was
into the Gods River country below Hudson Bay. She
learned how to cope with the wilderness as she went, and
she liked this new life and wanted more.

They made another trip to Hudson Bay. They canoed
together on half a hundred other rivers. And of course
she had traveled with Ben for more than twenty years on
his lecture tours.

Finally she related their recent adventure in canoeing
the canyons of the Rio Grande in the Big Bend country
of Texas. We listened enthralled as she took us on a trip
which began in a December heat wave and ended in numb-
ing cold and a freak snowstorm.

In coming down Santa Elena and Mariscal Canyons,
gorges a thousand feet deep along the Rio Grande border

with Mexico, they could not turn back. They came
through, the first canoeists ever to do so. But they advised
officials of Big Bend National Park, on the Texas side
of the river, not to let anyone else try. The water was
too rough, the risk too great.

Now it was late and the Sipperly children had gone off
to dreamland. We got to our feet and turned toward our
campsites and bed. Across the river the fire still flickered
and crackled in the darkness.

I woke up smelling smoke. A morning breeze brought
us a whiff of last night's fire.

When we shoved off after breakfast, the sun was shining
through a white cloud of smoke rising from the ridge
beyond the river. The backfire had spread over and out
of sight, joining and stopping the original blaze. But
for miles in the woods down the right bank, nearly all
the way to Big Creek, we saw blackened ground, dead
stumps smoldering and smoking.

Now we met several local people on the river; they
had come down a primitive road to put in at the mouth
of Big Creek. Most of them were fishing.

Beyond Big Creek we paddled along pools nearly two

hundred feet wide, now that the river was approaching its end. Below each pool, though, the rapids were narrow and swift, giving us a good run.

One channel between pools was long and deep, hardly twenty feet wide, a shady green canal rippling along beneath a low archway of trees . . . and the morning sun highlighting the limbs and young leaves laced overhead. Here, for a few passing moments, was rare delight.

We remained together. Jo and Tricia had begun to sing—

Michael, row the boat ashore
Hal-le-lu-jah . . .

From behind us came a burst of wild chortling—a pileated woodpecker. I turned to see it. The bird was somewhere beyond the trees——

Sister, help to trim the sail
Hal-le-lu-jah . . .

Something was moving in the water by the left bank—splashing, splashing, splashing in rhythm. We looked closely. It was only a stick hanging down into the water, bending under with the current, snapping back, bending under again . . .

River Jordan is chilly and cold
Hal-le-lu-jah
Chills the body but not the soul
Hal-le-lu-jah

Two miles below Big Creek. A curious thumb of rock on the right-hand ridge. It stood even above the tree-tops. Why was it there?

River Jordan is deep and wide
Hal-le-lu-jah
Milk and honey on the other side.
Hal-le-luuu-jah.

We pulled in to another gravel bar for the morning break. Some had put up thermos bottles of coffee at breakfast; these were now brought out and the contents enjoyed. There was the usual chatter of conversation, and treks to the woods. Tricia and Jo had gone in swimming.

I found Margaret March walking around the gravel bar alone, picking up pebbles. She thought they were pretty, some of them. Searching for a moment, I located a rock that was honeycombed with fossil crinoid fragments—not at all uncommon in this chert gravel. But Margaret hadn't seen this before, and she was fascinated. Fossils, right here on a gravel bar!

I cracked the rock on another one, exposing sharper, cleaner fossil imprints in the broken faces. I showed these to Margaret.

For her this was all new discovery. Through the remaining minutes of the break (and part of the lunch hour as well) I saw her strolling about, picking up rocks, cracking them, carefully studying each piece.

The swimmers climbed back into *Atarexia* and we were again underway. I noticed that the younger members of our crowd were swimming even while the older folks kept wearing jackets and long sleeve shirts. Tricia and Jo and Dave Royal and Joe Grajek and the Kingsburys had all taken to the water. The sun was warm, but to me this mid-April river felt a mite chilly. Maybe they were used to colder northern waters . . . .

Tricia, Jo, and Dave who had hitched a ride with them, were quietly slipping up behind Werner in his kayak. We watched——

With quick flips of their paddle blades, they showered him, drenched him with water—and he scurried away out of reach.

The water fight was on. Werner bided his time, waiting his move, then came swooping in, nimbly swinging his double-blade paddle, giving all three of them a good dousing. Skimming away out of danger, he moved faster than any canoe . . .

We all had a laugh, and by lunch time the battlers had pretty well dried out. Werner did complain a little; they'd drowned his pipe.

We had come to Cow Creek, and the river turned to the right into Cow Creek Shoals. In the girls went—Waaaahoo!

Two hundred yards downstream we floated past the Elephant Head, a massive bluff rising on our right. The

Battle

elephant's trunk, a heavy column of rock almost separated from the cliff behind it, hung from the main bulk of the head just above. Two dark spots on the head were the eyes.

Beyond the Elephant Head we ran another rapids called Jumping Shoals. Joe remarked that most of the Buffalo, though, was quieter water than the small swift rivers he and the other Muir canoeists had been running in Wisconsin. The big advantage here was in the quality of wildness. So many of the Wisconsin streams were lined with resorts and summer cottages.

Not far below Cow Creek we stopped for a leisurely lunch in the bright warm sun. After we ate, the children sprawled on a patch of sand and built crumbly castles. The grownups sat and talked, or lay back and dozed.

No one much wanted to leave. But we had been discussing the next few days of floating, from Mount Hersey to Gilbert, and that meant we should shuttle cars tonight. Eventually some of us talked the loungers into getting started again, to keep us all on schedule.

For the first time I would see these last miles to the White, and complete all 123 miles of the Buffalo float stream. Joe, too, would soon fulfill his desire to canoe the entire river.

What would these last miles be like? I had wondered, and imagined the valley becoming wider, with no river bluffs at all. I guessed wrong. Even here, high bluffs fronted the river bends . . . one such bluff, I now recalled, would be at Lone Rock Damsite, 3.6 miles above the White. Lone Rock Dam is another Corps of Engineers proposal, one that would have a fluctuating impoundment backed up all the way to their Gilbert Damsite near Highway 65.

The greatest change in the river appeared to be in the size of the stream itself, in the broad pools where we could spread out in loose formation from bank to bank. With the greater length of the pools, of course there were fewer rapids. And now, at last, the rapids had become deep. We passed a fisherman who had motored upstream from the White; the likes of that would have been impossible on the upper or middle Buffalo.

Within the river bends there had been open bottoms, but now, in the last mile or two, the ridges ahead were closing in . . .

The Buffalo was proving itself beautiful, full of life and interest all the way to its end. The water was as clear in the shallows, as incomparably green in its depths as it ever was upstream.

On the left, a little creek flowed down its bed of solid rock to the river. Up the hill, woods coming into leaf stood before the westward-moving sun, their pale greens glowing in the backlight.

Between the hills ahead we saw a low sandbar island. We followed the Ferriers toward the left bank, toward

Noon break

deeper water along the base of the hill.

Suddenly Ben and Marion disappeared around a sharp bend. In a minute Joe and I rounded the same corner, and I saw we'd reached the White River.

Ben motioned us all into closer formation, and called back that we should follow them up the left bank to avoid the main current of the White. We moved up together and dug in with our paddles.

I felt a slight chill. Absently, I stopped paddling a moment and dipped one hand in the river. Cold! And I

remembered. We were on water released from the bottom of Bull Shoals Reservoir. Trout water. Great fishing, but Lord help anybody who falls in.

We had to paddle harder, for we were catching some of the current. The work lasted only a few minutes, however, for half a mile or less until we pulled across the White to Buffalo City landing . . . .

Now we were pulling out on the muddy beach, walking up to back the cars down to load . . .

And with that, we began talking again about tomorrow.

Iceledo:
Ruins of the Ward cabin
and (left)
the John Hill place

The Land

1 HEADWATERS COUNTRY

THE LITTLE WOODEN SIGN by the gate simply said "Elevation 2578 ft." There was nothing more to show that it stood on the highest point in the Ozarks. Closing the gate behind me, I looked up again.

From four heavy foundation blocks the spidery steelwork of Buffalo Fire Tower tapered a hundred feet skyward to the lookout's cab. Within the tower's open frame a steep stairway went zigzagging up, flight upon flight, landing to landing. I began to climb.

That afternoon the wind was sweeping over the mountains from the south, bringing rain squalls across the eastern sky, with dark clouds and white mingling in vast, ever-changing pageantry. At the first landing above the treetops, I paused.

I had come again to the tower, very near the beginning of the Buffalo, very near the end of my wanderings along the river. I had been traveling by car and canoe and on foot since January, and this was May. In these months past, I had gathered material for a book, a scenic inventory of the Buffalo River and its watershed. My notebooks and photo files were now well filled, and the country had become as familiar as home. But while standing there on the landing facing the balmy rush of the south wind, I was taken by doubt and uneasiness. Maybe my collection of facts would not yield room for the poetry . . . .

Below me and beyond, the sea of trees rippled under the sweep of the wind. Northward-moving clouds shadowed the waving foliage in deep green. A moment later the sun returned, and the sea became vibrantly green-and-gold. I began to climb again.

Now I could trace the furrow of the ravine lying a half mile west where I had found the Buffalo's tiny headstream trickling from under the fallen leaves. From the tower road the hollow ran south, joining other hollows and becoming the valley of Bear Creek. This, the longest of three major forks at the river's headwaters, was labeled 'Main Prong Big Buffalo Creek' on an old Forest Service map.

I reached the last landing, close below the padlocked door of the cab. The rippling green sea stretched away from under the tower, gradually becoming blue-green in the distance, then a series of ridges in paler and hazier shades of blue to the nearly flat horizon. Here were the Boston Mountains: a high plateau, many deep wooded valleys, a few isolated hills or knobs rising above the general level of the ridges. And Buffalo Knob, beneath the tower, a little higher than all the rest.

Starting down, I paused to look once again. Beyond the nearer ridges to the south, Bear Creek and the other two tributaries would become Big Buffalo Creek. Within some miles the creek would become the Buffalo River, turning northward in an ever-deepening valley.

To the east, before it became lost among the hills, I could see a small portion of the Buffalo's canyon, and I remembered . . .

I had first visited the headwaters canyon with Dexter Curtis of the cafe at Ponca. Deck had grown up in that neighborhood east of Fallsville, and he had promised to show me the Buffalo he had known as a boy. So one winter morning we picked up Troy Fowler, a Boxley cattleman who also had known the country since boyhood, and drove down to the river from the mountain west of Edwards Junction.

We went lurching and bucking down an old wagon grade in Deck's jeep, with tree limbs scraping and slapping the side curtains. Troy was sitting in front with Deck, and I hung on as best I could to the cushion that served as a back seat.

The road switched back on itself. Deck wheeled sharply and seemed certain to plunge off the outer bank, but stopped just in time, roared back until we crunched into the upper embankment, cut the wheels to the right again and moved ahead down the hill. I was still thinking about this little maneuver when we reached bottom and rolled out into an old pasture planted with pine seedlings. Deck steered the jeep among the pines and stopped.

Headwaters country from the Buffalo Fire Tower

"Now," he announced, "this is the Sherman Reed place."

We followed him over to the edge of the clearing. A creek babbled somewhere nearby. Suddenly I realized we had come on the ruins of the homestead. The first tumble-down pile had been a log barn; the next, a chicken house. Beyond these I saw the main dwelling, now only a mound of decaying logs and split shingles with a heap of chimney stones at one end. Beyond the house was a smokehouse, still standing but also near collapse.

Deck and Troy picked over the debris, finding and reminiscing about an old wagon wheel hub, a rusty plow point, a bit of iron scrap from some other farm implement. I strolled around to get the lay of things. The house had had a fenced yard, with flowering shrubs and even a walk of flat stones up to the front porch. It faced a lane along the creek.

"That's Terrapin Branch," Deck called to me. "Only we named it Devil's Den Canyon up the hollow there. It really gets rough up there . . .

"Hey, come and look what I found."

He had pulled a weathered relic of a wooden armchair from the smokehouse. It had been long used, broken and tied together with wire.

"Now, ol' man Sherman Reed used to sit up on the porch in this chair. Many's the time I've walked by out there"—Deck motioned to the lane beyond the front fence—"and he'd be sittin' in this chair. 'Come on up, boy, and rest a while,' he'd say. And I usually would."

Tenderly, Deck replaced the chair in the smokehouse. We walked back to the jeep.

The pasture ended at the tree-lined bank of the Buffalo. Down the slope we went, with Deck gunning the engine, roaring through the river and up the other slippery embankment, leaving a great muddy wave behind us. The Buffalo here was a fair sized creek.

We stopped again. Back across the river I spotted the mouth of Terrapin Branch. Deck was telling us this homestead had been owned by Sherman and Freeland Marshall, father and son.

There wasn't much left. The frame house was gone except for a decaying hand hewn sill beam lying on the ground. Troy paced its length, thirty-four feet.

The tall rock chimney was still there, its base now entwined with a rambler rosebush. Deck and Troy peered into the fireplace, commenting on a rats' nest up inside the flue. I noticed the chimney top was beginning to come apart.

Had people farmed these little clearings—made a living

The Marshalls' chimney . . .

here on only five acres for a big family?

Not entirely. They'd had gardens, maybe field crops in the flat along the river. But their cattle and hogs had roamed the wooded hills for miles around, living off the land. Some years the menfolk cut timber, maybe at first on their own acreage, then hiring out to work on tracts belonging to lumber companies.

Again we forded the river to another homestead, the Searl Collins place. It had a larger, longer clearing, also planted in pine. And a log barn, falling in. And a log house, still with roof. The house consisted of one big room plus a one-room lean-to in back. There must have been an attic or sleeping loft above the main room, but the ceiling had vanished. Deck told me the family had several children.

"When did these people leave?" I asked him.

"About . . . well, in the late 1930's," he answered. "They all sold out to the Forest Service about twenty-six or -eight years ago."

"So these places have gone down in that time," I said, thinking aloud. I was amazed at how fast the buildings were decaying. In another thirty years there would be nothing but piles of chimney stones.

Downriver, the hills moved in even closer to the Buffalo.

So they'd sold out to the Ozark National Forest and now their fields were in seedling pines.

The Ozark National Forest, I knew, dated back to President Theodore Roosevelt, who reserved it from the public domain in 1908.

Public domain?

Land that no homesteader would take. The roughest, poorest ground. Acreage with most of its virgin timber stolen, then repeatedly burned over to encourage pasture for free-roaming livestock. Public land already well worked over for private gain.

In the early years of the National Forest, management was pretty sketchy, and people resented even the few controls that were attempted. Old abuses continued. But change was on its way.

Change was coming because people like the Reeds and Marshalls and Collinses were reaching the end of their resources. After a wave of in-migration and settlement before 1900, the land became overpopulated. Every bench and hollow had its families of homesteaders eking out their living on a few sloping acres. The soil was going, the timber was going, sons and daughters were growing up with no new land available. People had to get out.

From 1900 to 1940 the population loss was gradual, mostly a siphoning off of the restless and homeless. Some came back from the cities during the 1930's depression. But with World War II there began a massive exodus from these hills. Caught between diminishing resources at home and rising desires for a better way of life, whole families and even entire communities picked up and left. And finding few other buyers for their depleted land, the emigrants usually sold to the Forest Service. From the 1930's onward the Service acquired hundreds of old homesteads and tracts of cut over woodland to fill in around its original holdings.

People are still leaving, but the population trend is toward stability. Private holdings now within the Forest are often those best lands which yet produce a living—crops, cattle or timber—for their owners. Selling land to the Forest is a voluntary thing, and inholders nowadays are more disposed and able to hang on to their acres. So the National Forest is becoming stable, too, in terms

and the Collinses' cabin

of area owned within its authorized boundaries.

Today the Ozark National Forest includes the first sixteen miles of the Buffalo below its source as well as 70 percent of the land in the headwaters region.[1] Management of the Forest affects the entire upper watershed. Because of this, I arranged to see and hear first-hand what the foresters were doing.

My guides were to be Jim Hughes, forest ranger for the Pleasant Hill District which includes the Buffalo headwaters, and Bob Jackson, Jim's assistant ranger. One cloudy morning in May, we climbed into their pickup truck for an all day tour of the headwaters country. Bob drove us out Highway 16 from Fallsville, then turned north onto a dirt track with a Forest Service sign: Dixon Road.

Soon Bob stopped the truck. Already we had passed several old fields in seedling pines like those I had seen

[1]And to the east, the Forest also includes the headwaters of several major tributaries—the Little Buffalo River, Big Creek, Cave Creek and Richland Creek. All together, National Forest lands comprise about an eighth of the total area of the Buffalo watershed.

with Deck and Troy. Now Jim pointed to three or four broken and hollow oaks which had been deadened with a beaver girdler, a machine which chews a groove through the bark around each tree. Pines had been planted among the dead oaks. It was part of a widespread program of 'timber conversion' to replace slow-growing scrub hardwoods on dry south and west slopes with faster-growing pines that would yield larger financial returns.

"Girdling is OK for the big trees," Jim commented, "but it can't compete with chemical injection on smaller stuff."

"What poison do you use for injection?"

"We use 2,4-D. It's actually not a poison like the insecticides; it's a growth stimulant. Trees that are injected just sort of burn themselves out in a sudden spurt of growth."

Nearly four hundred acres along Dixon Road had been converted to pine. The hardwoods were killed three years ago; pine seeds planted two years ago. Seedlings were just beginning to show above the grass. Several cows were grazing among the pines.

"There's another problem," Jim said. "Cattle and hogs. These cows will kill some of these young pines, trample them and pull them up. Hogs are worse; they'll root up anything that's planted."

The old tradition of open range was coming in direct conflict with the new forest management. Jim emphasized that these young pines would be the future livelihood of local timber workers, and it would be to their advantage for everyone to keep hogs out of the forest, and at least control the numbers of cattle. The Forest Service was moving toward requiring it. I imagined such restrictions would not be universally welcomed.

We continued down a long hill toward the Buffalo. The Forest Service had bulldozed this narrow road the year before, partly along old wagon ways. Bob explained that truck trails were being built to provide access for Forest employees and timber operators, and for hunters. "When we build roads now," he added, "we have the 'dozers scoop out a few small water holes for wildlife, along these dry ridges."

Then we forded the Buffalo. The stream was up a little from recent rains, and slightly cloudy in color.

"You know," said Bob, "most of the muddy water in these streams comes from roads. When they were rebuilding Highway 16, you could really tell the difference down here."

"What about logging tearing up things along the river?" I asked.

"We don't allow clear cutting of trees within two hundred feet of any major stream," Jim answered. "We require loggers to cut only the trees we select, and to disturb the ground as little as possible.

"Now we're planting pine in old field gullies and along abandoned roads. That should help to keep these streams clear, too."

We drove up another long, winding hill from the river, following a ridge overlooking the wooded valley of Nuckles Creek. Presently we came onto a gentle open slope with a southern exposure. Through more deadened scrub oak, I glimpsed the Buffalo Tower a couple of miles to our left.

"This is the Valley Grove spray area," Bob explained. "We sprayed this last June—nearly a year ago. In this case we used 2,4,5-T, another growth stimulant, and put it on with a helicopter. We covered 664 acres."

We stopped and got out to walk across an old clearing that had grown up in brush, field pine and scrub hardwoods. Spraying had killed nearly all the broad-leafed trees and bushes, but the pines seemed unharmed. The slender pine needles had not absorbed a lethal dose.

Grass was also immune to the spray, and with the overhead foliage knocked out, it had literally gained a place in the sun. Both Jim and Bob were pleased to find a heavy stand of good native grasses crowding out the coarse broomsedge which usually takes over uncultivated clearings in the Ozarks.

Suddenly there was a chorus of howls, wailing from down in Nuckles Creek. Then silence. "Must be a couple of coyotes after something," Jim commented.

Farther up the road we stopped again. A hillside beneath the deadened oaks was brightened with bunches of pink and white phlox. "Unfortunately we do kill some of the flowering shrubs—dogwood and redbud," said Jim. "We're hoping, though, that dogwood can recover; we've already seen some sprouting from the roots of old stock. But we don't spray near public roads because people enjoy seeing these in bloom."

I wondered what effect these sprays might have on animals, on cattle and wildlife. Jim and Bob had not heard of any.[2]

A more immediate problem was that the cost of labor for girdling, injection and planting pine seedlings had been steadily increasing. The Forest Service felt forced to mechanize, to spray by helicopter and to broadcast seed from the air or with a cyclone seeder. Surveying, aerial spraying and seeding the Valley Grove area, for example, was costing less than half that of doing it by hand. Even with that, converting the area to pine would run around twenty dollars an acre.

Aerial spraying had its limitations, too. The sprays were death on crops such as corn, so they could not be used within half a mile of any farm. And of course the chemicals could be harmful to man, so they had to be handled with considerable care.

On the Buffalo headwaters, timber conversion was already underway on some 2,000 acres, and in ten years or so the foresters hoped to have about 10,000 acres of old scrub hardwood lands in pine. By that time, much of the land favorable for pine would be converted.

We had turned eastward on another road, along a moist north slope that would remain in hardwood. Here a crew had been doing 'timber stand improvement', girdling trees of low commercial value such as elm and ironwood, and crooked and hollow ones including many beeches. In a few years these would decay and fall down; the idea was that eventually their space and sunlight would be taken by trees of better quality.

So much of this government forestry took the form of investment for the long, long run—much farther into the future than I as an individual would ever plan my own life, farther even than large corporations can plan. But then it would take a long pull to bring this forest, so much over-cut and abused in the past, back to its productive prime.

[2]In *Silent Spring*, Rachel Carson cites ways that these chemicals, particularly 2,4-D, might endanger the lives of cattle, birds and deer. More obviously, hardwood spraying alters the animals' food supply. Acorns are eliminated, grass increases. After the pines grow tall they shade out the grass.

Jim Hughes talked about this. "In time we hope to create tree stands of even age—every mature tree about the same age—so we can harvest in blocks or units of at least twenty acres. Already we're taking out older trees to leave younger ones more nearly the same age. It'll be a hundred years, though, before the Ozark National Forest will be operating under an even-age system. Up here in these hills, it takes that long for a tree to reach maturity.

"Right now we have a good many stands of trees thirty to thirty-five years old. These are on land that was clear-cut and sold to the Forest in the 1930's. Someday these young trees will be fine timber—but it will be fifty to seventy years from now."

We had lurched through mudholes and scraped high center and come to the road's dead end on the mountain side. Leaving the truck, we hiked down through the woods toward our final goal of the day's tour, a proposed Forest Service scenic preserve on the Buffalo.

About three hundred yards below the truck we came out on top of a chain of bluffs along a side hollow of the river. Then, when we were almost upon them, we saw the waterfalls. A small creek poured over the bluff to a shelf, ran down a few feet and dropped again.

The lower fall spilled into a pool before a dark grotto below the overhanging shelf, and the deep ravine was filled with foliage almost tropically lush and green, an effect now heightened by the darkening storm clouds. The stream disappeared under the giant leaf clusters and white blossoms of an umbrella magnolia, but I could hear it rushing on its way to the Buffalo.

We moved farther along the bluff to a viewpoint overlooking the river. The narrow valley bottom and the steep hills beyond were clothed in dense, unbroken woods, a jungle of trees hiding the river except for one short segment of rapids, just enough to prove the Buffalo was there. I saw not one sign of man's activity in the whole wild panorama.

I pulled out my map, and on it Bob drew the tentative boundaries of the scenic preserve. It would have about 625 acres, including old growth timber along one and a half miles of the Buffalo, plus the side hollow with the waterfalls, plus the watershed of one more small tributary. Development plans called for improving the road down to where we had stopped, a picnic area near the viewpoint on the bluff, and a trail into the canyon and along the river.

"But," Jim added, "we're talking about recreation de-devolpment only in our long range plans, ten years or more ahead. The important thing now is to locate these natural beauty areas and protect them for the future."

At that moment the crack and rumble of thunder sent us running to the truck; we would explore no more that day. However, from my map I had learned one other

In the scenic area

81

thing. Just out of sight, at the downstream end of this scenic area for the future, lay those three relics of the past, the abandoned homesteads at Terrapin Branch.

Below Terrapin Branch the Buffalo flows through wild, rough country for six or seven miles until the valley widens, land is cleared, and the river nears Highway 21 above Boxley. From there northward to Ponca, the Buffalo valley presents a pastoral scene, quietly beautiful.

Wooded hills flank a narrow bottom land given over to pasture; farther back on each side are the higher ridges of the valley rim, often capped with long bluff chains. The river here is a wide shallow creek brawling down its bed of cobbles between tree-shaded banks, small enough to nearly disappear in drouth, large enough to become an un-fordable torrent in flood.

The community of Boxley consists of a steam sawmill and a country store, a rural postal station, a well-kept church and cemetery next to an empty schoolhouse, and several miles of neighboring farms along the valley. White frame houses stand beside the road, and despite television and other latter-day distractions, people still sit in creaking swings on front porches and let time and the world go by. In other words, the settlement has a definite flavor of the past.

Pioneers first arrived in the valley in the 1820's, followed by many more in the 1830's and 40's. Straight up the river they came, riding in high-wheeled wagons pulled by massive oxen, fording the river at each bend, breaking and trampling through the cane brakes which covered the alluvial bottoms.

Most often they came from Tennessee and North Carolina. The great majority of these people were moving from worn out land in the southern Appalachians; they had come looking for a fresh start in the Ozarks. Soon the cane fields became plowed fields, and the first families of the valley lived well off the virgin land.[3]

By 1850 the settlement had grown large enough to support a grist mill on the stream from the big spring just north of Boxley. Samuel Whiteley's water mill served as a neighborhood center, and soon the community was being called Whiteley, or Whiteley's Mills (the name Boxley came later, in the 1880's).

While this country didn't figure importantly in the Civil War, troops and partisans of both sides roamed through the region, and Union and Confederate forces met in a brief skirmish near Whiteley's Mills in April 1864. Most of the fighting took place near the present junction of Highways 21 and 43.

The valley's most unusual Civil War story centers around Bat (or Saltpeter) Cave, on Cave Mountain a mile south of Boxley. There in 1862 the Confederates began mining nitrogen-rich earth from the cave floor and extracting potassium nitrate or saltpeter from it for making gunpowder.

Workmen hauled cave earth out to daylight and dumped it into wooden leaching vats, and water was added to dissolve the nitrate. The solution was drawn off, boiled, and run through wood ashes, then boiled again in large kettles. As the water evaporated, crystals of saltpeter formed in the kettles. The saltpeter was collected and taken away in wagons, over the mountains to the Arkansas River for shipment to arsenals of the Confederacy.

Soon the Union Army heard of this enterprise. On January 9, 1863, a detachment of the First Regiment, Iowa Cavalry, numbering three hundred officers and men, set out from Huntsville for the Buffalo River. Joseph W. Caldwell, commander, later reported

> At 4 o'clock on the following morning [January 10] I had the column in motion, and by daylight reached the saltpeter works on Buffalo River . . . where I completely

[3]The local creeks bear the names of some of these early families: Arrington, Clark, Edgmon, Whiteley. But the most prevalent name in the valley is Villines, pronounced vil-LINES. Five or six Villines families, possibly of French Huguenot extraction, came here from North Carolina and Virginia before 1850. Today, among their greatly increased numbers, one finds Villines neighbors who realize they stem from a common ancestor in the dim past, but who are unable to explain how they are related.

surprised the small force there employed, and captured 17 of 20; the lieutenant in charge and 2 men engaged at work in the timber a short distance from the buildings, succeeded in making good their escape.

The buildings, 14 in number, very extensive, entirely new and of good workmanship, together with two steam engines, three boilers, seven large iron kettles, weighing, according to the bill for the same, 800 pounds each, besides a half-ton of saltpeter, a large fire-proof iron safe (Hall's patent), three Concord wagons, two carts were completely destroyed by fire or otherwise.

That ended the Confederate saltpeter operation.

After the War the natives commenced a piecemeal removal of anything salvageable. The broken steam engines, the boilers and the iron safe all disappeared. As for the kettles, it turned out that they were only broken along the rims—they could still hold plenty of water. Soon the local farmers were setting them in springs for watering troughs, and in back yards for boiling clothes on wash days. One fellow put his in the barnyard for scalding hogs at butchering time.

In 1959, after reading about the seven saltpeter kettles in Walter Lackey's *History of Newton County,* and hearing that several were still in the valley around Boxley, I became curious. Would I be able to find all seven, nearly a century after they were last inventoried in a Union Army officer's report?

The first one, at the Bill Duty place a mile north of Boxley, was a big black cauldron four feet eight inches in diameter and nearly two feet deep. The next four, none difficult to find after I had asked people along the valley, were of varying shapes and sizes, the largest being six feet across. But after locating the fifth kettle I ran out of clues.

My young companion, Gene Primrose of Ponca, then recalled that an elderly neighbor had a broken kettle, though it was smaller than the ones we had seen. But sure enough, the wash pot in Susie Villines' back yard had come from Saltpeter Cave. Mrs. Villines also put us on the trail of Kettle Number 7, which belonged to her cousin Dewey Clark on the Crossroads Mountain.

Mr. Clark's home stood on the ridge at the head of Whiteley Creek, almost overlooking Boxley. His family had moved up from the valley about 1915, bringing the kettle with them. Since that time it had served as a rain barrel under a corner of the house roof.

I felt a bit smug after photographing Dewey Clark with his rain barrel. Seven kettles, the commander had said. Seven kettles, I could reply, all present and accounted for.

Six weeks later Gene Primrose wrote me that he had found another broken kettle!

Kettle Number 8 belonged to the Grover Beaver family who lived on the same mountain road we had driven to Dewey Clark's. One of the Beaver forebears had taken

At Boxley

it from Bat Cave to use as a wash pot. Number 8 also proved identical in size and shape to Dewey's Number 7.

What had happened? Had the soldiers overlooked a kettle in their hurry to move on? I then recalled a remark Susie Villines had made: One kettle, now a watering trough at Troy Fowler's, hadn't been broken until long after the Civil War. Maybe Troy's was the one that escaped the raider's notice. No one really knows.

Bat Cave, scene of the Civil War raid, lies just off the Cave Mountain road a bare quarter mile up the hill from Highway 21. In the past hundred years, many hundreds of people have tramped through its passages. For a while one of its rooms accommodated public meetings

Boxley: The mill pond . . .

and square dances, and became known as the Dance Hall. In 1964, an attempt to mine bat guano and cave-dirt for fertilizer resulted in a truck trail being bulldozed to the mouth of the cave itself.

Whatever stalactites and stalagmites the cave ever contained have long since been marred or stolen by vandals. However, the cave's intrinsic form, with big tunnel-like passages, high rooms, great domes and carved walls, largely makes up for the lack of formations.

For the first-time caver, Bat Cave is basically two-passaged. A hundred feet inside the entrance the cave forks. The right-hand passage extends about 1,000 feet, down large hallways, through the expansive Dance Hall room, then by a low duck-walk to the last large hall, which is blocked at the end by rockfall.

The left fork runs back about 300 feet from the entrance —and drops off into a gaping black pit. Many a Sunday afternoon explorer has stabbed the void with his two-cell flashlight beam and concluded both width and depth are beyond estimation. Actually the hole, called the Big Room, is about 75 feet across and 30 feet deep. Spelunkers have rigged ropes and ladders, climbed down to the floor of the pit and from there have explored the cave's lower level.

The lower passages are neither as large nor as long as those of the upper level, but they do present a challenge in being more difficult to reach and follow. Also, the lower-level cavers can better appreciate the cave's interesting drainage system. Underground streams from the upper level reappear in and flow down the lower passages, finally coming together and trickling into a crevice too small to explore, but raising the inevitable question: Where does the water go from there?

Samuel Whiteley's grist mill continued in use for a few years after the Civil War, but by 1870 the community needed and demanded a larger mill. In that year they put up a two-story frame building and Robert Villines became the miller.

Although a number of others operated the mill at different times, through most of the years the millers were Robert, then his son James Larkin Villines, and finally Jimmy's son Clyde. About 1950, Clyde Villines shut down the old mill. By then nearly everybody was using store-bought meal and flour, and the machinery was in bad repair. "And when the flume caved in," Clyde says, "I just quit."

North of Boxley, the stream from the big mill spring meanders among the trees along Highway 43, spreading into the backwater of the mill pond. Cows occasionally

and the mill

wade belly-deep into the cold water to gorge themselves on the luxuriant green water cress.

A little farther is the broad, tranquil pond, with its inverted mirror image of trees, barn and hills beyond. At intervals a fish jumps. A muskrat swims across the surface, trailing a wake of broadening ripples. The pond becomes still again, and the image returns.

From the far end of the pond's earthen dam, a stone-and-concrete flume conducted the overflow to the mill. The old building sits back about two hundred yards from the road, inconspicuous against a grove of trees. People seldom notice it.

Clyde Villines took me inside one time and showed me how the mill worked.

Obviously it lacked a water wheel, the kind I'd often seen in pictures of old mills. Clyde told me then that this mill did have such a water wheel at first, but the miller soon replaced it with a more powerful undershot turbine. Water came down the flume from the pond and poured into a ten-foot pit next to the end of the building, turning the turbine wheel set in the bottom of the pit. The rotating turbine shaft was connected to another shaft which ran under the building floor, and from there various pulleys, belts, shafts and gears transmitted power to the mill machinery.

Clyde then explained how the millstones turned against each other in grinding corn and wheat, how the revolving screens separated flour from bran, how the hammermill ground corn into feed. We traced the courses of conveyors and chutes that carried meal and flour through the several operations.

Mr. Villines has sold a few minor pieces of the mill equipment, and the silk flour screens have rotted on their frames. Most of the machinery remains in place, and the building's heavy hand hewn framework appears to be as sturdy as ever.

The building, however, is a fire trap. If that isn't reason enough for Clyde's keeping curiosity-seekers away, then the upstairs floors are, for they're so rotten that you walk them at your peril.

I hope, though, that the mill of Boxley escapes fire and further decay until the day it can be put to rights and run again; when we can step in and peer through the haze of flour dust and see the screens turning, or watch the grains of corn slipping down through the bottom of the hopper onto the millstones. When we can again feel the old building shaking a little as the mill noises flow into our ears . . . the soft grating of the stones, the thumping and squeaking and creaking rattle and rumble of antique machinery being turned by the force of water

Cob Cave in Lost Valley

roaring down into the pit outside.

I've never heard a water mill. Imagining isn't enough.

Three miles north of Boxley, Highway 43 fords a small stream coming down from a minor side valley of the Buffalo. The hurried outsider drives across the concrete slab and continues on his way, knowing and learning nothing of the surprises that lie just beyond sight up the valley of Clark Creek.

Local people, of course, have known what is there since the first pioneers went hiking up the creek to find waterfalls and a cliff with a big shelter cave underneath. For many years the settlers kicked up little Indian corncobs lying in the dust of the cave. But people who spend their lives amid such sights don't long remain excited about them.

Mrs. Susie Villines, the same 'Aunt Susie' of Kettles 6 and 7, is a granddaughter of Abraham Clark for whom Clark Creek was named. And she wrote a revealing bit of history about the shelter cave up the creek:

> I was born here . . . have lived here all my life and had never gave this spot any thought . . . till three men come from Michigan to do some surveying for the government and my father told these men of the place. So they wanted to go see the place and they gave it the name Corn Cob Cave. They took some corn cobs and pieces of gourds and pieces of potry and pieces of baskets made of bark. That was in the year of 1898.
>
> There was no one seem to think much of it till a well known man Thomas Ryker he heard of the place and come to see it. So he announced that there would be a Sunday school and all day singing [at Cob Cave] on the following Sunday with a basket dinner. And so Boxley Sunday School and Beechwoods Sunday School went to gather and we had a real nice time. And there were people in the surrounding communities came and joined in the service and in the site seeing. That was in the year of 1902.

Even after the organizational efforts of Mr. Ryker, 'Cob's' Cave, as it was called, remained only a picnic-place for local Sunday schools, a curiosity to be shown to neighborhood newcomers. There was to be little change for three decades, until 1931.

In that year S. C. Dellinger of the University of Arkansas was running an archeological survey of Indian caves and bluff shelters on the White and Buffalo Rivers. Somehow he heard about Cob Cave and its litter of corncobs and pieces of split cane. Dellinger and his assistants found their way to Clark Creek.

Hiking up the rocky creek bed toward their destination, the startled members of the party beheld a huge black hole at the bottom of a sheer 200-foot bluff. Through the ages the creek had been cutting, scouring, undermining the cliff until it had hollowed out an enor-

mous bandshell, 150 feet deep, 50 feet high, and 260 feet from end to end. The cave's broad stone ceiling was half as big as a football field!

Clark Creek still swept 50 feet back under the roof, but at one end the shelter had a high, dry shelf that was protected even from wind-blown rain. The ledge was covered with dust, a clutter of dead leaves and slabs of limestone which had dropped from the ceiling. And here the Indians had left some things behind. In fact Cob Cave turned out to be a classic Ozark 'dry' shelter. Mr. Dellinger once described to me what they found—

Inevitably there were corncobs, little ones four and five inches long. His crew also uncovered pieces of gourds, sunflower and other native seeds the Indians had gathered, and woven work and basketry. All had been preserved by the extreme dryness.

Other artifacts were much like those from shelters through the entire region. Dellinger had been finding dart points, stone and bone knives, stone and shell hoes and flint axes at many sites. He was disappointed not to discover any Indian burials in Cob Cave.

Dellinger and his crew worked for three weeks excavating in the shelter, carefully removing layers of dust and leaves, gravel and stones, lifting away heavy slabs of limestone and tunneling under others, trying to avoid damaging artifacts, recording positions and descriptions of things they found. A cache of baskets and basket fragments turned up, buried under dirt and then leaves. Dellinger systematically recorded how deep they were buried, from what part of the cave they came, even the position of each basket in the pile.

But that was 1931, and since 1931 archeologists have made enormous progress in digging methods and handling of data. Mr. Dellinger himself concedes that carbon 14 dating, microscopic analysis of plant pollen in the dry soil, and other new techniques would yield much more information than he was able to obtain.

We have only a vague notion, then, of when the Indians occupied Cob Cave. Apparently they were there between one and two thousand years ago, this assumed after comparing the cave's artifacts with similar ones of known ages from other sites.

And we are not likely to learn any more about the Indians in Cob Cave, because since 1931 the site has been repeatedly searched by a wide assortment of professionals, amateurs and outright vandals. "If anything further is found," Dellinger comments, "it should not be of any more importance than splint cane or cobs."

Dellinger's discoveries did focus some attention on Cob Cave as an Indian site, but little was said about the canyon's other attractions, the cliff and waterfalls. The scenery hadn't yet fired anyone's imagination.

Lost Valley: The natural bridge . . .

Then in the spring of 1945 a *National Geographic* photographer, Willard Culver, came to Arkansas to illustrate an article on the state. His trip-planner and bag-toter would be the state's publicity director, Glenn Avantus 'Bud' Green. Together they embarked on a ten-week tour around Arkansas.

In April someone in Harrison told them about Cob Cave. Culver wanted to go see, but at first they couldn't find anybody who knew how to get there. Only after some delay did they locate two men who could take them to the Cave. Green planned an expedition.

One morning in May, Green and Culver, their two guides and a group of Harrison High School boys and girls arrived at the Clark Creek crossing of Highway 43. Leaving their cars parked beside the highway, the group started hiking up a lane along the creek.

For nearly a mile they tramped through the woods, following the creek up its little valley. In a lengthy letter to me, Bud Green related what happened:

As we walked farther up the creek, the hills drew in closer. Finally we found it easier to wade the creek, even though it was high from a rain that morning, than to try to negotiate the steep banks and heavy undergrowth. Then, shortly after taking to the creek, we heard the unmistakable sounds of waterfalls.

We rounded a bend in the creek, and there was our first thrilling sight. The sun had come out, highlighting a glistening column of water falling from a 30-foot bluff.

Leaving the waterfall, we started to clamber up the rock-strewn creek—and were almost immediately confronted with another thrilling spectacle. Directly ahead, the bluff turned across the creek to form a high barrier. Through this there was a dark passageway, out of which came another torrent of water.

The stream had cut through fifty feet of massive lime-

Cob Cave and lower Eden Falls (Look for the other boy.)

stone to form a natural bridge. After Culver posed the students on ledges around the cascade and took pictures, everyone climbed up into the tunnel and walked through. The opening was fully ten feet wide, with a safe dry ledge above the stream. And near the tunnel's upper end, they came upon a large spring gushing from the wall to join the creek. The hikers joyfully drank their fill of its cold sweet water.

Green continues:

> Once beyond the bridge, we saw that it formed a sort of entrance to the upper reaches of the canyon. We soon found that the greatest array of beauty and astonishing sights lay beyond this gateway.
>
> Less than 150 feet above the bridge we discovered a cave. A low passage went into the bottom of the bluff, and we hurried up the creek bank to look. Two of the boys had flashlights, and they went in to explore.
>
> Soon we heard them coming back. They had found

an underground stream only yards inside, but the passage was so cramped and wet that they had not gone very far.

We went on into the heart of the canyon, following the creek and climbing over huge boulders and slabs of rock. After a fourth mile of this we reached Cob Cave.

The explorers looked around the Cave's vast interior. The two guides were showing everybody the Indian excavations, but Green's attention had been drawn in the other direction. Beyond the upstream end of Cob Cave he had discovered a beautiful series of waterfalls, four of them coming in steps down a 200-foot gorge.

Then somebody spied still another waterfall coming into the gorge from the left-hand hillside—

> Up we went, clutching at trees and bushes to keep from falling back, hurrying now because this new stream appeared to be coming out of a cave. And so it was,

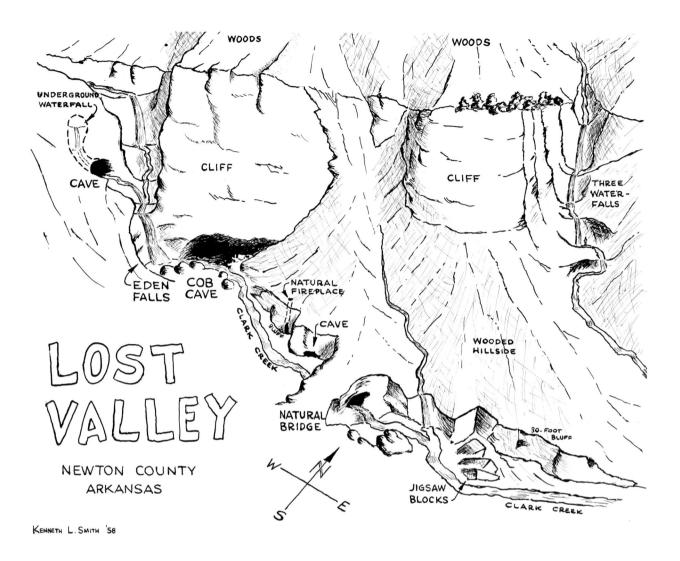

LOST VALLEY

NEWTON COUNTY
ARKANSAS

Kenneth L. Smith '58

another cave, 10 or 12 feet wide and with standing room. We followed the stream a short distance inside—and began to hear another waterfall.

We tried to go farther back, but found our way blocked. After two or three tries we finally discovered a narrow passageway. We had crawled about 200 feet back from the mouth of the cave when the passage narrowed to a still lower crevice. As we squirmed through, then at last could stand erect, we were nearly overcome with the spectacle. Here we were, deep within a mountain, probing with flashlights around the walls of a circular room perhaps 40 feet high. Over a ledge near the ceiling came a splendid waterfall.

Its roar reverberated through the high-ceilinged chamber. Its sprays filled the air with icy cold mist. We stood shivering in our awe.

When the group retraced its way down the canyon, Bud Green stopped and looked again at the waterfalls coming down the shadowy gorge above Cob Cave. In his mind he likened the beauty of this secluded scene with the Bible's Garden of Eden, and even before he left the valley he had given the falls a name . . . Eden Falls.

Bud's religious feelings then gave way to the demands of his job. "To help advertise its great attractions and bring in tourists," he says, "I named the area, from the natural bridge to the canyon's dead end, The Lost Valley."

Or simply Lost Valley. Strictly speaking, neither lost nor valley. Hidden, yes. And a deep narrow ravine or gorge. Not that it matters. The name is appealing and it has stuck.

It didn't matter, either, that Willard Culver's pictures never appeared in the *National Geographic*. Bud Green had gotten busy publicizing Lost Valley in other ways, with newspaper features, guided tours, pictures in travel folders. The outside world had at last begun to hear about the hidden canyon up Clark's Creek.

In 1958 I visited Lost Valley to collect information for some newspaper stories of my own. Though I had known

the area for several years, I needed to expand my knowledge of it, to take a 'tape measure tour' and learn the true size of the natural features.

Several friends helped me, and we even cataloged a few things I'd overlooked before. For example, Bud Green had seen three massive blocks of stone lying beside the creek near the natural bridge. Bud named them the Jigsaw Blocks, for like pieces of a jigsaw puzzle they fitted a notch in the bluff behind them, from which they had fallen long ago. We measured the largest block: 28 feet long, 20 wide and 11 high. Probable weight: more than 300 tons.

And in the bluff beyond the bridge we found an oddity called the natural fireplace. An entrance three feet wide by six high opened into a small chamber bathed in subdued light reflected down a 20-foot chimney.

We measured the width and depth of Cob Cave, and the four steps of Eden Falls. From the top of the gorge, the creek first plunges about 80 feet (though some of that is on a slope, not clear fall). It next drops an estimated 40 feet, then 10 feet, and finally another 40 feet into the pool at the upstream end of Cob Cave.[4]

Clark Creek is an interesting phenomenon in itself. The stream is unusually short, only three miles long from beginning to mouth. And extremely steep, for it falls 400 feet per mile in its leap-and-tumble down the mountain to the Buffalo. For a small stream, it flows with considerable speed and force—with power enough to cut and carve the canyon that is Lost Valley.

In times of flood the creek appears to take a course entirely above ground, but let it recede to normal size and strange things happen—

First, in the ravine above Eden Falls, it disappears among the boulders, soon to reappear as the underground waterfall that so impressed Bud Green.

[4]We only guessed at the height of the underground waterfall, but recently it was measured by cave explorers who set up an ingenious sectional climbing pole beside the fall and scaled it to the top, 35 feet above the floor. Moving into the passage upstream, they found it short, lacking decoration, and studded with loose boulders threatening to drop on them at any instant. They quickly retreated and shinnied back down the pole.

[5]The trees here are of many species, including a number that are unusual: several kinds of oaks, American elm, beech, shagbark hickory, chinkapin, white and blue ash, blackgum, American basswood, yellowwood, cucumber magnolia, carolina buckthorn, pawpaw. In the deep narrow valley many wild flowers have been found on the forest floor: crested dwarf iris, trilliums, white and purple phlox, yellow trout lilies, Jacob's-ladder, hepatica, wild hydrangea. Parasitic 'beech-drops' grow only on the roots of the beech trees. A rare and dainty orchid, the nodding pogonia, was once found here, as well as the large twayblade orchid, here near the western limit of its range. On the rocks and bluffs are other plants: columbine, pink stonecrop, Arkansas penstemon or beard-tongue, bulblet fern, walking fern, and smooth lip fern.

Then it flows out of the cave, down lower Eden Falls and past Cob Cave to disappear into another bed of boulders. Down to the natural bridge the surface channel is usually dry, and the cave stream found by the high school boys in Green's party is no doubt a reappearance of Clark Creek. That stream reaches the surface as the spring in the tunnel of the bridge.

The creek remains in sight for about two hundred feet below the bridge; then for the third time it sinks into a bed of gravel and boulders. It finally reappears (for the third time) at Highway 43 and the river.

All this is because the stream flows over and through the Boone formation, massive beds of limestone which are honeycombed with crevices, caves, sinks and springs. The creek has simply sought and developed the lowest possible channel to the Buffalo, sometimes on the surface of the ground and sometimes not.

Our exploring took place early in April, the time I had chosen for best visibility. Fall leaves had been beaten off by winter rains; beyond bare limbs the cliffs loomed impressively.

At the bottom of Lost Valley a grove of beech trees spread across the hillside, and a few still had last year's leaves. Slanting sun rays filtered through the sprays of pale yellow beech leaves, adding a cheerful golden note to the scene. Days were getting warm, the redbuds were beginning to bloom, and here and there the first bits of green were appearing in the woods.[5]

But in only a month these sunny pathways so open to the sky would be in deep shadow under a dense canopy of foliage. The still, moist air would then be laden with the sweet perfume of azaleas, mingled fragrances of myriad other plants . . . and a feeling of mystery. The green canopy would hide from view all that lay ahead; hikers wouldn't see the natural bridge, the cliffs and waterfalls until almost upon them. The old-growth woods, the big trees giving deep shade would set off and enhance all the other beauty, and add to the newcomer's joy of discovery. . . .

And yet, in 1960, loggers invaded Lost Valley, bulldozing a road and mauling these woods to within sight of Cob Cave. In 1963 another timber cutter worked his way up the trail to the natural bridge. In each case they were after trees having stumpage value of only hundreds of dollars.

Slowly the wounds are healing. Someday, if the place is left alone, it will be difficult for any casual observer to assess the change. But for this generation and maybe the next, the pristine setting of Lost Valley has been badly damaged.

It makes one pause to think about what is happening to the natural world, and the values that different people place on beauty.

2 CANYONS, CAVES AND CABINS

ON OUR FLOAT down the river from Ponca, Harry Pearson and I had to pass up one of the most interesting side trips, the hike into Hemmed-in Hollow.

No matter. I had visited the Hollow three weeks before, and Harry would have the opportunity a few weeks later.

For my visit early in April, I had purposely chosen a morning following an all day rain. First I rounded up two neighborhood boys, fifteen-year-old Kenneth Farmer and his thirteen-year-old brother Larry, to help me with picture-taking. Next we headed down the Sneed Creek Road, a bumpy, plunging three mile grade to the Buffalo. Reaching bottom, we drove along the river bank and parked beside Sneed Creek.

We took our shoes off, waded the creek, put shoes back on and started walking. The logging trail soon became a cow path, and that very soon dwindled to nothing. Each of us went scrambling his own way across the steep hillside, and then finally down to a swampy flat beside the river. A quarter mile below Sneed Creek we reached the mouth of the stream from Hemmed-in Hollow.

For some distance up the ravine we could follow a dim wagon track, the same one the O'Neill family had used when hauling in the lumber for their cottage. I told the boys about the O'Neills living here in the Hollow. Immediately they wanted to know whereabouts.

I couldn't say. So we watched for signs of a home site, and presently we thought we had found it—a suggestion of a clearing on a small natural terrace overlooking the creek, shaded by big beech trees. At the base of the hill a few yards distant there was a noticeable depression, maybe an old excavation, a root cellar. We saw nothing more.

The wagon trail disappeared, and again we went scrambling along a steep hillside, trying to stay close to the creek. About a half mile in from the river, I recalled, there would be a waterfall, a broad spill dropping ten feet from a ledge. The boys now told me they had never come here before.

The waterfall was not only going strong; it was in full sunlight. There had to be pictures. But we were anxious to get moving again. Already we could see something much better——

After another minute of scrambling we reached the canyon's end. Ahead, to our left, and to our right, we were half surrounded by a towering cliff overlooking the expanse of stream-washed bedrock where we were standing. Into this natural amphitheater, from a deep cleft in the brink of the overhanging wall directly in front of us, there came a waterfall.

Even now in flood it was a thing of airy grace. Dropping free from the top of the precipice, the stream came down in a long, wavering, wind-blown column, swinging randomly from place to place as it splashed on the stone floor.

The great height to be encompassed here in this confined space makes for photographic problems. I moved as far back as possible, onto a boulder in the middle of the creek with the waterfall spray blowing in my face. Using an extra-wide-angle lens, I barely caught the fall from top to bottom. For half an hour the boys patiently remained at their stations almost under the shower, getting drenched while I worked.

"How high is this waterfall?" Larry asked.

Nobody knows exactly. In 1955 Dr. Dwight Moore from the University of Arkansas did let a 200-foot rope down from the cliff nearby. He estimated that he stood about twenty feet higher than the head of the fall, and the rope touched bottom on the talus about twenty feet higher, he guessed, than the foot of the fall.

As with Big Bluff, this waterfall is the highest feature of its kind in the Ozarks. It is also undoubtedly the highest in all the broad American midland between the southern Appalachians and the Rockies.

Harry was to see the Hemmed-in Hollow waterfall in late June when its flow was much diminished. ". . . the spray was like diamonds in the sunlight," he wrote, "thousands of falling diamonds, weaving, curving, curling down to the canyon floor . . . beauty . . . delicacy . . . the gossamer web of here and now."

Three miles below Hemmed-in Hollow, Harry and I had floated past the mouth of Indian Creek, an inconspicuous dry wash coming into the river at the shoals above Gray Rock. We were much too busy with the rapids to notice Indian Creek, too busy for me to mention then what I had seen up its canyon.

One frosty March morning young Bill Dill of Harrison and I had started hiking into Indian Creek canyon from the stream's headwaters west of Mount Sherman. We followed the creek down its rough, steep ravine toward the Buffalo, half-sliding down slippery banks, climbing over boulders, detouring around the more abrupt drop-offs in our way of descent.

Presently we came to waterfalls, first a small one and then a 50-foot cascade down a steep rock face. And then a third, lesser fall that spilled twin streams around a boulder wedged at the brink. Just below this last waterfall the creek flowed into a still pool . . . and mysteriously sank out of sight.

We kept going down the dry channel, and very soon we came to a natural bridge. The bluffs on either side of the creek leaned inward against each other to form a slit or needle's eye some fifty feet high. We could stand in the creek bed at the bottom of the slit and look over another considerable drop-off into the canyon downstream.

There was no way to climb down through the bridge, so we pulled ourselves up the steep north bank of the creek and moved around the bluff, across the hillside and down a steep pitch through a break in the cliffs, finally reaching the stream bed in the lower canyon. From there we hiked back upstream to view the natural bridge from below.

Flood waters had worn a smooth, curving channel down through the needle's eye. Above that on the left, the rough, uneven wall loomed more than a hundred feet, leaning against a grotesque horn of rock projecting from the other side. What an odd, fantastic structure! Shadowed, dark, mysterious, it could well have been the creation of strange elfin people who dwelled in the underworld.

Bill had climbed up the ledges to the right to look into a hole in the bottom of the bluff. Now he was calling me.

When I reached the crevice he had gone inside, along a narrow tunnel. He stopped in the dim twilight about thirty feet ahead. I caught up, and he leaned aside so that I could look farther.

A stream came flowing from a low side passage. Could this be Indian Creek? It must——

Handing me the flashlight, Bill stepped back. I leaned out and peered ahead and to the right. The creek went

Hemmed-in Hollow
(Look for the other boy.)

94   *Natural bridge, Indian Creek Canyon*

racing down a trench and over a waterfall into darkness. The brink was only ten feet or so from where I was standing, but beyond the edge I could see nothing. Apparently the waterfall chamber was fairly big. I listened to the echoing rumble of the fall . . . . It might be **thirty** feet high.

This was another disappearing stream in the Boone limestone. Where would it surface again? Would we find a cave there, so we could reach the foot of the underground waterfall? And what else could we discover in the remaining two miles to the river?

Alas, we were not to find any answers that day. Bill and I had run out of time and had to turn back.

Later with some friends I took another hike into Indian Creek, this time from the river. For nearly a mile we followed the creek's bed of cobbles and gravel, seeing not a drop of water; it was all flowing underneath. Eventually, when we reached solid rock bottom, we also found the stream. Now the canyon walls had moved in close, and I was hoping, actually expecting, to show my companions the natural bridge almost around the next bend. Already we had discovered the creek emerging in full flow from under a ledge of rock.

The going only got rougher. After picking our way along a slippery side hill and coming to a cluster of monstrous rocks blocking the way, all but two of us turned back. The creek was flowing in the surface channel again, indicating that the natural bridge was still some distance ahead.

My canoeing partner Boyd Evison and I climbed over the boulders and kept going. But not for long; within five minutes we were boxed in by a waterfall coming down the crevice straight ahead and side walls that appeared too steep to climb. We might have backtracked and gone around, but there wasn't time.

Rivulets of water came spilling from a bluff beside us, from a mossy overhang a few yards above our heads. I moved away to see over the shelf, and there, some twenty feet above us, the water was coming from a great dark hole in the cliff. The cave was big enough to walk into, but it was beyond our reach.

We looked, wondered what lay inside the opening and wished we were able to see. Now, though, we had to go back and rejoin the others, failing to see the natural bridge, failing to find the exit of the creek below the underground waterfall. All we'd done was stumble on another mystery.

Hemmed-in Hollow and the mysterious canyon of Indian Creek form part of the roughest topography of all the Buffalo River country, part of the river's deep and rugged trench-valley just before the Buffalo flows out of the Boston Mountains. Nowhere in the river's watershed is the change in elevation so abrupt and so impressive as here from the summits of Gaither and Sherman Mountains to the bottom of the Buffalo's canyon twelve hundred feet below.

On the summit of Gaither there is a spectacular overlook of the river emerging from the mountains onto the Springfield Plateau. One morning I hiked out the spur of Gaither that lies between the Buffalo and Cecil Creek to the north, until I was walking along a narrow, slivering ridge of sandstone. Finally, as I neared the end of this rocky spine, the hill fell away below me, the pathway along the bare crest cleared the treetops, and the view became almost full circle.

I looked straight off the last point of rock, down past Erbie at the foot of the mountain and on down the Buffalo. A patchwork of fields and two or three bits of river were visible before everything merged into the far distance. On the horizon were flat-topped Boat Mountain and her sharp-pointed sister peaks. Away off on the horizon to the right of Boat, the faint hazy outline of a ridge ended abruptly in Point Peter, twenty-five miles down the valley in Searcy County.

Below and to my right, the Buffalo came flowing from its Boston Mountain canyon; Sherman Mountain loomed just beyond. Below and to my left was Cecil Cove, nearly encircled by the slopes of Gaither and the long irregular line of cliffs following the mountain's summit.

Clouds were piled along the horizon and the wind carried others across overhead, putting me in sunlight, then shadow . . . and the cloud shadows moved across the vast woodland below, brightening and then darkening the patches of clearing. . . .

Buzzards came circling, sailing effortlessly on the air currents sweeping up the mountainside. First I counted five. Then a sixth, from over the ridge behind me. And then eight . . . nine . . . eleven. All sailing, circling, not far above. Now I heard soft rushes of air as the big birds swooped and dived in the sky.

This continued for a while, but eventually they moved their circling pattern off to the north, nearly out of sight. Occasionally a stray would come back, sailing close, and I would see its shadow dancing across the treetops. I sat down on the rock.

From far below in the Cove woods there now came the eerily-accented *hoohoo-hoohoo . . . hoohoo-hoohooaw* of a barred owl. Then silence. Another eight-hoot. Then an eight-hooted answer from a quarter-mile down the hollow. For some minutes the owls' conversation went on. Then from 'way down toward the river I heard the faint but recognizable bellow of a bullfrog. Did it come from the river? Or from a spring, down on the mountainside? I could **not** tell.

From Gaither Mountain, a long view down the Buffalo

Again from the Cove woods, the wild chortling call of a pileated woodpecker. And from the woods just below me, bird sounds I could not identify.

From down among the valley farms, sounds of human activity—trucks, and a tractor. Now I heard a truck laboring along the mountaintop clear across Cecil Cove.

I listened to insects' droning, on and on and on . . . a hawk's shrill cry from the trees, and twittering birdsong from below. And the wind's faint breeze . . .

A dog barked—twice. Twice again. Was it close, down below the point? I decided not. Possibly it was barking there where I glimpsed the road among the trees, along the bench.

Then from the same direction came frenzied barking, maybe two dogs, giving chase . . .

. . . and the deep, far-away notes of the bullfrog. And the drone of insects. And the wind-song . . .

      *   *   *

The first time I had come out to this overlook was with Jim Schermerhorn, who wanted to show me Cecil Cove. We had stood and looked, and Jim had talked about walking and jeeping down the Cove's wagon trails, about visiting ruined buildings on its abandoned homesteads. He had stumbled on its long-neglected cemetery, resting place of those who had lived out their lives there.

But Jim's main interest in the Cove was in its abundance of caves. The same Boone limestone that causes streams to disappear in Lost Valley and Indian Creek Canyon lies hundreds of feet thick under the lower slopes of Cecil Cove. In the valley's nine square miles, Schermerhorn had located more than twenty caves and sinks.

One cave dominated his interest over all the rest, and that was Beauty Cave. While we were there on the overlook, Jim pointed out the general course that the cave followed under the mountainside beyond Cecil Creek. I told him I had visited Beauty Cave myself, on two quick

trips in the mid-1950's. Jim, though, had gone in on numberless occasions, more often than any other person, to explore and map and photograph this largest known cave in Arkansas.

I remarked to Jim that I had always heard it called Fitton's Cave, for an attorney in Harrison who had once owned the land. Jim replied that ever since its discovery (probably about 1925 by a man named Newberry), the natives in the area had been calling it Beauty Cave. Thereafter I noticed Jim mostly used that original name, especially when describing what he had seen inside.

Actually the cave has two widely separated entrances with different names. Beauty Cave entrance, the one most used, is a small, unimpressive hole in the side of a ravine. If you're a first-time visitor, though, you get a large surprise when you crawl in—you find yourself at one end of an immense room, over 700 feet long, up to 110 feet wide and 50 feet high.

From there you have to follow a tortuous passage down over rockfalls, down one vertical drop of 12 feet and along agonizing belly-squirms, eventually to reach an underground stream at what is called the T-Junction. By this time you have traveled nearly 2,300 feet from Beauty Cave entrance.

The stream flows in from the surface at the other entrance, Bat Cave. About 700 feet inside, it drops over a 47-foot waterfall. To go beyond that, you have two choices, neither one appealing. One is to wade down the creek in cold water sometimes chest deep. The other is to take a hazardous upper passage, crawling along on ledges and thin shelves of rock projecting from the walls as high as 80 feet above the creek.

Both routes lead to a spacious chamber known as the Round Room. To go farther, you again have two choices —wading the creek, or taking another high passage which requires jumping twenty-one times from ledge to ledge across a chasm that reaches as much as 30 to 40 feet down to the water.

For all your trouble, you only end up at the T-Junction, a little over 4,500 feet inside Bat Cave entrance. As said before, Beauty Cave entrance is the one most used; now you can understand why.

Two routes, more or less parallel and called the East Passage and Crystal Passage, go on into the depths beyond the T-Junction. For traveling to the 'back' of the cave, spelunkers use the East Passage. While Crystal Passage contains many of the most unusual formations, much of it is extremely difficult to get into.

Schermerhorn was one of the first ever to go through Crystal Passage. He and his companions traveled a long distance without seeing a single footprint in the soft floor. Finally they wiggled through a crevice into a room having footprints; they were in the familiar East Passage. Then,

in moving around, they lost the hole back to Crystal. . . .

In 1958 Jim and other cavers began mapping Beauty Cave, and at intervals over the next eight years they surveyed some 39,000 feet, or nearly seven and one half miles of passages. But by 1966, Jim could estimate there was at least that much more to be surveyed in areas already explored.

How much had *not* been explored? That was a foolish question, but one evening Jim and I spread his huge map of the cave across his living room floor, and he talked about areas for future investigations—

"The Labyrinth, there off Crystal Passage, hasn't been covered. . . . There are several passages taking off from this passage. And there are tremendous domepits and stuff down here; they look like they go all the way up to the surface. . . ."

Schermerhorn, acting as guardian and caretaker for the cave's owner living in Oklahoma, holds the keys to a locked iron gate at the Beauty Cave entrance. For a while, he would loan a key to almost anyone experienced in caves. Then he discovered that even those able to take care of themselves did not always take care of the delicate and irreplaceable formations. Several of the most unusual, including fantastic shapes which had been named 'the possum', 'the reindeer' and 'the unicorn', had been broken and lost. Regretfully, he began refusing entrance to all but those doing mapping or scientific work.

What are the formations, worth enduring a long, tiring trip to the rear areas of the cave to see?

First there are the familiar calcite growths—stalactites, stalagmites, columns—making one of the best displays of any cave in the Ozarks. Moreover, there are many of the rarer calcite helictites, growing in curves and corkscrews, protruding from the walls and ceilings at all angles. Helictites are found in every shape and description, and some approach the size of the largest known to exist.

Rarer yet are the speleothems (cave formations) of gypsum—every type described in cave literature, plus a few varieties which haven't been found anywhere but in Beauty Cave. Jim and his companions discovered these gypsum formations in an extremely dry passage far back in the cave. Clusters of delicate needles up to fourteen inches long grew from the sandy floor. Tufts of white flexible 'angels hair' hung from the ceiling. Other tufts resembled cotton. Pure white gypsum 'flowers' sprouted from another part of the ceiling; some of these, they later learned, were among the largest known.

Caving enthusiasts have made long pilgrimages to see the decorations of Beauty Cave, and a number of the rare forms have attracted national attention. Photographs of gypsum needles in Beauty appeared with an article on caves in the June 1964 *National Geographic*.

But the rare embellishments of Beauty Cave are so

*Beauty Cave: Rare gypsum stalactites
and (below) gypsum 'flowers'*

fragile that it is feared they cannot long survive the presence of visitors, however few may come. What is left for the next caver to see and enjoy will always depend on each person's self-control, on how well he abides by some common sense ideas of conservation, on how well he refrains from cutting, marking, taking or breaking or even touching the delicate formations. In Beauty Cave, and in every other cave, there can be only one true philosophy:

> *Take nothing but pictures.*
> *Leave nothing but footprints.*

Altogether the massive beds of the Boone limestone constitute the largest and most fascinating section of the region's rock formations. Streams disappear in the Boone, and there are caves in the Boone. And once in the past at least, the Boone sheltered a great deposit of bones. . . .

On the Boone a few miles east of Beauty Cave, an Englishman named Waldo Conard once owned a farm. Most of his land was poor. The limestone lay at the surface, and on that he could raise little but hope.

Conard's fondest hope was to discover lead. In April of the year 1903 he went digging and probing in the natural fissures of the rock-scabbed hill above his house. One place looked promising and he went down farther, heaving out clods of clay, blocks of limestone, and bones.

Ten feet deep, and still no mineral. Just bones, bones, bones—what was this? Conard wiped the thing on his pants leg and looked again. It was a tooth, a piece of a big sharp tooth, nearly four inches long!

Waldo had a partner, a Dr. R. R. Teller from Oklahoma, who was much taken by the collection from the prospect hole. Sensing that the bones might have some value to science, he wrapped up a few, plus the big tooth, and sent them to the American Museum of Natural History in New York. Teller invited the Museum people to investigate.

In the fall Barnum Brown of the Museum came down for a look. Sifting through the dump from Waldo's excavation, he was surprised to find about three hundred jawbones, and many scattered limb bones and vertebrae. The next spring Brown returned, employed Conard and one or two other local people to help him, and proceeded to dig.

The more they excavated, the more impressed Brown became. The fissure had evidently been an animals' den for tens of thousands of years. Bear and lynx and panther had holed up here, and they had dragged in peccaries (wild pigs) and deer. Weasels and other animals living in holes and pockets in the fissure walls had left thousands of small bones—those of mice, rabbits, wood rats and many other creatures. Owls had perched on ledges and eaten shrews and mice, dropping tell-tale portions of the skulls. Wood rats may also have nested here, for some of the remains seemed to be a pack rat's collection of odds

and ends: a horse's tooth, jaws of a raccoon and other fragments.

The entire deposit was one grand mixture of disassociated bones. Sometimes Brown did find an entire limb or part of a vertebral column, but never a complete skeleton. And though Brown constantly watched for signs of ancient man, he found none. There were no human bones, no artifacts.

Digging deeper, they discovered that water seeping from one wall had left a large stalactite deposit. As the fissure had slowly filled with rocks, clay and bones, the stalactite material had cemented much of it into a solid mass. Eventually they were forced to blast it loose. Many bones were broken in the explosions, and many more were broken while being removed and washed. All were extremely friable, and the ones that were saved had to be soaked in a solution of gum arabic to harden them.

Finally, as digging became more difficult and the bones seemed to be thinning out, Brown stopped excavation. The old prospect hole had been enlarged to a pit seven feet wide, 12 feet long and 25 feet deep. Brown returned to the Museum with a large collection comprising several thousand jaws, skulls, limb bones and vertebrae.

Over the following months, Brown and others of the Museum staff examined each specimen, analyzing and comparing, identifying species and even discovering ones unknown before. In his published report,[1] Brown wrote that the fissure had yielded "a wonderful assemblage of mammals, representing 37 genera and 51 species, of which four genera and 24 species are considered extinct."

A number of the animals were northern species. Near the bottom of the excavation, for example, Brown had uncovered bones of an extinct relative of the arctic musk-ox. Undoubtedly these northern animals had lived here when the climate was much colder, when they had been forced southward by one of the great glacial advances late in the Pleistocene or ice age. The total evidence from the fissure suggested that it was occupied over several different time periods, possibly from as little as 10,000 years ago to well over 100,000 years past.

And what of Waldo's big tooth?

After some study, the Museum people found that it and a few other fragments were of the long-extinct saber-toothed tiger. The tooth was easiest to identify; it was one of the saber canines. Moreover, this was a new species of saber-toothed tiger, and Barnum Brown named it *Smilodontopsis conardi*, remarking that "I take pleasure in dedicating the species to Mr. Waldo Conard. . . ."

[1] "The Conard Fissure, a Pleistocene Bone Deposit in Northern Arkansas: with Descriptions of Two New Genera and Twenty New Species of Mammals." *Memoirs of the American Museum of Natural History,* Vol. IX, Part IV, February, 1908.

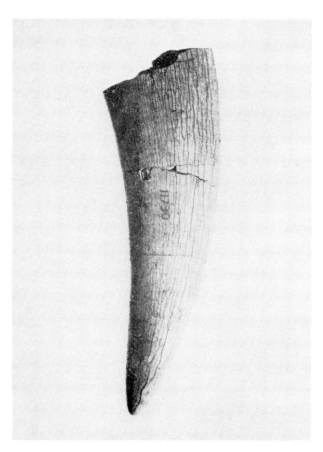

American Museum of Natural History

The Tooth

In the spring of 1965 I found the Conard Fissure, locally more often called the Bone Hole, at the end of an unmarked trail through the woods.

Barnum Brown's excavation had partially filled with dirt and leaves, but the stalactite he described was still in sight near the bottom. Next to the pit was a weather-rounded mound of reddish clay.

Scattered over the pile were bits and pieces of bleached bone, discarded scraps from the excavation. I could hardly believe these whitened fragments were tens of thousands of years old. Absently I picked one up, pinching it between thumb and forefinger.

It broke, and crumbled to bits like a dry crust.

In addition to mountain scenery and the underground attractions of the Boone, this reach of the watershed has one other prime fascination—the remains of a pioneer architecture. Through this portion of Newton County there may well be more log buildings than anywhere else in the Ozarks.

It may remain so for only our generation. Many of the old cabins are going to ruin. Take, for example, the Henderson place on the Sneed Creek Road. When the

boys and I returned from Hemmed-in Hollow, I stopped once again to see it.

A homesteader had cleared this bench on the hill behind Big Bluff and built the house around 1900. Several families—the Hendersons, Bryants and others—had lived here at different times until past 1950. Then the last of them moved out and the house began to go to pieces.

I remembered it as it was in 1959, with wallpaper hanging in tatters, the roof with a hundred pinholes of sky. With the chimney coming apart and dumping stones and crumbled mud mortar into the fireplace.

In six years the decay had progressed visibly. Now the porch roof was gone. Inside, the wallpaper had disappeared, and so had the inner walls and ceiling. More distressing, the basic log structure was beginning to rot.

Decaying log cabins seemed to be everywhere, but sound ones were hard to find. I had been looking for outstanding examples of pioneer buildings, at the same time developing some thoughts about what the ideal log cabin should be like—

First, of course, it had to be well built and in good condition. It had to have its original appearance; it could not be covered with siding, as so many were, nor could it have any later additions out of harmony with the original style and materials.

And it had to be someone's *home*—not just a dwelling for transients or renters, but a long time home for owners of the house, for people who were settled in a log cabin

way of life. As much as to see the house, I wanted to talk with its people.

These were difficult criteria to meet. The cabins having some semblance of their original appearance were invariably empty, abandoned. The lived-in cabins were almost always of the 'covered up' or 'tacked onto' variety.

In time I located two good log houses. One, at the Ponca low-water bridge, was a fine example of axmanship with cedar logs. 'Beaver' Jim Villines had built it about 1880. The other, on the road south of Erbie Ford, was a one and a half story cabin with an unusual cut-stone chimney; I heard it belonged to a bachelor named Graydon Hickman. But the Villines cabin was occupied by a renter and I couldn't catch Mr. Hickman at home. Continuing my rambling, leisurely search, I moved into the valley of the Little Buffalo.

One chilly winter afternoon I drove up the Little Buffalo to Parthenon, through a lovely scene remindful of the valley from Ponca to Boxley. Mountains crowded close along the cleared bottom lands, and bluffs fronting the river were lesser likenesses of cliffs on the Big Buffalo.

Parthenon has a scattering of houses and two or three old store buildings on the level valley floor, and a deserted stone schoolhouse on the hill beyond. I stopped at the general store, a boxy two-story building on the village main street, and went in.

Sure enough, the cavernous interior was heated by a glowing wood stove, and that was surrounded by half a

The Conard Fissure

dozen elderly men toasting their toes, warming their backsides and talking. After a proper interval, I edged into the circle and began asking questions. What was there to see hereabouts?

We talked, and they told me of the Chimney Rock, about five miles up the Little Buffalo. I knew it well: a 65-foot tower of stone overlooking the river, a massive boulder balanced on top. What else was there, right here in the neighborhood?

Two or three of them knew about the Hannah Rock, lying in Hannah Hollow a mile or so above Parthenon. Walter Lackey had told me that a Mrs. Hannah had once tilled a garden on top of this great block which had broken away from the rest of the mountain. Today my informants agreed that Mrs. Hannah had used a ladder to reach her garden, and that on leaving she had pulled it down to prevent trespass by wild animals. . . .

One of the men then told me of the War House Cave, somewhere under the bluff at the head of Hannah Hollow. The Cave had been a Civil War hideout . . . for whom, no one seemed to know for sure. Why not go and see it?

But I didn't think that I could cover Hannah Hollow in a brief winter afternoon's hike. And I had saved for last my most important questions of the day. Where were the log cabins in this part of the country?

They obligingly told me what they could. After noting their suggestions, I went on my way.

First I traveled up Dry Shop Creek, only to find the one cabin in ruins. Doubling back to Parthenon, I turned up Wet Shop Creek. Several miles up its narrow wooded valley, I came upon two log houses. One was occupied, but it was covered with white clapboards. The other was being 'restored', complete with green plastic skylights, by a new owner from out-of-state.

Where next? It would be a beautiful drive for six or eight miles farther up the Little Buffalo—but I'd not seen any log houses up that way. Instead, I took the road which turned south up the mountain, toward Deer.

On the mountain I stopped to inquire at the country post office of Wayton. Were there any log cabins thereabouts? The postmaster suggested that I try a side road about a mile south. Going as he directed, I turned off to see.

Never had I found so many old log buildings in so short a stretch of country road. In barely three miles I counted seven log houses and three barns, plus three other small dwellings that surely belonged in the 'covered up' class. But only the three houses encased in composition siding seemed to be occupied. The rest were either in ruins or were being used as cattle barns.

The log cabin road became narrower and muddier.

The Henderson cabin in 1959 . . .

and in 1965

Now a gate loomed ahead; I'd have to turn back.

No! There was the perfect log house, with smoke coming from the chimney . . . .

I opened the gate and walked into the yard, greeted by the loud barking of the owner's dog. A middle-aged man opened the door and came out on the porch. I explained why I had come to call.

He was Cecil Murray. Yes, he and Mrs. Murray (who by now had come to the door) had lived here for a good many years. They invited me in.

The Murrays were heating with the fireplace, and it felt mighty good on that cold afternoon. I got right in

Cecil Murray tending fire. ". . . most of the heat goes up the chimney."

front of it and stood there, warming first one side and then the other.

How old was this house? Neither Mr. Murray nor his wife could recall. It had been built by his father—oh, maybe seventy years ago.

Wasn't it a little chilly here inside? It was quite cold out-of-doors . . . . They both agreed, and were soon telling me of their hopes to build a new home, to get out of their log house.

This fireplace, for instance, was such a poor thing for heating. Most of the heat went up the chimney.

Then Mr. Murray pointed to the bottom of the front door. I saw a crack of daylight. These old houses were probably put together without so much as a yardstick for measuring things to fit. Even though the rooms here had been sealed with wallboard and wallpaper, they were chilly. I thought of the shingle roof—probably it was laid directly on wood strips nailed to the rafters. No sheathing. A thousand unsealed cracks and openings. Watertight but not airtight.

And newer homes must have had a hundred things dear to Mrs. Murray's heart. Bigger windows to let in more sunshine. Modern kitchens. Closets and cabinets.

What would become of this house if the Murrays moved out? I imagined it standing empty, the roof beginning to leak—and then the sure way to ruin.

But I was beginning to understand that others must take a different view of these things.

The Little Buffalo

3 A SAMPLING OF THE PAST

FROM SCENIC POINT at the highway summit south of Jasper, you can see in one brief glance a vast territory, the result of building up and wearing down of the land through an immense length of time. You can stand on the northern rim of the highest plateau of the Ozarks, the Boston Mountains, and look across hundreds of thousands of acres of a lower landscape, the Springfield Plateau.

The word 'plateau' suggests flatness, a tableland, and here the term seems out of place. These Boston Mountains are a maze of ridges, stream valleys, canyons and hollows. The Springfield Plateau is also rough country, a thousand hills and ravines. But the ridges and summits of the Bostons are remarkably near the same altitude over large areas, and isolated flats along the mountain tops are the remains of a surface once nearly level everywhere. And down on the Springfield Plateau, the ridgetops and expanses of upland prairie also lie on a fairly uniform level.

To your left and right you can trace the irregular northern 'front' or escarpment of the Bostons, from the northeast flanks of Gaither and Sherman Mountains to the northern face of Judea Mountain sweeping below Scenic Point and on to the east toward Redrock Point. From Redrock, the boundary of the range extends eastward beyond sight, along the northern ends and faces of Lick Mountain, Horn Mountain, Point Peter . . .

To the north you see a group of peaks standing out by themselves, separated from the Boston Mountains by several miles of lower country. But they're obviously as high as the Bostons; in fact Boat Mountain, the flat-topped one, stands even a little higher than Scenic Point. Boat and the peaks around it are 'outliers' of the Boston Mountains. Millions of years ago, they were joined to the main mountain range as part of a higher land mass covering this whole vast area lying below Scenic Point. Erosion, working over a span of time we can hardly comprehend, has taken it all away, down to the present level of the Springfield Plateau.

All, that is, except the peaks of the Boat Mountain group. They lie on the divide between the Buffalo's watershed and that of Crooked Creek to the north, so they have escaped being worn down by streams. The hard rock capping their summits has also helped prevent erosion.

The rocks of this region originated in sediments laid down in ancient seas, and everywhere the formations lie nearly flat. This is readily apparent wherever layers are exposed—look over to Gaither and Sherman and Boat Mountains and you will see the similarity between the bluffs along their summits and the one just across the highway below Scenic Point. These sandstone bluffs are all of the same material lying at the base of a massive complex of sandstones and shales called the Atoka formation. The Atoka (or Winslow) rocks were formed early in the Pennsylvanian period of geologic time, some 300 million years ago.

Drive down the highway toward Jasper and you will cross layers of rock increasingly old, often exposed to view in the road cuts. First below the Atoka are the Morrow Group of sandstones and shales, thin limestones and conglomerates, also of Pennsylvanian age. Then you move across the Pitkin limestone and the Fayetteville shale, the top layers of an extensive series of rocks from the Mississippian period, 310 to 350 million years ago. The black Fayetteville shale lies in areas about half way down the mountain.

Below the Fayetteville and a thin layer of the Batesville sandstone, you reach the Boone formation. The Boone, which dates from early Mississippian time, extends most of the rest of the way into Jasper. Here in the road embankments the Boone limestone shows itself mostly as a mixture of orange clay and broken rock. The limestone has weathered and dissolved away, leaving the clay and many 'lenses' or pockets of chert, a compact and nearly insoluble rock composed of silica as in quartz sand.

Beyond Jasper, the Buffalo River cuts into lower and older layers of rock as it moves downstream. The oldest

The Boat Mountain group, outliers of the Boston Mountains

formations in the Buffalo watershed are those at the lowest elevations near the mouth of the river. There, the dolomites of the Salem Plateau belong to the Ordovician Period of about 450 million years ago.

The entire length of time when these sedimentary rocks were being formed falls within the Paleozoic era, the age of ancient life. Land animals had only begun to evolve, and primitive marine organisms dominated the scene. Warm seas covering this region teemed with life—shelled animals, armored fishes, corals, ancient sharks. When they died, their bodies often became trapped in the sediment slowly building on the shallow bottoms . . . today we see their fossil remains in the rocks.

Pick up a piece of Boone chert and you may discover the lacy imprints of colonies of bryozoans, animals so tiny that one alone would not cover a period on this page. Very often you will find the chert honeycombed with little cylindrical bits of crinoid stalks, for crinoids were extremely abundant through the Mississippian period.[1]

Most of these rock formations have their own assemblages or combinations of fossils. Some few 'guide' or 'index' fossils are peculiar to one formation and no other. Thus only the Pitkin limestone contains the screwlike stems of bryozoan colonies of the genus *Archimedes,* and

only the black Fayetteville shale has one of the region's largest fossils, an animal with the formidable name *Rayonnoceras solidoforme*.

Dr. David Russell of Jasper showed me my first *Rayonnoceras,* a 14-inch specimen that a patient of his had pried from the Fayetteville on the mountain above the village of Mount Judea. Neither of us knew what it was. Dr. Russell had whimsically named it 'Proconsul.'

Later we learned that the long, tapered cylinder of rock was once part of a squid-like marine animal known as a nautiloid. Its body and tentacles had disappeared, leaving the compartmented shell to become fossilized.

Still later, when the John Muir canoeists and I went floating down from Mount Hersey, we stopped to camp on a gravel bar below Woolum. As I was unpacking, Al Kingsbury came over with two oddly-shaped chunks of stone in his hands.

[1]Crinoids were simple animals, somewhat like starfish, that attached themselves to the sea floor by their stalks and then waited for nourishment to drop into their open, upward-facing mouths. They grew in patches, resembling beds of lillies swaying gently with the currents.

Their stalks were strengthened with limy plates, like buttons on a string but connected with muscular tissue. On the death of a crinoid its stem-plates usually came apart, so we seldom see more than sort stem fragments in fossil form.

Atoka sandstone cliffs on Sherman Mountain, Newton County

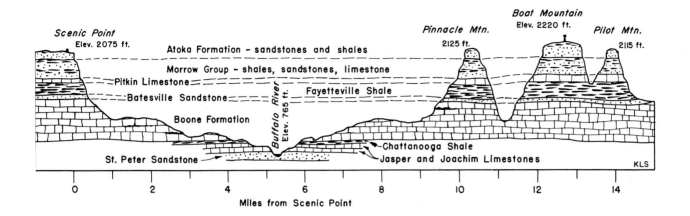

Geologic cross-section of the Buffalo valley from Scenic Point to the Boat Mountain group. In this sketch, heights of the mountains are greatly exaggerated.

What were they? He'd picked them up on the gravel. I looked. They were fragments of *Rayonnoceras*. The novelty of it then began to wear off.

Jack McCutcheon is a fossil-hunter. At times he is a cave explorer, an amateur geologist, or an Indian archeologist. As a cattleman, his schedule is fairly relaxed and more often than most of us he can pursue his hobbies. And on Cave Creek, his home in eastern Newton County, the raw material is all close at hand.

In January 1965, Jack decided to explore the sink hole in the Boone formation behind his house. He had put it off for some time because first he had to fashion a ladder; the hole was 32 feet straight down.

While his good wife Lois watched from the edge of the pit, he eased down the ladder (rope, with broom handle rungs) to the bottom. He looked around. A room opened off one side of the sink. From the room, two passages went farther under the hill.

He crawled and duck-walked down the larger tunnel—then realized he was traveling on a bed of dried clay. Maybe it would be good for pottery. He gathered samples.

The other passage was much smaller. After thirty feet of squirming, he started to turn back . . . .

Something was lodged in the dirt floor; he pulled it loose. It was an animal's jawbone, badly discolored, with teeth missing. It looked old.

He crawled a few feet farther, finding another bone protruding from the floor. Then, as he moved back toward daylight, he picked up a tooth, one from a fairly large animal.

When Jack showed Lois the clay and bones and described the passages and the pretty stalactites in the room, she was all for going down herself. No, said he; the ladder was too dangerous. On hearing that, she marched off to the house.

But very soon she returned, carrying a yardstick. And what was she going to do?

"Why, you keep talking about how pretty it is, and if I can't go down the sink hole, we'll dig a tunnel."

Beginning at the mouth of the pit, she moved down the hill, sighting over her yardstick in three-foot steps downslope. Presently she announced that she was 32 vertical feet below the mouth. She took a few steps down the hill—allowing for the rock pile Jack had descended into the room—and pointed to a low shelf of rock. "See? It's just dirt under that ledge. If we dig there, we'll dig into the room." Womanly logic prevailed, and Jack started digging. He was thinking, too, about developing the clay deposit.

Within two weeks he had burrowed a 15-foot gopher hole under the ledge and had broken into the room. It went uneventfully, except that halfway through his digging he found two more bones. One was a tusk that apparently came from a hog. The other was a jawbone resembling a deer's. Lois of course had picked the perfect spot for the tunnel and she crawled in right away to see the cave.

Not long after that, I first met Jack and Lois McCutcheon. At the time they were experimenting with the cave clay, trying to make dishes and ash trays. They weren't having much success. The pottery usually cracked when it was fired.

Then Jack laid out his bones. They were yellowed and mottled with age, and extremely brittle. One that had been accidentally broken had shattered into splinters. Jack didn't want to dig any more in the small passage for fear he might destroy something of scientific value.

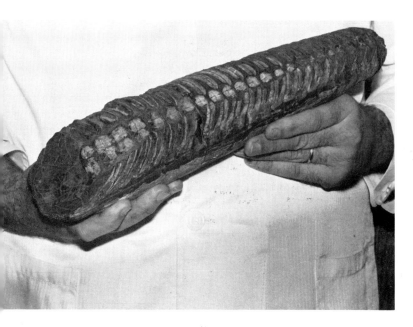

Fossils:
(above) The remains of Rayonnoceras
solidoforme, an extinct marine animal
found in the Fayetteville shale.
(below) Fragments of crinoid stems
in a piece of Boone chert.

"I want some advice from an expert," he said.

The expert we contacted was Dr. James H. Quinn, chairman of the geology department at the University of Arkansas and an authority on fossils. A friend of ours from the University carried Jack's bones to Dr. Quinn and set them before him.

Quinn became excited—these bones seemed to fill a gap in the fossil record of Arkansas. He immediately identified a jawbone and the tusk; they belonged to the peccary, the pig-like javelina of the Southwestern deserts, probably an extinct species here and certainly long absent from the Ozarks. The other jaw did appear to be a deer's, while the large tooth and the femur or leg bone might have come from *Canis dirus,* the extinct dire wolf.

Some days later Dr. Quinn, three of his students and I drove to the McCutcheons' on Cave Creek. Jack took us to the cave. One at a time we wormed through the tunnel, stretched full length and pushing along on toes and elbows until we could get up to our hands and knees, and then stand erect in the room below the sink hole.

I had the feeling of being at the bottom of a well, able to look up the pit at daylight but trapped in eternal twilight and darkness. The quality of the light reflecting from the mossy walls of the sink, and the noisy dripping of water coming down from the surface, heightened that impression.

For nearly an hour we all dug in the earth floor at the back side of the room—finding nothing. The students and I then crawled back into the passage where Jack had discovered the peccary jawbone. The dirt-floored tunnel was narrow and scarcely two feet high. Jack and Dr. Quinn remained working in the room.

The boys began scratching and raking the crumbly dirt with their geologist's picks, and before long they were finding bones, chunks and fragments and occasionally a whole one . . . .

Another peccary jaw! Unlike the one Jack had found, this had the big tusks intact. We made way; Jack and Dr. Quinn were coming in to see.

Soon we had gathered a six- or eight-pound sack of bones, and we returned to the house. While Jack arranged the collection on a table, Dr. Quinn talked about our findings.

To begin with, Jack McCutcheon had discovered the only cave preservation of vertebrate fossils, other than the Conard Fissure, that was known in Arkansas. "Two or three sites something like this occur in southeast Missouri," Quinn remarked, "but I think this is the only one we know of with so late an assemblage."

He picked up a fragment, lit a match and held it to the bone a moment. We smelled smoke, the acrid odor of burning bone. "When bone chars like this," Dr. Quinn

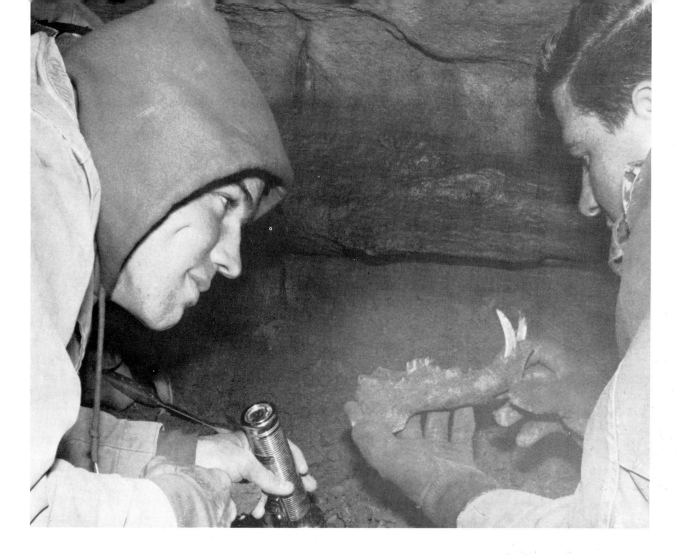

In Peccary Cave

explained, "it's not entirely fossilized. That burned-bone odor we smelled comes from the proteins that were in the bone to begin with. When bone fossilizes, these proteins disappear. That's what fossilization means—replacing the organic substances with mineral.

"I've tried this flame test on bones of different ages, and the ones I knew were more than about 6,000 years old didn't respond at all—they didn't burn, char or smell. So at least we can say these bones are less than 6,000 years old. I would say much less—about 3,000 years . . . These are much more recent than anything from the Conard Fissure."

How did the bones get into the cave?

"Those animals didn't fall into the sink, if that's what you're thinking. That sink opening looks much too recent—that roof might have fallen in only a hundred years ago.

"No, I believe the cave had another entrance, and it was about where Jack dug his tunnel—remember the bones he found when he was digging? We could say the old entrance was sealed by a landslide . . . oh, maybe one to three thousand years ago.

"We think we have the remains of a dire wolf; that would almost certainly mean the wolf denned in the cave. And the wolf could have dragged in the peccaries."

Quinn looked over the assortment on the table and picked up the largest, heaviest piece we had found. "And maybe the wolf dragged this in, too, though it's probably from a horse, or bison . . ."

Presently Dr. Quinn, his students and I said our good-byes and began our long drive back to Harrison. Dr. Quinn carried the bag of bones; he was now much interested in trying to identify everything we had found.

Within a few weeks Dr. Quinn obtained a small research grant from the University so that Jack could be paid wages for a short period of excavation. Jack had already agreed that the University could have any bones he unearthed, and so he went to work.

Since that time Dr. Quinn has sought a foundation grant to pay for complete excavation of the cave, plus carbon 14 dating and the research of identifying all the

Perfect!

species represented by the bones. "Our talk about the age of the bones, for instance, is pure speculation," Quinn admits. "We'll know for sure only when we get a carbon 14 date."

Identification of species must be done in large museums where extensive collections of fossils are on hand for comparisons. In the meantime, Quinn has identified a few animals on his own.

By far the greatest number of bones belong to the extinct peccary *Platygonus compressus.* Several hundred skeletal parts of peccaries of all ages have now been unearthed, and from these the cave has been named Peccary Cave. A full grown animal—with six-inch tusks—would be twice the size of the present peccary of the Southwest.

Teeth of the dire wolf were scattered throughout the dig, and a host of other bones ranged from those of fish to the jaw of a porcupine and the teeth of a large bovid. Many species of course aren't yet identified.

More recently, Jack McCutcheon's discoveries in Peccary Cave have taken a new dimension. In the fill of the cavern he has unearthed charcoal, and what appear to be bits of worked flint, and a human tooth.

What did Jack think of these latest discoveries? He would only write me that "there are a lot of questions to be answered . . ."

And, said he, "I expect each answer will suggest two more questions."

Almost from one one shovelful to the next, Jack had progressed from unearthing wild animal fossils to turning up evidence of prehistoric man. I made the same sort of progression, from scratching in Peccary Cave to excavating for Indian remains, though not in as direct a fashion.

Mine began very soon after my first visit to Peccary Cave, when I came to know Gene Waters. Like Jack McCutcheon, Gene is a Newton County native with a great curiosity about what lies in his home ground. Gene's greatest interest is archeology, and I had asked him to show me where and how the Indians had lived along the Buffalo. Thus one winter afternoon we drove down to a field along the river not far from his home. Gene had the owner's permission to search there for arrowheads.

"Saaay, this looks good——" Gene remarked. "They've plowed since the last time I came here, and I'll bet that rain the other day cleaned off anything they turned up."

I learned there's no trick to looking for arrowheads; all it requires is normal vision and thorough, persistent searching. Finding them, and especially knowing what I found, was something else again. There I needed help from Gene.

"See this—" he called, "it's a scraper." He held up a fragment of flint I would have mistaken for a useless something from the Indians' trash heap. "This was used for scraping hides," Gene explained. "Only it's been broken, maybe by the plow."

Here the Indians had set up a temporary hunting camp, and on a rise of ground about a hundred yards from the river we found where one of them had sat making arrowheads. He had left many flinty chips and flakes about his workplace. Gene briefly scanned the waste material. "Nothing here," he commented, "—just this broken corner-notched point.

"Now today . . . today I'm looking for one that's perfect." Gene slowly moved away, eyes to the ground, gradually working toward the lower edge of the field. I strolled off in another direction, eyes down. Minutes passed.

"Hey, come see what I've found!" I turned and ran to where Gene was kneeling.

The plow had brought a perfect arrowhead to the surface and the rain had washed it clean. "It's worth hunting all afternoon to find something like this," Gene chortled. I fully agreed.

Gene Waters had searched this field many times, accu-

Projectile points from the surface at Gene Waters' site No. 55. These are all dart and spear points; the bow was unknown to Indians before 1000 B.C. Ages of these artifacts are estimated by comparison with similar objects from other sites having carbon 14 dates. Descriptions and ages by groups:

1 Four serrated side-notched points, three with tips broken. Each has a 'twist' or bevel—the first one is on edge to show this. These oldest points are from the Early Archaic period of Indian prehistory, around 6000 B.C. Site 55 was then a camp for nomadic In-dians who lived by hunting and food-gathering.

2 Two broken corner-notched points, Middle Archaic.

3 Two stemmed dart points, Middle to Late Archaic, 5000 to 500 B.C.

4 Four contracting-stem points of the Woodland period, about 500 B.C. to A.D. 1100. In this time Indians acquired the bow and arrow, pottery, agriculture. But they lost skill in making projectile points —compare these with the earlier ones.

mulating nearly a hundred artifacts. One evening when looking over the rest of his extensive collection, we decided to gather all the pieces from this one site (which was easy, for he had plainly marked each piece with a site index number 55) and attempt to analyze them for the Indian story of this place alone.

The best we could do was sort through the projectile points. Though many were broken, nearly all could be laid out by type and approximate age, and they did yield (to me) one astonishing revelation. The points were of types covering a time span from 6000 B.C. to past A.D. 1000—so their makers had been camping here at intervals for well over five thousand years![2]

Most of the Indian sites along the Buffalo were field camps like site 55. Of course there was a limit to what could be learned from them, for only the stone implements remain. Gene told me that the same was true for the

[2]Indian projectile points (a term including arrow, dart and spear points) have been classified by shape and geographic distribution into more than a hundred named types. Points found with charcoal have been dated by carbon 14 testing, so that now each type is known to have been developed and used within its own fairly well defined span of time during Indian prehistory. For example the Dalton type of point is one of the oldest found along the Buffalo; it dates from several thousand years before Christ. The tiny Scallorn point, one of the most recent, was used by Indians until the coming of the white man.

Other stone artifacts from Gene's site 55:

1 Axe, Woodland period, 500 B.C. to A.D. 1100.

2 Three knives. Large knife is Middle Archaic, about 3000 B.C.; others are Late Archaic.

3 Three scrapers. The two smaller ones are end scrapers or celts. The larger one is believed to be from the Woodland period.

4 Two roughly flaked pieces, age unknown, probably unfinished projectile points or knives.

camp sites in caves and bluff shelters.

Gene went on talking. "You say you want to know more about *how* the Indians lived. Really, to do that, you have to excavate in a bluff shelter. I mean a dry one that has perishables—baskets, and mats, and rope . . .

"Trouble is, dry shelters are scarce. I know of only a few, and they've already been excavated, or torn up by pothunters."

"Aren't there any of these dry shelters left?" I asked. "Isn't there some place we can have a weekend or two of excavation, so I can see how it's done? A dry shelter would be the best——"

"Well," he replied, "I do know of one dry site. It hasn't been *all* torn up . . . I'd like to work in it, and I have the owner's permission, but I'd rather get help from someone who's more experienced. I want to work that site just like the professionals do."

Why, that was what I wanted—to see how the real

archeologists worked. With Gene's assistance, I began contacting the most experienced archeologists in northwest Arkansas, asking for their help.

One of our volunteers was Don Dickson, then president of the Northwest Arkansas Archeological Society. He needed perishable materials from a dry shelter for his educational displays. He hoped that we might find perishables together with stone and pottery artifacts, for then carbon 14 dating could establish the ages of non-perishables of the same types from all sites, moist or dry.

We agreed that Don would take any material we might find at the site, analyze it and write a report on the project. If there were many artifacts, he would divide the lot into representative collections for Gene Waters and for the University of Arkansas Museum, plus a sample of perishables for his displays. The other crew members we had rounded up would be in it for the experience. Jack McCutcheon, for example, told us he wanted no artifacts.

"I come to learn," said he.

One Sunday in February we all met at the site for our first day of digging. There were six of us: Gene and I, Don Dickson and Jack McCutcheon, and Jack Gregory and Stuart Towns from Fayetteville. We had agreed to keep our group small for better control of operations. Don, with the most experience by far, would direct the work.

This Newton County dry shelter of Gene's was a cave-like room hollowed in the base of a bluff. I'd noticed a spring flowing close by; Indians would have picked this place for sure.

The rear of the cave was so dry that little puffs of dust rose at our every footstep. Pothunters had scratched out little foxholes over much of the floor, and Don emphasized that we'd not come to repeat the likes of that. Under his direction, we began preparing for a dig that we hoped would be more meaningful.

We would only excavate within two five-foot squares, with a three-man team working each square. One man would excavate while the other two screened the earth he removed from the pit. After a brief inspection of the room, Don decided that a fairly undisturbed area near the right rear wall would be as good a place as any to dig.

First the squares had to be laid out in relation to a permanent datum point which Don produced by chiseling a cross within a circle on the rear wall of the shelter (If our work were interrupted, the squares could always be measured off again from there.). Beginning at the datum point, we set a line of stakes at five-foot intervals running due west toward the mouth of the cave. This was our base line, and from it we laid out a grid of several squares toward the right rear wall, including two for the area we wanted to excavate.

Still we weren't ready to dig. Don was drawing a sketch map of the shelter. On his map I saw we would be excavating squares 1W1S and 2W1S, numbered according to their positions west and south of the datum point. Then, after setting up the screens at the mouth of the cave, we stopped for lunch. Sitting and eating our sandwiches, we talked about the work ahead.

Don explained that each man in a square would dig with a trowel within measured six-inch layers. Both he and his teammates at the screen would have paper sacks to hold anything of interest they might find. Each sack was to be marked with the appropriate square number and layer, for instance Square 2W1S, 18″ to 24″. Important items would go into separate marked envelopes. If anything important were found in its original resting place, Don would have us taking measurements, making sketches, taking photographs.

What might we find? What should we look for?

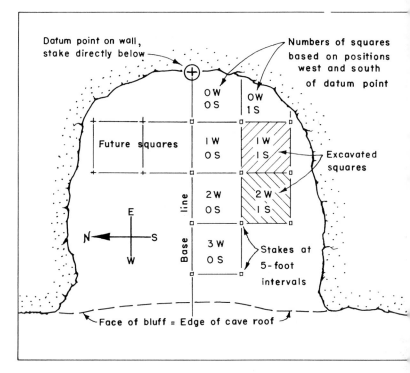

Sketch map of the dry shelter

"This site is extremely dry," Don replied, "so we should find many perishables. Remember, we want to save everything—plant materials of all kinds. Leaves, stems, grass . . . Watch especially for seeds.

"And save every chip of flint—it takes an expert to know a small flint knife when he sees one. Just save all worked flint of any sort. Just save *anything* altered in any way by man."

Did we have to save periwinkle shells? The pothunters' dirt piles had them by the thousands . . . .

"No, we don't need to save them all—but get a representative sample from each layer."

Don believed that the Indians had boiled and eaten the periwinkles. Most of the shells had their tips bitten or broken off, so that the snails could have been pulled or sucked out of the shells.

Were periwinkles a delicacy, as snails are today to some people? Or had living been pretty hard, so that Indian women had to scour the creek bottoms for these tiny snails to make a meal? We did not know, but the sheer number of shells on the cave floor suggested that snails were often on the Indians' menu.

We had finished lunch, and Don and Gene were to dig in the two squares. They began to move dirt, a handful at a time with 6-inch trowels.

And with every turn of a trowel, clouds of gray dust billowed up, enveloping all of us. Don had put on a respirator and we thought he looked amusing, sitting

in the dust and breathing through a rubber snout. But he wasn't inhaling the stuff, and we were.

Stuart Towns poured the first bucket of dirt on the screen, raising a choking fog of dust—we hastily backed off.

The cloud settled and we began raking the material across the screen. Again we were enveloped in dust. There just wasn't any avoiding it.

We had to face another not-too-pleasant fact—the cave had long been a shelter for domestic animals. After the dust sifted through the screens, half of what remained was dried goat droppings.

Dust and goat droppings. All afternoon. Dust and goat droppings. That wasn't all, though. We were finding a great variety of things the Indians had left, and Don was getting his plant material in abundance. We were saving grass fiber, seed heads, broken hickory and walnut shells, acorns, many tree leaves and bits of wood. Often there were pieces of peeled cane; the peelings had been used in making baskets. I picked three or four large melon seeds off the screen, and those went into special envelopes.

To the uninitiated it would have all been just so much trash; we were creating birds' nests of grass in open paper sacks. But for a while, at least, even the smallest, most insignificant-looking things were treated as important discoveries. We watched the screens very closely, and I was considerably thrilled on finding a grain of Indian corn.

There were broken mussel shells, and pieces of deer and wild turkey bones the Indians had cracked to remove the marrow. There were many, many, *many* periwinkles—none over an inch long. I was becoming impressed at how the red men had used every bit of food the land afforded; they seemed to have wasted nothing. Then I discovered the tiny toothy jawbone of what must have been a mouse. I couldn't help speculating that the animal had ended its days in the stew pot.

Though we picked out and saved flint chips by the hundreds, we found only half a dozen arrow points through the whole afternoon, and most of those were broken. Each point was around an inch long, exquisitely made, and the one or two whole ones had tips almost needle sharp. These 'bird points' were of the Scallorn type, and Don told us that Scallorns were used widely

in this region from about A.D. 700 to 1500.

We were all quietly at work late in the afternoon when Jack Gregory, at one of the screens, shouted in excitement. We rushed to see what he had found.

He was holding a broken Scallorn point. Twisted around its stem was a rare and perishable fragment, a bit of the sinew the Indian had used for tying the point to the arrow shaft.

We came upon a few other perishables including a small piece of cane basketry and several short lengths of twisted and braided cord. But except for the whole Scallorn points which I suppose some brave dropped and lost, I am sure no Indian would have given any of this stuff a second glance. We were delving through their trash heap, the rubbish and dinner scraps they had thrown on the floor of their living room. From time to time even they must have objected to the mess—and the women had figuratively swept it under the rug by covering it up with fresh dirt they carried in from outside. Then they all began building a new layer of litter on the floor . . . . We could thank them, centuries later, for their untidy habits.

The second Sunday nearly became an all-day repetition of our first afternoon of digging. However, some of the excitement of discovery had passed, and the annoyances seemed without end. Through hour after hour we hoped to reach bottom of the disturbed surface zone with its dust and goat droppings, but it did not appear.

We moved from one layer to the next in the pits, changing sacks and beginning to build new grassy birds' nests in the new bags. We found bits of turtle shells and a beaver's tooth and more Indian twine, and we took sample after sample of periwinkles. It was becoming a long day.

Most of us now had respirators. At first I thought mine extremely uncomfortable, but supposed they were just made that way. Then someone informed me I was wearing it upside down.

How old was this stuff we were saving? Don guessed that it might be anywhere from 500 to 1100 years, and that caused new stirrings in my mind. I picked a leaf off the screen, a sycamore leaf, gray with dust. Had it actually been here since before Columbus?

Finally we reached bottom of the disturbed zone in the rear square. Don then collected bits of charcoal for possible carbon 14 testing, and soil samples for microscopic examination. The soil, he told us, contained tiny seeds, plant pollen and minute snails, all of interest to the specialist.

Today we had found a few more Scallorn points, broken and whole, and in the afternoon one of us discovered a perfect point with some of the tying string attached.

Somehow there was more excitement in finding the first one.

Around four o'clock Gene uncovered a fragment of basket in the rear square, then a piece of bone about three inches in diameter and slightly concave. Don became a little excited, for the bone appeared to be a portion of a child's skull. Both Gene and Don carefully worked over the area with trowels and a camel's hair brush, but nothing more appeared. They kept at it, working down a spot about a foot across. In half an hour they'd taken out three or four inches of fine dirt, but nothing else, until . . .

Now they were uncovering a little mound of resistant material, matting of some sort. Don kept sweeping the dust with his brush, exposing several square inches. He scraped dirt again with his trowel, then removed the rest with his brush. The bared hump of matting was now six inches across, and draped over something. Don looked up at us. "I believe this is a pelvic bone," he said. "We've found a burial."

Don resumed his meticulous troweling and brushing, enlarging the uncovered area, soon working several inches down beside the hipbone. At that time he made another discovery—the bone beyond the edge of the matting still had a thin covering of dried flesh and skin. The burial

and screening 115

was at least partly desiccated, preserved because it had been so dry.

What should we do now? We couldn't possibly remove the burial today; it was nearly sundown. "No," Don admitted, "it's awfully fragile. We'd tear it to pieces if we tried to take it out now.

"This is a recent burial—recent in prehistory, I mean. It seems to be well preserved, which could make it quite important to science. Look at this matting; it had feathers woven into it. That *is* unusual.

"I don't feel competent to remove this," Don continued. "We need people from the University Museum. We need packing materials, and a litter for carrying it out, and preservatives——"

Who should have the burial once it was removed? We talked about this, and finally agreed that no one of us should keep it, nor could we. It would have to be treated with preservatives and protected from all shock and movement; otherwise it would rapidly disintegrate. The University Museum was the logical place for keeping and eventually displaying this burial.

Before leaving the cave we covered our find with paper, then with earth and a carefully-placed large flat stone to keep wild animals from disturbing it. We would return in a week with others to help us remove the Indian.

Next Sunday morning we had fourteen people at the shelter, an enlarged digging crew plus several advisors and onlookers. Jim Scholtz and Mike Hoffman had come from the Museum, and Don had also rounded up several of the area's best amateurs.

By noon the burial was nearly all exposed, and I saw that it lay on one side, knees pulled up under the chin and arms tucked somewhere underneath the matting. It took so little space—only about 24 by 40 inches—that I guessed out loud that it must have been a child. Someone immediately corrected me. Our experts, who had often seen Indian burials in this compact flexed position, believed this one had been a full-grown adult. The Indian was not of robust size, however.

Most of the body was covered with a fiber mat, and a heavier mat, the one having feathers, was draped over the upper portion. The feather mat was skillfully made of bundles of small stems tied one against another; what little that remained of the feathers protruded from between the stems of the bundles.

A portion of the head was uncovered, revealing a small patch of skin and thin brownish hair adhering to the upper side. Except for a little of the hip which we had seen first, the only other uncovered part was the feet. On the upper foot, portions of the toes, toenails, and even the whorls of the skin on the bottoms of the toes and the

ball of the foot were preserved. The lower foot also had a few patches of skin intact.

Our plan was to dig a trench around the body until it lay on a pedestal of earth, then to dig directly under it until it could be lifted free in one piece, matting and all. We would then place it in a shallow wooden litter for transporting to the Museum.

We took most of the afternoon just in digging the trench. It had to be done with trowels to avoid damage, and every bit of earth was sifted for artifacts that might accompany the body. Nothing turned up, though, either in the trench or on the screens.

When the trench was finished, Scholtz, Hoffman and Dickson began troweling deep hand holds in the crumbly earth pedestal supporting the Indian. This delicate work took nearly an hour.

At last they were finished. About eight of us slipped into the trench around the burial and huddled like football players listening to their quarterback—in this case Jim Scholtz. He emphasized that everyone should get his hands as far under the burial as possible, then lift and move slowly in unison. Others would position the litter close to the edge of the pit for receiving the body and its clod of earth.

Everything went well, but our handholds hadn't been quite low enough. We found the pedestal littered with loose bones, principally of a hand which had lain on the underside of the body. The lower portion of the burial obviously wasn't as well preserved. We hurriedly picked up whatever bones we could find and placed them in the litter. All our equipment was ready to go; it was nearly dark.

With great care and anxiety, four of our crew carried the burial litter down the hill toward the cars. Don planned to load it in his Chevrolet for the trip to Fayetteville and the Museum.

Don opened the trunk. We lifted the litter to slide it in. It wouldn't go! It was at least six inches too long.

And so it was, too, with Scholtz's Ford, and with the other cars. We had a burial we couldn't transport!

Stuart Towns' Volkswagen, parked off to one side, had been ignored. It looked so small.

"Stuart," I asked, "have you ever taken the back seat out of your VW?"

"I have it out right now."

"Come on, let's try Stuart's car. Bring the litter over here."

It worked. After shoving the front passenger seat forward against the dash, we could shoehorn the litter onto the back-less back seat. Stuart still had room to sit and drive. One of the others would ride on a corner of the back seat to watch over the Indian.

The Indian burial. It lies face down, head to the left.

On one more visit to the shelter, we sifted the loose dirt in the pit for any stray bones, then decided we'd reached a logical stopping point. We had planned this as an exploratory or test excavation to begin with; none of us had time to do any more. And Don believed that the ground below the burial was too damp; there wouldn't be any more perishables. The poor preservation of the lower side of the burial was evidence of this damper soil.

Through the following months, Don Dickson sorted and cataloged the material from our layer sacks and began the longer task of analysis, identification, and writing a report.[3] Soon he could offer some tentative conclusions—

The dry stratum containing the perishable remains which we excavated appeared to result from a single occupation in the late Woodland period by Indians similar to Caddoan peoples who lived to the west and south. With no carbon 14 date yet available, Don 'guess dated' the occupation as somewhere between A.D. 600 and 1100. That means the burial is probably about 1000 years old.

[3]When examining the plant remains, shells and broken bones, Don listed the things the Indians ate. He identified most of the common animals of the area; wild fruits including pawpaw, persimmon and plum; acorns and nuts of course; and domesticated plants including beans, squash, gourds and sunflowers. He found lamb's-quarter or pigweed, one of the Indians' pot herbs and of the same family as spinach and beets. There were probably several varieties of corn. Many plants remained unidentified; he would ask trained botanists about these.

Apparently the cave was abandoned at the end of this occupation, for there was no evidence of the Mississippian cultural pattern which extended from the close of the Woodland around A.D. 1200 to the arrival of white men with their trade goods after 1600. The 'pureness' of this Woodland site having no intermixture of Mississippian artifacts is itself of value to archeology.

At the University Museum, Mike Hoffman painstakingly removed and screened the dirt we had left piled on and around the burial. He found no artifacts, but now the skull, which faced downward, was in view. The lower jaw had dropped open, giving the macabre impression that the dead Indian might be grinning or talking.

In time, the overworked Museum staff would finish cleaning and treating the burial with preservatives, and they hoped to then place it on display. There it would be for the public to see, face to grinning face.

In this sampling of the past we have taken long leaps through time, from talking about fossil marine animals 350 million years old to searching for 3000-year-old peccary bones, and then to finding an Indian 1000 years old. Now we take one more step, to the pioneer past of only a few decades ago.

Lois McCutcheon's father, Walter Christian, had grown up along the ridge between Cave Creek valley and Rich-

George Ward's two barns:
(above) Squared logs, carefully
dovetailed, from the old
Mount Hecla schoolhouse.
(below) Round logs, put together
with much less care.

land valley to the east, in and near a community called Iceledo. By one account, Iceledo was someone's way of spelling 'isolated'—an intriguing name for a mountain community. Jack McCutcheon and I wanted to take Walt there and have him show us around.

One May morning the three of us climbed into Jack's pickup truck and headed across the wide Cave Creek bottom land through Bass, up the mountain to the south, then east along the ridge to Iceledo Gap. From the Gap we turned into a shady byway along Taylor Bench, a gently sloping shelf running northward along the mountain side. Neither Jack nor I had ever come this far before. From here on, it was Walt's day to show us places he had known as a boy.

About half a mile down the lane we stopped at the first homestead. Little remained of the house but piles of rotting laths and shingles. Walt began talking.

"This was . . . as fer back as I can recollect, George Ward lived here. But I don't think that'll go back to when it was built.

"I wouldn't doubt if this old buildin' here—I wouldn't doubt if it ain't a hundred. It was an old buildin' when we moved in on Devils Fork, fifty two year ago. It was a real old buildin' then."

A hand-hewn wall plate lay on the ground. Somehow this long beam had stayed while nearly everything else had decayed or gotten carried away. Jack told me that its rectangular holes had been mortised by hand for fitting other beams at right angles into the plate.

Though Jack was only in his forties, in his youth he had helped put up log buildings himself (Log construction persisted in Newton County until World War II.). He picked up a lath about three feet long and showed me how it had been split by hand, with portions shaved flat for nailing it to the rafters. Hand-split shingles were nailed in turn to these laths.

This yard had once been some woman's pride. Iris and peonies were in bloom, and deep dark red rambler roses. And always the settlers had planted daffodils. Here they grew along the stone walk . . . .

Walt and Jack had moved to the rear of the house. They were studying a heavy piece of wood lying in the grass, a hewn flat about five feet long, 16 inches wide and four inches thick. Suddenly Walt spoke. "I'll tell you what that's been, Jack. That's been the old meat bench in the old smokehouse."

We strolled down to the barns. The two buildings were now only pens of logs with the roofs fallen in. One was of pine logs, carefully squared and notched and fitted together. The other had round logs loosely laid one atop another.

Walt told us the squared logs had come from the old

Mount Hecla schoolhouse. About 1917, the school board had decided to build a new building, a "board school," as Walt put it. "They let George Ward have the logs if he would tear the old school down . . ."

We moved over to the other barn, the one with round logs, and Walt talked about the art of log construction.

"They jointed barns different to what they did the houses. They jointed just two sides of the barn logs.

"Then, later on, they knocked the house logs like these . . . the later house logs were just kinda sized two ways. The barn logs weren't even scalped. From 19 and 20 on down, barn logs were just cut and notched and put together."

Walt now pointed to a door frame in which there were several square wooden pegs. "Puncheon door facing was split out and then hewed out and dressed with a drawknife," he said.

"—and then pegged in," Jack added.

"They made their pegs of a night," Walt went on. "They split them out and whittled their pegs of a night. Then, when they had a house-raisin', they had their pegs ready."

We walked back to the truck and drove down the lane, bumping past the Jesse Bolin place, and the Henry Hill place, and the sites of two or three other homesteads whose families Walt had known. The buildings were gone. No one lived in Iceledo any more.

By the time we reached the site of the Mount Hecla School, I'd learned to pronounce it as they did: Hecly. The frame building, Walt's "board school," had been taken away, leaving only the foundation, broken remains of homemade pupils' benches, and the stone well. Walt sat on the well box and reminisced about his days here in school (relatively few, since he was a cutup), and about the games they played in the now-empty schoolyard (baseball, usually, with the teacher playing catcher).

I pulled out my topographic map, and we pored over that. The rough country around Iceledo had many features named on the map—mountains, knobs, ridges, peaks. Barlow Christian Mountain, not far north of us, had been named for Walt's father.

Walt jabbed a finger at the sheet, pointing to a name set between Barlow Christian Mountain and Iceledo Mountain. "Now, that Lawyer Gap . . . I don't know if you've heared how it got its name. There was some fellers stoled a yearlin', and beefed it. They had their trial there in the Gap."

Across the road was a modest cottage with brick-pattern composition siding and a tin roof. This had been the home of Uncle Ben and Aunt Emmaline Taylor, an old bachelor and his spinster sister. The door stood open, so we stepped in and surveyed the clutter of odds and ends: a cane bottom chair without the bottom, a cracked coffee cup, faded magazines from the year 1950.

Behind the cottage stood a sagging cabin that had been the earlier home of Uncle Ben and Aunt Emmaline. Walt well remembered visiting them here in his childhood. In looking over the cabin, we found three oddly-shaped sticks jammed between the logs. Each was about 30 inches long and pointed at both ends. What were they for?

These were gammon sticks, Walt explained. "They were used for hanging hogs at butchering."

The cabin's log smokehouse had two more sticks pegged into the front wall at shoulder height. I asked Walt why they were there. He looked at them for a moment, then remembered. They had supported a hen's nesting box.

The Taylor barn was also of logs; in fact they had come from the first Mount Hecly schoolhouse, antedating the one that had become a barn on the George Ward place. Jack and I climbed the open-jointed front wall and peered into the loft. There on the floor was a section of hollow tree trunk with a hinged lid; again I asked for an explanation. It was a mountaineer's beehive, a 'bee gum', so called because hollow gum logs were often used for that purpose.

We crept in low gear up the rocky, rutted track beyond the schoolyard. Then we passed the Rufus Taylor place, an unpainted frame house which had been the last Iceledo post office, until around 1950. A quarter mile beyond that, we had to stop; a fallen tree blocked the way. We would walk a short distance down the lane to one more log house, the John Hill place, built about 1900.

It was nearly in ruins. The front porch had collapsed and the house roof leaked so badly that everything else was decaying from the inside out. The cabin had a second-story loft with one outside door. The stairway to the door had vanished, but someone had set the head of an old iron bedstead against the wall below the opening. First Jack and then I climbed that and peeped over the threshold. Save for piles of rubbish, the loft was empty.

I climbed down and the three of us turned back toward the truck. We had come as far and seen as much as we could that day.

4 LONG LONELY RICHLAND

LEAVING the tin-roofed village of Snowball, a county road climbs past the school buildings, winds across the foothills and ascends the flank of Rollins Mountain to McCutcheon Gap. From there the road switchbacks down through the woods into Richland valley.

This was the most direct of all the ways I had traveled into Richland, but it, too, was not to be taken casually. Rollins Mountain was yet another barrier; the road seemed to become narrower as I drove up and over the Gap. Going down the long hill into Richland that gray March afternoon, I sensed a difference in the surroundings . . . .

Calf Creek valley and the lands farther east had been more open, more populated. Here, as I peered ahead through the trees, I could glimpse only one irregular strip of cleared fields along the valley floor. Another high wooded ridge lay beyond. There wasn't a house in sight.

At the foot of the hill I did come upon an old farmhouse, and the road forked. I decided to first take the right, and so followed it north for a quarter mile, turned left along the creek—and stopped. Richland Creek had no bridge. The ford would have been easy in summer, but now the flood ran broad and deep. One of the people living across the creek had parked his car here on the near shore and waded home.

Beyond the far bank, I knew, the road continued for four miles down the valley to the Buffalo at Woolum Ford, with only two occupied dwellings in the whole distance. Jack and Lois McCutcheon and I had come over the back way from Cave Creek to see that lower end of Richland.

Along the valley road we had passed abandoned houses, quite often large ones. And the ruins of a one-room school, and one or two empty, tumble-down country store buildings. All had been part of the once-thriving Point Peter community.

And there were miles of broad and level fields, some of the finest crop land in the Buffalo River valley. The old farms were now in a single large holding, and a few tenants with modern equipment were managing the entire spread.

Oddly enough, the last, largest field down Richland Creek had been in cotton, that same crop so important in the valley long ago before the Civil War. I could hardly believe it; cotton hadn't been grown anywhere else in this country in twenty years. The nearest gin was a hundred miles away.

But we had stopped and looked, and there they were, the bare winter stalks of last year's crop of cotton.

Turning back from the creek, I drove up the valley through what was left of the Eula community. Along the dirt road there were three or four houses being lived in, three or four others abandoned, the empty Hall School, the well-filled Hall Cemetery.

The School, a squarish shed-like building having one big room, still housed a collection of plank benches, children's desks with 'Sears Roebuck' cast into their fancy iron scrollwork, and the teacher's high desk near the recitation platform up front. Walls were papered with the *Arkansas Gazette* of the early 1930's.

Less than two miles above Hall School, another deep ford of Richland Creek blocked my way up the valley. I had to return by Snowball . . . though not before having another leisurely look around.

Richland worked a strange spell, compounded of quiet loneliness and the beauty of producing farm lands set below the timbered ridges. And of tangible reminders of the past, for though many had disappeared, many others remained. Old farmhouses reflected a bygone day, and along the roadside I had found a dozen spans of rail fence. And now I had walked out to a neglected family graveyard set beneath big trees in the center of a field.

Returning to the car, I stopped and listened. The steady drone of a tractor came from across the bottoms. Slowly the farmer dragged his harrow past the far hedgerow, trailing a cloud of dust.

In the deepening twilight, I left him with his work.

120

Spring branch near Harriet, Searcy County

THE LAND

The Boston Mountain escarpment, from South Mountain near Marshall westward to Point Peter.

*"No, I don't carry that,
but the salesman wanted to put up a sign anyway."*

What's there to see in this country?

It may not impress you,
   this low range of mountains
   breaking off to a lower plateau.
And in winter, drab woodlands,
   and fields with broken chert
   lying among the dead weed stalks.

But look to her people.
Kindly, unaffected,
   they hold to a slower pace,
   and in their language
   and on their lands,
   you will find ways of the past.
Look quickly, before those ways are gone.

Some newcomers talk about quaintness.
Look for the deeper beauty.

The Murrays' log house

Redbud *(Cercis canadensis)*

Return in the spring,
   winter's end, and a new beginning.
In every corner of the land,
   you will find a floral procession
   of beauty and immense variety,
   a continuing parade of life and bloom
   on to the climax of autumn.

J. M. Clark

Celandine-poppy
(Stylophorum diphyllum)

Umbrella magnolia
(Magnolia tripetala)

124

Fire pink *(Silene virginica)*

May-apple *(Podophyllum peltatum)*

Early azalea
(Rhododendron roseum)

125

Sink opening into Peccary Cave

Helicitites, Beauty Cave

Search.
Find the hidden places,
  and discover
  the strange and mysterious.
Find memorable experiences
  and a deepened awareness,
  closer to the land.

J. H. *Schermerhorn*

126

Pioneers' wall along a little-used road near the Buffalo headwaters

At John Eddings Cave

Hemmed-in Hollow

In Richland valley

The ford above Eula blocked me from that even more isolated part of Richland upstream until I had traveled a long, roundabout road over the mountain from Bass past Iceledo Gap and the Round Hill Tower. It was all to see only one more mile of Richland valley. Still another impassable ford prevented my going farther up the creek.

This I regretted. My map showed the road continuing up the narrow valley past the last fields and farmhouses, past the abandoned Wasson School where the hills close in and the really wild country begins. Someday, possibly in the summer when the creek is low, I want to visit that part of Richland.

The creek's headwaters are in the Boston Mountains, within the Ozark National Forest. Richland's farthest source lies at one of the southern extremities of the Buffalo watershed, and the creek flows more than thirty-two miles from beginning to mouth. It is the longest of the Buffalo's tributaries.

Two well-graded National Forest roads cross upper Richland Creek, and one of them, the Falling Water Road, is perhaps the loneliest in all the Ozarks. For eleven miles along that road I didn't see a single house, nor any sign that people had ever lived there. Driving down the forested canyon of Richland's tributary Falling Water Creek, I was struck by how rough, how truly primeval the country looked. Many yards below the road, the creek brawled noisily down the ledges and among the rocks and boulders. Beyond the creek and down the canyon were wooded ridges capped by rugged bluff chains of the Atoka formation. On the hill opposite, great isolated rocks stood alone against the storm-dark evening sky.

Halfway down Falling Water I had stopped to admire Falling Water Falls, where the creek plunged ten feet off an overhanging ledge within plain view of the road. A waterfall, any waterfall, holds me fascinated.

It had begun to rain. I'd climbed back to the car and driven on. Tomorrow I had an appointment to see another waterfall; the district forest ranger had told me about a much larger one up Richland.

The sprinkle of rain had stopped when I came to the concrete bridge across Richland Creek, but new clouds were moving in and now it was almost totally dark. After some searching, I located the Forest Service camping area some distance up a side lane. The campground consisted of a clearing in the woods, and two signposts. I pulled out my flashlight. One sign gave the rules for camping. From the other, Smokey Bear cautioned me not to start any forest fires.

As the night's rain began drumming on my car roof, I finished my simple supper, pushed a seat forward and climbed into my sleeping bag.

At six-thirty the next morning I started hiking up Richland Creek to look for the waterfall.

After wading across Falling Water Creek I stumbled on an old logging trail, but it soon vanished and I was on my own. There was no sign of man save an occasional rotting stump from the logging long ago. I picked my own way, for a while following the tracks of a stray pig which had come wandering, rooting along the creek bank. The tracks soon disappeared.

Richland Creek was flowing full from the rains; I would have to keep to this south side. And the stream was as

wild and beautiful as any I had ever seen. Green torrents roared among the boulders, and now the flood was flanked by monstrous rocks the size of small houses.

Only yards away from the roar and hubbub of the creek, I passed sheltered nooks and corners of the woods where the first tender wild flowers of April were pushing up through the dead leaves. Few were yet in bloom, but I recognized the distinctive stem and leaf forms of dog-tooth violets, *Dentaria*, the yellow merry-bells, and Dutch-man's-breeches. Perhaps there were rarer species, too, for here they would not be disturbed.

The hiking became more rugged. Several times the creek swung against the south hill, carving small bluffs, and I had to take long routes up and over. After what seemed to be endless scrambling and climbing (it was now nearly ten o'clock), Richland Creek began to bend south-ward, and through the trees and across the creek I spied the mouth of Devils Fork. The waterfall could not be far.

Another bluff blocked my way, and now I could hear the roar of Richland Falls. I looked across the creek. Here the stream was wide, a series of shoals dotted with little islands of rock. I decided to wade to the other, lower shore.

First I had to make ready: rolling up pants legs, then taking off boots and tying them together by the laces to hang around my neck. Finally I slung the tripod over one shoulder, picked up the camera box, and stepped in.

Ouch! The first shock was cold water.

I took another step. Ouch! There was broken slate all over the bottom . . . .

Slowly, painfully, cursing the rocks and leaning pre-cariously against the racing current, I worked my way from island to island and across . . . why hadn't I given those pants cuffs one more turn?

Richland Falls was only six feet high. But that could be overlooked because of its great width—fully a hundred feet of flood spreading across and spilling over the ledge-rock, brilliant white torrents of water disappearing into a line of foam that spread and dissipated across the dark blue-green pool. Again I was overcome by my weakness for waterfalls. I took pictures, too many pictures, until I finally realized it was past noon.

While sitting and eating the sandwiches I'd stowed in the camera box, I decided it would be better to hike the north side of Richland Creek back down to the bridge. The going couldn't be any rougher than the south bank, and besides, I'd avoid having to wade that creek again.

I began walking and boulder-hopping down the north bank, and in fifteen minutes reached Devils Fork, the trib-utary I had recognized when coming upstream that morn-ing. With my heavy equipment, I thought Devils Fork was just a little too wide to jump. Yet taking off boots

Falling Water Falls

Richland Falls

to wade only three yards or so seemed too much bother. I strolled up the creek, looking for stepping stones. There were few . . .

Two hundred yards upstream, I hopped across—and at that moment something caught my eye. Farther up the creek, a dark shadow under a bluff suggested a shelter cave.

On reaching the overhang, I found it was shallow, filling up with shale fallen from the cliff above. I turned to go—wait a minute!

If I'd not wandered this far, I'd never have seen them. I hurried up the creek. There beyond the trees, just around the bend, sparkling in the sunlight, were *two* waterfalls, side by side.

Here in the most pristine of settings, the falls dropped into a pool the color of jade, with thousands of shimmering silver wavelets. Who had ever seen this place? A few woodsmen, perhaps, and hunters . . . The forest ranger had told me about Richland Falls, hardly a quarter mile away, but not these. Had he ever seen them?

The streams above the falls came from different directions. I hauled out my map. Of course! This was the meeting of Long Devils Fork, on the left, with Big Devils Fork, the larger stream on the right.

Long Devils' fall appeared to be about 16 feet high,

and Big Devils' about 18 feet. Both waterfalls were deeply undercut; I could have walked around the pool behind both of them had I wanted. For a moment I stood in the swirling mist of the passage behind Big Devils' fall, glancing out through the bright curtain of water, scanning the floor and rear wall. The spray and deafening roar became more than I could stand and I retreated.

The cliff wall was dark shale, but along its base I found broken pieces of limestone fallen from above. They contained odd corkscrew fossils, about a quarter inch in diameter and up to ten inches long. I'd never seen the likes of these before.[1]

My picture session lasted until a shadow began to creep across the silvery curtain of Long Devils' fall. The sun was moving west, and I needed to be on my way.

Another long-abandoned logging trail appeared to lead homeward from the mouth of Devils Fork. But I soon found it turned back up the mountain, so I struck off through the woods. First I tried to stay high on the hillside, taking a cross-country route above the bluffs fronting Richland Creek.

[1]Unknown to me at the time, they were stems of bryozoans of the genus *Archimedes*, index fossil of the Pitkin limestone. The Pitkin for this reason is sometimes called the 'Archimedes' limestone.

The waterfalls on Devils Fork

This proved exceedingly rough, slow travel. Gradually I worked down to a low route along the creek itself. Now I had to thread around, behind, over and between innumerable boulders, and this also proved exceedingly tiring and slow.

The sun was nearly touching the western mountain top when I looked across Richland and saw Falling Water Creek flowing into the main stream. Before long I had climbed onto the roadway, trudged across the bridge and to the camp area. By my watch and map, I had taken two hours to hike those last two un-level miles.

During the long drive home, visions of the day's travels swam through my mind . . . scenes of wilderness, sounds of green water spilling among the boulders. Sunlight sparkles on that incredible jade-green pool below the Devils Fork waterfalls.

I settled into deep, weary satisfaction. Today I had seen all the best of upper Richland valley.

Or had I?

Walt Christian, who lived as a boy at the head of Big Devils Fork below Iceledo Gap, would soon tell me about another waterfall. It spilled into a box canyon on Long Devils Fork barely a quarter mile above the twin falls.

I hope it, too, will wait until another day.

(Map on page 168)

LAND OF ROCKS 5

WITH MANY stops and distractions, we have been gradually working our way down the Buffalo River watershed, until now we can move into the reach of country east of U. S. Highway 65. Here, since the Boston Mountains only skirt the southern edge of the drainage, our travels will be wholly within the Springfield Plateau . . . again in Boone limestone country.

And here, where the Boone formation spreads far and wide over the land, we are faced with its one overwhelming aspect—its mantle of rusty orange clay and flinty chert gravel. More than anything else, this is a land of rocks.

The Boone chert is to be seen nearly everywhere. Motorists drive on it, for it is both foundation and surfacing for countless miles of gravel roads. Hikers and hunters walk on it, for it covers the ground through untold acres of woodlands. Farmers even cultivate it, for the broken rock may comprise half of all they touch with their plows. On the Springfield Plateau, 'flintrock' is the most basic fact of existence.

Beneath its covering of clay and chert, the Boone limestone goes hundreds of feet deep, and the very appearance of the landscape is the result of the Boone's peculiarities.

The typical Boone topography begins with major ridges lying between the perennial streams; and from the major ridges many lesser ridges extend like fingers; and from those in turn still lesser ridges extend in a dendritic or branching pattern in all directions; and between the ridges are a maze of ravines, hollows, and feeder valleys. It is all very rough and complex. One such area northeast of Marshall was aptly named 'The Wilderness' on old topographic maps.

Many of the smaller hollows and ravines are 'solution valleys' created more by dissolving, honeycombing and collapse of the underlying limestone than by the normal work of erosion. The solution of limestone has taken place partly at the surface of the bedrock beneath the chert mantle, and partly along drainage lines or crevices of the rock. Solution valleys contain no streams except after rains, and then only small ones in their lower parts. These ravines open out into the perennial stream valleys all over the Boone limestone area.

Even the largest streams are often choked with chert gravel that has washed down from nearby hillsides. Creeks may seem to flow only after rains, but usually there is water running under the gravel, and it may continue through all but the driest times.

The larger stream valleys do have some fine alluvial farm land; Bear Creek has the best in this area. And scattered upland prairies may have good crop land or pasture. But most of the region's farmers live on the widespread chert, and there a man really can't make a decent living at farming.

Out among the ridges you are apt to see the strawberry patches, steep gravelly slopes plowed straight up the hill— the only way a tractor can be safely maneuvered. Berries are the one big money crop on the gravel, a sort of make-it-while-you-can venture. The denuded slopes grow good strawberries, but only for a few seasons. There isn't even enough topsoil to visibly erode away, but the fertility goes.

The wildest, least populated part of this country is that nearest the Buffalo, where the larger creeks come down narrow valleys in entrenched meanders like those of the river itself, and smaller streams divide the land into many rough ridges and ravines. Farther back from the river, the road from St. Joe to Maumee and Highway 27 from Marshall to Harriet both wind along the highest gravel ridges. State 74 east of Marshall and the road up Sellers Creek to Campbell both follow open valleys bounded by gravelly hills and threaded by gravel-choked streams. South of Highway 74, the land gently rises toward the foot of the Boston Mountain escarpment, and the surface gravel is replaced by overlying sandstone and shale.

This land is poor and it lacks that element of the spectacular which we find in the scenery of the Boston Mountains, or along every portion of the Buffalo River itself. Yet in a hundred ways the country is beautiful. Beauty can be found in summer's soft folds of green that cloak the rocky ridges, or in October's glory of color

133

Land of Rocks: 'Pasture' on the Boone chert north of Marshall

through the woodlands. It can be found in the redbud-brightened hills of April, or in the warm golden glow of late afternoon sunlight on the summer countryside. It can be found in the cold silent flow of a spring welling up from under a bed of water cress, or in the dappled shade of a little-traveled country lane down a back hollow. So much depends on what we choose to see.

Here as elsewhere, the Boone lime contains numberless caves. Some have been known for generations. Blowing Cave, across the creek from the hamlet of Zack, served as a fruit shippers' warehouse through the years when Zack was a flag stop on the old Missouri and North Arkansas Railroad. Other caves in the area have names suggesting past ownership (as for Pruitt's Cave near Marshall); location (Davis Creek Cave); past use (Saltpeter Cave on the Buffalo below Gilbert); or natural phenomena (Wind Cave southwest of Marshall). But many others are only anonymous holes in the ground, and the true extent of even the better-known caves is yet unsettled. This general lack of knowledge has stimulated a new curiosity, a quest for caves coupled with a desire to find and record what lies within.

For example, Haunted Cave in southern Marion County is one of the county's largest, and long the most talked-about. The name Haunted (or 'Hainted') comes from several vague legends, the most widespread one being the 'fiddler' story: Once a country fiddler ventured into the cave, and he never returned. The tale persists that the fiddler can still be heard playing weird ghostly tunes somewhere back in the darkness of Haunted Cave.

For all that talk, the cave wasn't thoroughly explored until 1964, when a group of high school students from Yellville became curious about it. First they followed the main corridor as far as they could, about 1500 feet. Then they systematically checked out the one lengthy side passage and all the short, paralleling alternate routes. They brought in climbing equipment, scaled two small waterfalls in the side passage and went on into lesser tunnels and crawlways no one else had ever seen. Finally, when the crawl space became less than spelunker-size, they turned back.

With the help of their teacher-advisor Dan Marsh, they then produced a detailed map of Haunted Cave. Apparently none of the cavern's interior features had been named, so the boys thought up their own, some a bit adolescent but mostly in keeping with the cave's name and legend. The spacious, curving entrance room, some 30 feet wide by 200 long, became Mystery Hall. Further inside, other parts were named the Doom Room, Skeleton Passage, Fiddlers Rock.[1]

How could those boys 'map' a cave? You may think

Strawberry patch

it's easy—just go in with pencil and paper, and when the passage turns left . . .

But how much left? Or to begin with, how far until the passage turns left? Remember, everything beyond reach of your feeble light is in pitch blackness. And in Haunted Cave, several of the passages were nothing but muddy crawlways. Try crawling around in the dark for a while on your hands and knees—and then try to estimate how far and in what direction you've gone. Ten to one you'll exaggerate. I'm sure the first person who traveled that fifteen hundred feet to the rear of Haunted Cave called it a mile.

In a Searcy County cave that did turn out to be a measured mile in length, I was given a lesson in mapping by George Connell and three of his fellow-spelunkers from Harrison. In barely two years since the Arkansas Speleological Survey had begun in 1963, these fellows had assisted the Survey in locating nearly a hundred caves in this portion of the Buffalo watershed. Now three of them, equipped with a 100-foot measuring tape and a sighting compass, were actually surveying a cave.

Surveying proved to be a matter of teamwork, with each of the three—lead man, rear man and recorder—having specific duties. Typically, this is how I saw them work—

The lead man moved a short distance ahead and set a sighting point, merely a small metal disc that he laid

[1]The map subsequently appeared in their Shawnee Caving Club's mimeographed bulletin, *Trails Below*. The Club, incidentally, was the first high school caving group to ever become affiliated with the National Speleological Society.

Haunted Cave

on the passage floor. At the same time, the rear man moved up to the last disc the lead man had placed previously. Lead man and rear man then stretched the tape between the discs to find the distance between the two points.

Next the lead man set his carbide lamp on the floor, squarely on the metal disc that marked his sighting point. The rear man then stood on *his* point and sighted his compass on the lead man's light, a bright spot of flame in the dark passage ahead. Thus he found the azimuth or direction from one sighting point to the next. Then the lead man and rear man moved forward along the passage to repeat the process.

The third man or recorder took notes on the distances and directions from point to point along the passage. He also embellished his notes with other information such as the width of the passage at each point the lead man set; estimated heights of the ceiling along the passage; locations of openings to side passages; positions and types of major formations. Anything that would help in drawing the map, he put in his notebook.

On paper, the map was developed first as a zigzag line representing the distances and directions between sight-

ing points. Then all the other information was used to delineate the passage walls, the formations and so on. Each side passage could be surveyed and mapped in the same way, and all passages could be put in their proper relationships on one map sheet to show a multi-passaged cave.

This cave was almost entirely level. For one that isn't, mapping gets more complicated. A profile map (to show the ups and downs) may require additional surveying equipment and know-how. It can involve vertical climbing, with another set of equipment and techniques. This I learned when I accompanied Jim Schermerhorn and five other cave climbers exploring a vertical cave named Copperhead Sink, in a hillside overlooking Highway 14 east of Big Creek . . . .

"These pits aren't like ordinary caves," Jim remarked to me. "Usually they just go straight down and stop. And they're pretty common through this area—especially in Searcy and Newton Counties."

I looked again into the chimney-like hole, with an uneasy thought about what might happen to anyone lost out here at night. "How deep is it?"

"About seventy feet. But there's a talus pile at the bottom, and you'll touch the upper side about fifty-five feet down." David Taylor had answered my question. He had gone into the pit last September with the Alexander brothers, Jim and John, also with us that afternoon.

David continued. "We found several copperheads crawling around in the trash at the bottom. And frogs . . . Guess the snakes lived on the frogs. Maybe they both fell in and couldn't get out."

So that's how it came to be named Copperhead Sink. However, this was a cold, gray winter day, which took care of the snake problem. On hands and knees, I again peered over the edge of the pit. For the first ten feet down, the hole was reasonably small, but below that the cave belled out into a dimensionless black void. Just below me, a projecting ledge cut off view of the bottom.

The others were rigging the ropes and cable ladder. They were serious about this—decked out in hard hats with miner's lamps, and carrying flashlights and candles to boot. And I? At the moment I was more curious than serious; I had no hard hat, no carbide lamp, not even a candle.

Jim Schermerhorn suddenly looked straight at me. I would never do. He pulled a spare hard hat from one of his packs and made me put it on. Hard hats, he informed me, were absolutely essential when going into a pit cave.

They tied the end of the ladder to a good-sized tree, then let the ladder drop and unroll itself down the hole. Schermerhorn was looping and tying the safety rope around his chest. Hefty Jim Alexander seated himself on firm ground and prepared to belay.

Schermerhorn unhesitatingly scrambled down to the ledge, onto the ladder and down the hole; in a moment he was hidden from sight. Alexander busily paid out the safety rope, taking care to keep it fairly taut.

I watched the twitching, jerking ladder, and I could imagine Jim swinging wildly with every step, pitching from one side of the pit to the other. The rungs looked awfully far apart. And each was only wide enough to put one foot into, like a stirrup.

Taylor was next. He elected to rappel—let himself down on a rope—instead of taking the ladder.

Next was John Alexander, also rappelling. Then we tied Schermerhorn's pack of cameras to the safety rope, along with another coiled ladder to be used for a lower level, and let them down.

Jerry Gordon went in next, stepping down the ladder with great agility. Now Alexander was pulling in Jerry's safety rope. I was next to go.

Slowly I pulled the loop over my head and drew it tight under my armpits. I was next . . .

Alexander was talking. "Remember to keep your weight on your feet. Beginners always want to climb with their hands—but it'll tire out your arms.

"—and hang close to the ladder. Maybe you'd better wrap your legs around it; put your heels in from the other side. That'll keep you from leaning over backwards.

"And remember your rope signals——"

Slowly I crept down to the edge, overwhelmed by the thought that it was seventy feet to the bottom. That was as high as a five story building . . . .

Alexander gave a reassuring tug on the safety rope, and I stepped out onto the first rung. With a tight grip on the cables, I shifted my weight, lifted my other foot off the ledge . . . and onto the rung below.

Now I shifted weight, lowered the first foot down, down nearly three feet and into the next lower stirrup. I shifted my weight—and my foot pitched forward in the stirrup. Hang on for dear life!

Down a step, right leg behind the ladder, heel into the stirrup. Hang on . . .

Down. Down. Maybe ten more of those long, long steps. Ugh—now what's happened?

Oh. Snagged on a cable splice. After some gingerly raising up and pulling off, I got my coat loose. Now I could go.

Stop—stop and rest! My arms ached.

No. Just hanging there wouldn't help. Go down.

Cave surveying

Copperhead Sink: From the outside in . . .

and from the inside out.

Dutchman's-breeches

The safety line reassured. I could yell "Rope!" and Jim would pull tight. "Slack!" and he would feed out, and I'd go down a few rungs farther.

Bottom! John was steadying the ladder. No, down another rung. Finally I had one foot, and then the other, planted on the steep earth floor.

I looked around. The low side of the pit was indeed filled with trash—rocks, dead leaves, sticks. Up one wall were deep grooves eroded through the centuries by dripping water. Most of the interior was covered with elaborately fluted stalactites very slowly filling the cave with mineral. The entrance, far above us, was a bright-white spot of daylight, too small to do any more than dimly illuminate the shadowy gray walls of the pit. Now I saw my camera box coming down on the rope.

Gerald Wood, the last man to descend, rappelled in as

I tried for a picture. The others had climbed into a deep window in the wall eight feet above me, into a passage that went for two or three yards and then dropped off into another pit. They were fixing the second cable ladder for a descent.

Back in September, Taylor and the Alexanders had only looked down this second pit. Now we wanted to know whether any new passages led off from it. As Schermerhorn straddled the mouth of the pit to take straight-down movies, Jerry Gordon climbed down the ladder.

Jerry saw one opening in the wall halfway down, but it was hardly six feet deep. There was nothing but a sandy floor at the bottom. Jerry climbed out, and then they counted rungs as they pulled out the ladder. The pit turned out to be 29 feet deep. So much for that.

Now we began the process of ascent. The first man went swinging up the ladder, Schermerhorn illuminated the action with his photo floodlight, and cameras clicked. "You guys are doing more snapshooting than spelunking," said one of the non-photographers.

"Yeah, lemme see. One, two, three—five cameras down here," Jim replied.

Before long it was my turn to climb. The trip down had broken the ice; I discovered the climb back up wasn't so bad. It was tiring, but I had less trouble with the stirrups—and with my apprehensions.

For half an hour or more we were coming out and hauling up our coils of rope, the second ladder, the camera cases. The last two men then came up, and finally we were pulling in the ladder and rappel rope.

Taylor was stowing one of the coiled cable ladders in a pack. "Darn it," he lamented, "we should've taken the time in September to check out that lower pit. We wouldn't have had all this trouble."

"That's all right," Schermerhorn replied in soothing tones. "We've succeeded in finding out what's down there. It's another cave surveyed.

"And look what fun we had takin' pictures. Why, here's the most photographed pit cave in all of Searcy County."

The road which winds along the ridge into Buffalo River State Park also lies on the Boone—not that it matters. Summer visitors most often take the curves with all speed the law allows, slow down just enough to turn the corner inside the park entrance, and press the pedal again to hurry down the long hill to the swimming hole.

Why all this haste? Certainly a part of the answer lies in the almost magical allurement of water. The State Park swimming hole is a jewel in an appropriate setting, a tranquil pool which gradually deepens from the clear shallows along a spacious gravel bar to unseen depths

7:06 A.M.

7:07

7:10

7:14

7:18 A.M.

Family fishing, bright and early at the State Park

Panther Creek Rock House

at the foot of a sheer bluff and high hills looming above the far bank. The park's river frontage, then, is an outstanding combination of scenery with accessibility.

About April first, the season's early fishermen come to walk the gravel bar and try their lures. Before the first of May the water's warm enough for the more daring swimmers . . . and skin divers go poking around in the deepest places below the bluff, sometimes startling overgrown bass that the bank fishermen never see at all.

Families paddle up and down the lengthy pool in the park's rental boats, or their own, and before long the youngsters discover a rope tied to a tree on the south bank. From then on through the season, many hundreds of them grab hold, pendulum out over the water and—splash!

Life on the river often complements a camping experience; campsites are handily situated among the trees and along the meadow just above the gravel bar. Hardier campers, and those with trailers, come early, and by May the campground is alive with people roughing it in whatever degree each may choose.

Summer days are hot, but people continue to come—the river's always there for jumping in and cooling off. While families with children have to leave when schools open, September is still warm enough for swimming and October is the month of the color spectacle. November is often rainy and chilly; by then the last camper has packed up and gone home.

Even the most gregarious campers occasionally talk about getting away from it all, about going exploring. For that they can drive back up to the ridge and seek out the steep, narrow dirt road down into the park's 'back side', the ledge-rimmed canyon of Panther Creek. The road, colored and surfaced with the red Boone clay and broken chert, winds down the hill and along the creek, coming to a dead end on the shady floor of a quiet green hollow.

Visitors then see a gaping dark opening just beyond the trees. They walk up the slope and under the stone roof of Panther Creek Rock House, a shelter cave of imposing dimensions. The opening into the hollow is

168 feet wide; the roof arches to 40 feet in height; depth averages more than 80 feet. Among the rock shelters of the Buffalo River country, only Cob Cave in Lost Valley surpasses this in size.

At one end, the Rock House lengthens and deepens toward the rear, with a cave passage running even farther into the hill. A stream flows noisily from a crevice in the back wall and down a gully along one side, and then disappears into another crevice.

The Rock House lies at the threshold of other places to explore: Bat Cave, with its steep approach trail up a hillside among the azaleas, and smaller caves, springs and streams in the nearby hollows. Most of the country is second-growth woodland slowly recovering from the cut-and-burn era before the park was created in the 1930's.

Visiting the Rock House will always remind me of a trip I made down that road one afternoon early in April, for that was the day I got the notion of photographing all the wild flowers. Only a half dozen kinds were then in bloom, and the whole project looked deceptively easy. I spent an hour or two taking pictures of snowy white serviceberry and wild plum along the roadside, and Jacob's-ladder, Dutchman's-breeches, and one or two other flowers in the hollow near the cave. Then I made high resolve to take all the other species as they came into bloom.

But after the next ten days of warming weather I realized the futility of my plan—there were many more kinds of wild flowers beginning to bloom than I had time to photograph. I settled for taking the showier shrubs, and failed even to get all those. What I didn't know at the time is that the wildlands of the State Park and the rest of the Buffalo valley are host to some 800 to 1000 different species of flowering plants![2]

If nothing else, my short-lived picture project made me much more aware of the beauty and profusion of plants in the park and the other protected areas along the river. For the first time I took notice of the odd little wild ginger plant. And the smoketree, with its pinkish haze of feathery flowers. And the chaste white flowers of the bloodroot, the pink-veined blossoms of

[2]And the season of flowering is a long one. It begins with warm days in January when fragrant witch hazel bursts into bloom along the river banks, and runs to the last days of fall when dead-white Indian pipes flower in the mold of the deep woods.
Even in the Ozarks, a region noted for the richness of its flora, the Buffalo River valley is outstanding for its variety of plants and plant habitats. No one has ever counted all the kinds of plants to be found here, but estimates of the total (including non-flowering plants such as the ferns and mosses) run from more than 1000 to as many as 1500 species.

Wild plum

spring beauty, the rare flowering of the Jack-in-the-pulpit, and a host of other blooms lending brightness and variety to the fields and woods. Maybe in some other springtime I'll be able to take their portraits.

Between the river on one side and the back hollows on the other, there lies the park's center of development. A road runs straight down the cherty ridge, past a string of housekeeping cabins and all the way to the hill's rockiest extremity. There, a pleasant screened dining room overlooks the Buffalo.

From the dining room windows you watch the river, perhaps in that magical hour after sunset when the stream comes flowing from hills already in shadow, dusky ridges silhouetted against the golden after-light in the west. In the campground below, there are spots of yellow-white lantern light, and flickering supper fires. The river passes beneath your window, blocked from view; then it reappears downstream, moving to the right past high bluffs now faintly glowing in the last reflected daylight.

Gradually the light fades. A pale moon rises above the eastern ridges. The river flows on, curving to the left again under the dimly blurred folds of the hills, flowing beyond and out of sight.

(Map on page 169)

6 LOST CORNER

ALONG THE BANKS of Rush Creek are a half dozen weather-blackened buildings and the slowly crumbling stone walls and foundations of a good many more. Among the ruins stands a massive rock fireplace and chimney that once served as an ore furnace. The valley's few remaining residents, old people owning little but memories, watch over the relics and talk of better days.

Zinc was discovered in these hills about 1880, but things didn't really get moving until the early nineties, when the Morning Star mine was opened . . . and one day the miners pried from its ore face a single mass of pure zinc carbonate weighing 12,750 pounds.

The mine owners promptly recognized that their over-sized nugget of ore was worth its weight in publicity. They had Jumbo (as the miners called it) moved by wagon, White River flatboat and the railroads to the 1893 Worlds Fair in Chicago. Jumbo went on exhibit, won a gold medal, and sent speculators flying to Rush.

Through the next decade, the mines flourished; seventeen of them were operating in the Rush Creek District. Rush had become a swarming, noisy camp town of more than two thousand people. But the ore occurred only in scattered, irregular bodies, and the limestone, dolomite and chert hills overlooking Rush and Clabber Creeks were already becoming honeycombed with empty tunnels. Finding new ore often proved expensive.

World War I came, the price of zinc went sky high, and again Rush prospered. Then the war ended, prices fell, and Rush folded.

Today the abandoned Rush mines are a mecca for collectors, 'rockhounds' who search the diggings for bits of ore and pink dolomite and calcite crystals, plus the fun of exploring. They find the tunnel entrances by looking for their 'spoil banks', anthill-like piles and spills of waste rock here and there over the brushy hillsides. Many of the old passages appear safe enough to enter, but a number are beginning to cave in and some property is now closed to trespassers. At most of the mine portals,

though, the warning is only implied: Enter at your own risk.

The rockhounds' best friend at Rush, and a lode of information for all visitors, is a retired miner named Fred Dirst. I found him living in a trailer at the mouth of Rush Creek, and operating a landing there on the Buffalo, renting a few boats and canoes. I had heard that when people asked him, he would guide them through the old Red Cloud Mine across the river from his place. I asked him.

We climbed into one of his boats and motored a short distance upstream, then over to the wooded south shore. I followed him up the embankment into a small grassy clearing. Dirst paused and pointed toward the base of the hill. "Right over there," he said, "my mother and dad ran a hotel."

Dirst began talking about the lively days of the mining boom, about a neighborhood strongman and bully who insisted on taking other men and knocking their heads together—until one offended party leveled a gun at him and blew his brains out. That happened right here in front of the hotel. Only now there wasn't any hotel, or any sign of one. The frame building had disappeared without a trace.

We walked up the narrow roadway onto the spoil bank before the opening of the Red Cloud. We stepped into a half-lighted gallery where several partly caved-in portals opened to the surface. Dirst lit carbide lights and we moved farther into the mine.

High-ceilinged caverns spread into blackness beyond thick stone pillars left to support the roof. We moved past the pillars, turned corners, followed a path over rotting crossties, climbed up and down slopes. Eventually Dirst told me we had reached the deepest part of the mine. I guessed we had come three or four city blocks into the hill.

Taking another route in returning to the entrance, we stopped to look at bits of ore embedded in the walls, lustrous yellow-brown nuggets resembling pine rosin.

144

This was zinc blende or rosin jack—technically sphalerite or zinc sulphide—about 60 percent zinc.

The Red Cloud had also yielded a little calamine or zinc silicate, running about 40 percent zinc. But the most important ore, here and elsewhere in the district, was zinc carbonate or Smithsonite, also 40 percent zinc and ranging in color from white to yellow to light brown. The carbonate ore, with its glossy or pearly luster, was often called 'turkey fat' by the miners.

Present-day collectors usually pick up samples of the ores, but more often they're after the dolomite spar in which the ore is sometimes embedded. Choice specimens of dolomite have masses of little pale pink crystals, each presenting a lustrous face when turned to its best exposure to light. Occasionally the spar forms a matrix around amber-colored or clear crystals of calcite, and good examples of these are especially prized.

After nearly an hour in the mine, we returned to the entrance and stood blinking in the brightness of daylight. We walked out on the spoil bank, and Dirst showed me the locations of the Edith and Yellow Rose Mines across the river. As we started strolling down the hill, he began telling me of his first boyhood job, stoking a boiler at the Lonnie Boy Mine on the river bank opposite Rush Creek.

We paused a moment at the hotel site, where one of Dirst's cows was grazing among the trees. Then we went on to the boat.

The mined-out hills of Rush and the lands lying eastward comprise an isolated, deserted country, a hundred square miles of wild woodland with fewer than fifty living inhabitants. It is the lost corner of the Buffalo watershed.

In a sense the river has come full circle, from the forest at its headwaters through more open country at its midsection to the forest, again, here at its downstream end. And this country, with its lonely wooded ridges and creek valleys, and its bluff chains resembling those along the Boston Mountain summits, even *looks* like the land at the headwaters.[1]

Here too there was once a family living down every ridge and creek and within every bend of the river. The countryside is laced with the wagon trails that these families used for access and neighborly communication, and at times I tried to drive some of those that hadn't completely gone back to woods. It was jolting, punishing travel, threading along grass-grown lanes following the cherty ridge lines, dragging through ruts and over ribs

[1]But here the topland runs from 1000 to 1200 feet in elevation, at least a thousand feet lower than the Boston Mountains near the headwaters. And the valley bottom near the river's mouth lies within the lowest of the three divisions of the Ozark Highlands, the Salem Plateau. At the White River, the Buffalo is less than 400 feet above sea level.

Fred Dirst at the Red Cloud Mine

of bedrock on faint tracks that were hardly roads at all. Luckily I didn't ever get completely stuck, for it's a long walk out for help.

One May morning on the Cedar Creek Road, a deep mudhole stopped me a half mile short of the river, so I did get out and walk. Fred Dirst had suggested that I take a lane up the north bank of the Buffalo toward Rush, to find a long-neglected cemetery at the mouth of Cabin Creek.

The jungle along the river grew so lush and thick that I could only glimpse the Buffalo flowing quietly a few yards below. It was now becoming warm, humid, still. Now and then a bird would sing a little whistling song at its hiding place in the foliage, but the silence was noticeable. Presently I approached a gate, a small clearing hacked out of the heavy undergrowth . . . the graveyard.

There were maybe fifty graves. Of those, only a dozen or so had inscribed markers, all of one pioneer family with an unusual name: Laffoon. I had come up Laffoon Creek from the White River a few miles to the east.

In a way I was disappointed. Someone had recently cleared this cemetery of the encroaching undergrowth, rescuing it from total neglect. I wanted to find a graveyard that had been completely forgotten. I turned back down the lane.

Another rough truck trail led down to Cow Creek, to the creek's lower end near the Elephant Head Bluff on the Buffalo. Again I had to stop for a mudhole several hundred yards before reaching the river. Then, wandering through the woods toward the mouth of the creek, I stumbled on a lost cemetery.

About two dozen graves were scattered through the woods within a square plot barely defined by a ruined fence. All but one of the markers were homemade, lacking any names, just rectangular slabs of native sandstone driven into the ground.

In the deep damp shade of oaks and dark old cedars, all the plants of the forest floor were flourishing in profusion, a developing tangle of wild grape, Virginia creeper and poison ivy mixed with sprouts of redbud, sumac, wild plum, maple, walnut, oak, elm. Many of the gravestones were nearly hidden by the greenery.

The single store-bought stone was deeply weather-stained, but I could read the name

M. D. YOCHAM
DEC. 17, 1846
SEPT. 30, 1920

and below that

*Gone, but not
forgotten.*

Another day I traveled south of the Buffalo, looking for the way to the mouth of Big Creek. A good chert road through Cozahome continued out the ridge to the north, and a right fork, full of chuck-holes and half buried boulders, ran down a spur. Just before it plunged down the last hill into lower Big Creek valley, I saw a fine view and I stopped.

For some minutes I stood and looked across the valley at the ridges with their summit bluffs, and down the valley on the lonely clearings along Big Creek. The scene beckoned me to come . . .

On reaching the bottom of the hill, I decided to get out and walk. It was a good idea, for the road down Big Creek wallowed through many yards of mud, bumped over the cobbles along a gravel bar, and finally, not far from the river, plunged into a deep ford of the creek. Not caring even to wade across, I turned back.

The day was warm and drowsy and the creek was wonderfully peaceful. Finding a ledge overlooking a crystal clear pool, I sat down to watch the fishes.

Before long, two spotted suckers moved alongside a boulder on the creek bottom below my ledge. They hovered in the water, hardly moving. One fish was about fourteen inches long, the other about ten.

A third sucker, about twelve inches in length, came swimming toward the first two. The ten-inch sucker rushed out and drove it away, as if to protect the bigger fish still drowsing beside the boulder.

The Intruder soon returned. Protective Papa lunged out again, chasing it away from Big Mama.

In a moment the Intruder was back and Papa once more gave him the bum's rush. Again. Again. Finally the Intruder got wise and wandered off. Peace would prevail in the household.

In the Cow Creek cemetery

Saltpeter Cave

No. Now the kids, four or five little green sunfish, came barging in, and Papa was put to dashing after them. Get out of here!

He would lunge at them and they would dart away— three or four feet. Papa would rejoin Mama, only to find the sunfishes, every bit like inquisitive children, back and crowding close.

While Mama napped in her place next to the boulder, Papa lunged out to clear away the kids. But they wouldn't stay away; he had to do it again. Again. Again . . .

East of Big Creek, the country south of the Buffalo lies within the Sylamore District of the Ozark National Forest. The land isn't all government-owned, but enough is so that the Forest Service regularly maintains some of the roads.

The Push Mountain Road follows the watershed divide, staying high but usually affording only glimpses of other nearby ridges through the screen of trees. While the Push Mountain Fire Tower rises above tree line, its outlook is also on layer after layer of forested ridges, all of about uniform height, extending into the distance.

At times, though, the roadside glimpses are downright intriguing. The trees may part just enough for a view of some wild, uninhabited creek valley, or of a chain of rugged sandstone cliffs along a distant ridge. And one afternoon I climbed down from the Push Mountain Road into a ravine, finding little waterfalls plunging from the bluff into the deep hollow, all hidden from traffic on the road just above.

Here and there over this country are the highest landmarks, isolated knobs rising above the ridges and capped with a resistant sandstone that forms rings of cliffs around their summits. Jim Schermerhorn told me that one of these peaks, Almus Knob which lies north of the village of Big Flat, had a large cave in its sandstone caprock. Saltpeter Cave, Jim assured me, would be worth my seeing.

After a short steep climb from a forest road, I reached the base of the knob's summit bluff, and soon I found the cave entrance in a break of the cliff line. Jim had told me that the cave's one room was all within sight of the entrance, and that it was safe enough to explore alone. I walked down the slope into the mouth.

It *was* big. Jim's one room went back under the mountain like a highway tunnel. There were no formations whatever, just a wide, arched passageway into darkness.

Three hundred feet inside, I came to a small mountain of broken rock which had fallen from the ceiling. It appeared to be an old fall; there seemed to be no danger of being crowned by any more that might turn loose that afternoon. Nonetheless, in climbing over the pile I stepped softly. I moved on into deepening gloom.

Ahead of me now, I could see a pale, indistinct spot of light. I began to wonder whether Jim had missed seeing an exit to the other side of the mountain. No, the tunnel now came to a sudden end. The spot was only reflected daylight on the rear wall—daylight from the cave's mouth at the far end of the passage.

For more than an hour I moved up and down the immense corridor, taking pictures, making measurements. I learned the tunnel was 60 feet wide and 650 feet long. And as Jim had told me, there were no side passages at all.

How was this great passage created, here in the summit of a mountain? And why in sandstone, normally having few if any caves? And why was it named Saltpeter Cave, when there was no evidence whatever of nitrate mining?

I did not know. I'd let others do the explaining.

Friday, May 28.
My last trip to the lower Buffalo. I drove through Cozahome (by then I was using the local, logical pronunciation—Cozyhome) and out the ridge past the side road to lower Big Creek.

It was late afternoon. The road was deserted. I topped a rise and startled a deer; it bounded off into the brush. It was the first deer I had ever seen near the Buffalo.

The road climbed and then plunged along the uneven top of the ridge. Now I glimpsed the Buffalo both to left and right, far below. I had reached the neck of the seven mile bend below the state park. I pulled to the side of the road and stopped.

A view up the river seemed promising. With cameras and tripod, I hiked down through the woods, onto the open grassy slope down to the edge of the bluff. The river came toward me from the left, passing directly beneath my stand on the ledge, moving straight away and then to the right beyond the end of the ridge.

Here was one of the best views of the lower river, and the essence of all the Buffalo. A rapids murmuring down below, a placid pool reflecting the line of trees along the bank. A gravel bar inside the bend, this bluff towering along the outside. A bit of clearing along the left bank upstream—but it was not important in the scene. The dominating thing was the woodland, all the way from the river to the tops of the ridges.

The sun was sinking . . . . Over the past weeks and months, I had been fortunate. I'd had good friends and good luck, and so had seen much of this Buffalo River country. Now time was running out. Tonight I would be packing to leave.

The pictures were taken. I put the cameras back into the ammo box, gathered up and climbed the hill toward the car.

Ah, that I could do it all over again!

(facing page)
Last view of the river,
at the beginning of
the seven-mile bend.

PAST AND FUTURE

UNTIL TWO HUNDRED years ago, no white man had ever set foot along the Buffalo River. Even after 1800, the land and river still belonged to the Indians, and it was all unbroken wilderness.

We know very little about what this wilderness was like. Red men kept no records, and the first white men didn't take time to say much (if indeed they could write their own names). From the few sketchy accounts of early travelers, we have to visualize the entire natural world that was the original Buffalo River country.

From those travelers we hear of rolling upland prairies with big bluestem grass growing head high, and with acres and acres of wild flowers, and scattered roaming bands of buffalo and deer and elk. Park-like groves of great oaks spread across the hillsides. Ancient cedars shaded the drier slopes. Tall pines stood above ageless cliffs.

Game followed much-worn paths down the ridges toward water, passing below river bluffs where the buffalo took refuge from winter storms. In the rich alluvial bottom lands were jungles of pipe cane, bamboo-like thickets threaded with animal trails where the panther pounced on luckless deer, and where the bear padded along in endless search for food.

And the river? It was clear, rock-bottomed, teeming with fish. One wayfarer tells of the squirrels swimming across—thousands of squirrels, he said, in mass migration.

The first white men to come and stay were hunters and squatters, before and just after 1800. The Indians remained until they were pushed farther west with the Cherokee Treaty of 1828.

The first scholarly man to come this way was the naturalist Henry Rowe Schoolcraft who floated down the White River in January 1819. On passing the mouth of the Buffalo Fork, he noted in his journal "...it is a region much resorted to by hunters on account of the abundance of game..." The hunters were trafficking in bear hides and tallow which were exported down the White in flat-boats. Schoolcraft also mentions hearing of a hunter who surprised a herd of buffalo, and though he was loaded with the meat and skins of five bears, he killed three buffaloes purely for the pleasure it gave him. Within a decade of Schoolcraft's visit, both buffalo and elk were exterminated in this region.

From 1830 until the Civil War the settlers came, taking parcels of the choicest public land for $1.25 an acre, burning the cane bottoms and turning them to the plow. No less than pioneers elsewhere, they slaughtered any wildlife that failed to retreat, and for a while they lived through glorious days of abundance. One writer, Thomas Jerome Estes, told about growing up in Marion County in those times:

> ...game, fish, and nearly all sorts of wild beasts and fowls were plentiful, even after the [Civil] War. Deer and turkey were often seen in great flocks and herds, and old bear hunters had great times ... Talk about sport! If you think fishing, hunting, trapping, finding bee trees and eating honey, wild fruits, nuts and berries good sport, then we certainly had a sport paradise.

As wild game diminished, predator animals turned on domestic stock running free in the woods. Occasionally wolves or a bear would even attempt to make a meal on livestock penned near settlers' cabins. This unleashed another slaughter; all animals not directly useful were to be killed on sight. County officials placed bounties on wildcats, panthers and wolves, and everyone told and listened to wild 'scare' stories—the Big Bad Wolf and all its elaborations. In a book of memories called *Back Yonder*, Waymon Hogue of Searcy County wrote that in the years before 1900

> The mountain people pronounced the word [panther] "painter" ... equally as dangerous and deadly as the lion and tiger. Had we been able to eliminate the "painter" from our midst, we still would not have felt safe in the woods alone and unarmed. Other ferocious beasts denned and roamed about us, among which were the wolf, the wildcat, and the bear ...

And in his *History of Newton County,* Walter F. Lackey describes how the last bear in the county was dispatched, about 1885:

> ... with an army of hunters in pursuit, the bear was chased through Leatherwood Cove, across the river ... down the river to Roark Bluff, from there to the top of Bee Bluff where the bear made a halt, and sat hugging a cedar tree . . . One of the hunters shot the bear and it tumbled over the bluff. It took some time for the hunters to get down under the bluff and when they did, to their surprise the bear was still alive and sitting midway out in the river on the ice. One of the hunters shot the bear at close range . . .

The beavers went next. There below Ponca where they shot the bear, James Villines became 'Beaver Jim' for trapping so many beavers along the Buffalo . . . and by 1895 they were all gone.

And so the hunters pursued the wild beasts, taking what they needed, it is true, but all too often continuing to kill for the mere pleasure of boasting about it. Men talked, for example, of shooting as many as 40 ruffed grouse a day. In 1885 Arkansas passed a law prohibiting robbing their nests, but that did not stem the slaughter. By 1900, ruffed grouse had disappeared from this country.

Through the decades before 1900 the prospering settlers raised big families, sons and daughters who grew up and married and spread out to homestead the remote side valleys and hollows, the isolated benches along the mountainsides, finally the tops of the loneliest ridges. This younger generation saw the timber disappear.

Again we have only sketchy accounts of how great white oaks were reduced to staves for whisky barrels, and how thousands of prime logs were rafted down the Buffalo to become railroad ties. With the cedar-cutting we do better, for Daniel Boone Lackey, brother of Walter who described the bear chase, has written of those times.[1]

Young Daniel with his mule Going Joe snaked cedar logs off the high, dry slopes above the Buffalo River bluffs in Newton County. And massive logs they were, often 22 inches in diameter, with a few just under 30 inches. Daniel saw one cedar tree near the river above Pruitt that was 42 inches in diameter at the ground and 85 feet tall.

The cedar crew worked like horses from daylight till dark, cutting and hauling that cedar for a dollar a day, sleeping in the logging company's tents and eating the company's ample meals, going forth again to cut those trees and drag those logs down to the Buffalo. If the slopes were too steep they rolled them off the bluffs into the river; other crewmen would pull them back onto the banks.

On the first spring flood, Daniel spent three wet, miserable weeks helping wrestle the cedar raft down the river to Gilbert. There the logs were pulled up to the mill and reduced to uniform slats for shipment to pencil factories.

From 1903 to 1909 the cedar cutting proceeded, until the virgin groves were chewed up into pencils selling for ten cents a dozen, and the cedar was no more.

About 1910 the land began to yield diminishing returns. Much of the wildlife was gone; much of the original timber was gone. On many homesteads the soil was going, too. People began to move away.

Wildlife populations were dwindling. The rabbits and squirrels and quail did seem to stay, but deer and turkey were poached and exterminated so that, by 1946, more than half of Newton and Searcy Counties had unoccupied deer range, and wild turkeys were not to be seen anywhere. Cattle, hogs, and finally goats were running unchecked in the woods, overgrazing, eating everything within reach, even killing young trees.

There were more subtle changes, too, things fleetingly realized in flashes of rememberance. Orville J. McInturff, in his recent *History of Searcy County,* mentions the decrease in 'hole nesters'—bluebirds, purple martins, woodpeckers—all formerly plentiful. He blames starlings for the decrease.

And he sees that fireflies are disappearing. Years ago, he recalls, ". . . the numbers were so great a constant, soft moonlight-like glow could be seen at their mating time." He did not say what he thought had happened to them.

I have heard living men recall memories of streams flowing deep and clear where they are now dry and choked with gravel, and talk of the former abundance of fish and game where now there is little at all. On a ridge running down to the Buffalo in Marion County, I met a man who told me of his boyhood days:

> They's some things I'm kindly ashamed of now . . . .
> My father hunted like an Indian—keen as a whip. He wouldn't wait for a deer to stand. He'd get 'em on the run, behind the shoulder with his old 32-20. I remember one time he brought in three deer he'd shot. We only needed one . . . .
> And then a turkey hen took up in the field of oats down behind the house—had young ones in the oat field. Well, they got about half grown—crazy, like half-grown ones are. They'd come to any call. Dad came in one day with six of them. We only needed one.
> He should've waited, at least to take only one at a time.

---

[1] Daniel Lackey's account appears in the *Arkansas Historical Quarterly,* Winter 1960 issue.

Act of desperation: This Newton County hillside was bulldozed for pasture.

Most of this country had limited economic resources to begin with, mainly wildlife and a forest of slow-growing hardwoods that had developed on the thin rocky soils. Those resources, which must have appeared boundless to the first settlers, were largely wasted and consumed within a century.

Around 1905, there were 27,000 people living in the Buffalo's 1338-square-mile watershed. By 1965, out-migration had reduced the area's population by more than half. Even so, the eroded resource base can't support those who remain. The ones who stay are often those who aren't able to leave. Old age or the lack of skills for industry hold them to the depleted land.

The farm people have switched from cultivating crops to raising cattle. Often their landholdings are too small, too poor to carry the number of animals needed to make

anyone a decent living. Many of the farmers try to supplement their incomes by misuse of the land; they may be led by ignorance or greed but in the final measure they are desperate. They bulldoze steep hillsides, stripping away the trees and tearing into the chert gravel on which they hope to establish pasture. They turn loose their livestock to forage through the woods. In the spring they burn the countryside to encourage grass, laying bare more rocky ground. In their wood lots they lay low any tree that will cut out a crosstie; they can't afford to wait for their trees to grow to maturity. They need the income *now*.

'Desperate' hardly seems right for describing these friendly and well-meaning people. But desperate they are, or they wouldn't be choosing to take short-term gains resulting only in long term losses, as soil and water from their bulldozed and burned land goes slipping away.

Today there is only one natural resource left in abundance, and that is scenery. From the rugged and imposing cliffs along the mountain crests to the strange and delicate formations in caves deep underground, the Buffalo River country contains vistas and pockets of beauty everywhere.

The focus and most outstanding feature of this beauty is the river itself. Despite everything that men have done to despoil its watershed, the Buffalo remains today surprisingly much as it must have appeared in the days of the Indian. Indeed, with fewer people living along its banks and wild species like the beaver being restored, the river is—in some ways—more nearly natural today than it was a generation ago.

Most surprisingly, the *entire* river is of exceptional scenic quality. Every mile from headwaters to mouth contains extraordinary beauty and never-ending variety, much of it in surroundings having the flavor of wilderness. There just isn't any 'best' part of the Buffalo.

A large fraternity of johnboat fishermen have enjoyed the river for decades. And in the last few years, many people have discovered the fun of floating its pools and rapids in canoes. The modern canoe is moderate in cost, light and portable, fast and maneuverable. These factors all appeal to folks with modest incomes, interests other than fishing, or a distaste for handling heavier boats.

Also in only the last few years, many more people from outside the immediate area have begun to hear about the Buffalo's attractions. Like those who came before them, the ones who have come to see the river have often fallen in love with it.

Everything loved has its faults, but on a Buffalo River outing the hazards and discomforts—the worst of which might be sunburn or poison ivy—can usually be avoided. Also, in late summer, portions of the river are too low to float, and in severe drouth the stream disappears into freakish underground channels across two of its horseshoe bends.[2] Floaters adjust to these conditions by using lighter craft, or by floating the downstream portions of the river in dry times. Most of the year the entire river below Pruitt is open and floatable.

Those who know and love the Buffalo have long believed that it should be protected and preserved for the enjoyment of our generation and those to come. Taking note of this sentiment, in 1961 Senator J. W. Fulbright of Arkansas asked the National Park Service to look into the possibility of establishing a national recreation area along the Buffalo.

In 1963 the Park Service published its report. Their

study team had found the Buffalo to be the last major free-flowing stream in the Arkansas Ozarks, and one of the most scenic in the entire southeastern United States. The diversity of the river's plant life was noteworthy on a national basis. And while not present in great numbers, wildlife existed in great variety. The river and its tributaries constituted one of the richest areas in the nation in terms of total number of fish species. Archeological sites and relics of pioneer days were much in evidence, and geologically the area was outstanding.

The Park Service then suggested that the Buffalo be made a 'National River.' In summary, they commented

> The scenic grandeur of unimpeded rivers . . . is fast disappearing . . . Although man-made impoundments are causing the rapid disappearance of free-flowing streams in mid-America, the Buffalo River remains one of the few rivers still possessing exceptional wilderness value.

The National River would be a long, narrow reservation encompassing 132 miles of the Buffalo's twists and turns from above Boxley all the way to the river's mouth. Its area would be a maximum of 103,000 acres (this partly depends on Arkansas' donating its State Park lands). Boundaries were carefully drawn by the Park Service, to protect the river and its scenic shorelands while holding land acquisition to a minimum.

What would the National Park Service do for the Buffalo if it becomes a National River?

First of all, the Park Service would dispense information. Travelers would find handily-located visitor centers at Buffalo River State Park, at the river on U. S. 65 and Highway 7, and possibly also on Highway 123. They could stop in at these attractive buildings, look around, and ask questions.

They might ask about floating. Park rangers, with two-way radio coverage of the entire river, could give them the latest reports on rainfall and stream levels, access points and camping sites, side trips and points of interest.

Visitors might want to know more about the geology, botany, or historical features, and ranger-naturalists, experts in these fields, could help them. Each visitor center would also have exhibits to tell part of the river's story. And the visitor centers would be only one part of an extensive information program. There would also be folders, maps and other literature, signs and outdoor exhibits, and rangers and naturalists stationed in outlying areas.

The Park Service has divided the suggested National River into three general use zones—

That section upstream from Highway 7 might be developed on a 'see and go' basis, with nature trails to

---

[2]These underground short-cuts, below Sneed Creek in Newton County and from the Lookoff bluff to White Springs in Searcy County, are described in earlier chapters.

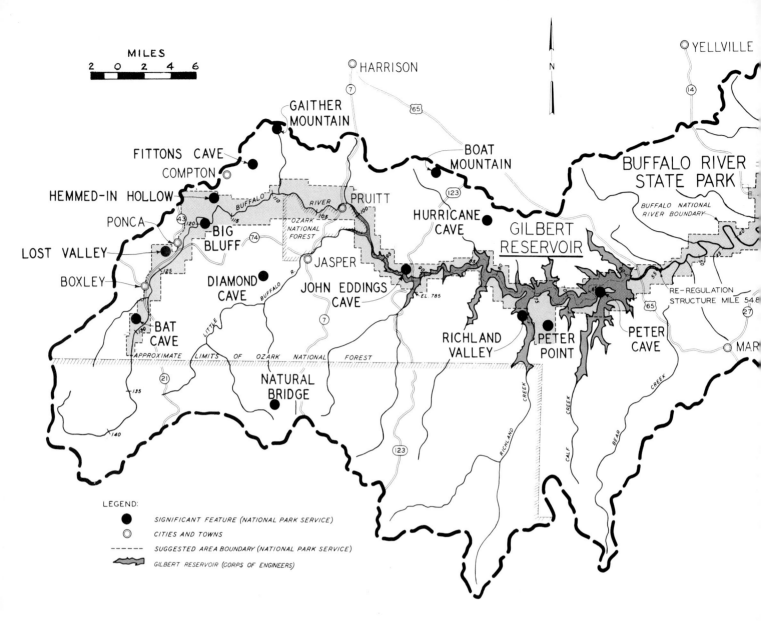

Based on National Park Service and Army Engineers maps

Lost Valley, Big Bluff, Hemmed-in Hollow. Development would be mainly oriented toward interpretation and enjoyment of the scenery.

The central half of the National River between Highways 7 and 14 is most easily accessible, so the bulk of the visitor-use and administrative facilities would be in that area. Developments for day-use—picnicking, swimming, short float trips—could most conveniently be located there. At one point the boundary could extend south from the river to include the landmark Point Peter, and its broad overlook of the Buffalo could be made more easily accessible. The Park Service also suggests reconstructing a pioneer farmstead, possibly in lower Richland valley, gathering and preserving log cabins and barns, furnishings and implements.

The portion of the Buffalo from the State Park to the White River is isolated, difficult of access and wild in character, and might best be set aside for the more primitive uses. This area would be ideal for hiking, trail camping, horseback riding and nature study. Developments would be kept small, scattered, and few in number.

The common backbone of these three segments would be the river itself. Along the stream there would be more than a dozen primitive camping areas having basic campsite and sanitary facilities. In addition there would be major campgrounds and picnic areas at the highway crossings. Existing access points for boating would be improved, and a hiking and horseback riding trail would be built along the river's entire course.

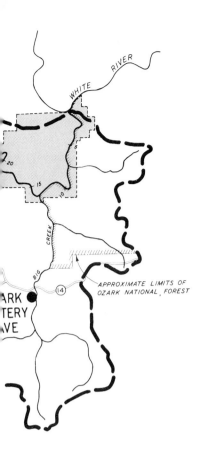

APPROXIMATE LIMITS OF
OZARK NATIONAL FOREST

Conflicting plans:
Gilbert Reservoir of the U. S.
Army Engineers would occupy the
midsection of the area proposed
in 1963 as a National River
by the National Park Service.

Park developments would be in keeping with the rustic beauty of the surroundings, and located to avoid detracting from the river, which would be left alone. Bottomland fields which now lend variety and pastoral beauty to portions of the Buffalo would remain as producing farms. Lands would either be bought and leased back to the owners, or 'scenic easements' only would be purchased to prevent inappropriate private development along the river. The second-growth woodlands which comprise most of the National River area would remain untouched. There the only agent of change would be Nature, working to cover old scars made by man, and gradually restoring much of the river's original, primeval setting.

Here, as in other recreation areas administered by the National Park Service, hunting and fishing would be allowed and regulated by the same state and federal laws that apply to the surrounding countryside. Hunting would be entirely prohibited only near the developed areas, for public safety.

The National Park Service hasn't been alone in making proposals for the future of the Buffalo. The U. S. Army Engineers, world's greatest dam builders, have been eyeing the river, too.

The Corps has centered its attention on two damsites. One, the Lone Rock site, is 3.6 miles above the river's mouth. Lone Rock Dam would create a fluctuating impoundment which would (when full) reach upstream to U. S. Highway 65. The reservoir would flood Buffalo River State Park, and that, the Corps realized, would be "strongly opposed" by the State of Arkansas, and by many sportsmen, wildlife groups and others. So the Corps more recently tried to get moving with the other dam, at their Gilbert site.

The proposed Gilbert Dam would be located about a mile above Highway 65, and its reservoir would (when full) extend to Highway 7 at Pruitt. And, about five miles downstream from Gilbert Dam, the Corps would build a low dam which they call a 're-regulation structure.' They publicized this as a device for releasing water to stabilize the flow downstream through summer drouth. More important, it would create a holding reservoir, part of a pumped-storage scheme for generating additional electric power.

Furthermore, water coming through the turbines of the main dam would be taken from deep in the reservoir—the water would be much colder than that from the surface. This cold-water release was supposed to support a trout fishery, like that of the White River below Bull Shoals Dam, from the re-regulation dam downstream to the mouth of the Buffalo and into the White.

The Corps announced this plan late in 1964, but public opposition to it mounted so rapidly that within a year Governor Faubus of Arkansas issued an official statement strongly opposing the dam and supporting the National River proposal.

With that, the Corps backed off. The Chief of Engineers wrote the Governor that he was withdrawing his recommendation for building Gilbert Dam. He was doing this "in view of the position of the governor and the fact that it is the general policy of the Corps of Engineers not to recommend authorization of projects which are opposed by the states directly concerned."[3]

However, this alone does *not* settle for all time the

[3]This letter was made public by Governor Faubus on April 15, 1966.

question of whether or not the Buffalo should be dammed. It is well worth considering what would happen to the river if Gilbert Dam were ever built.

Gilbert Reservoir would obliterate nearly fifty miles of the Buffalo's midsection. The river's pools and rapids, gravel bar camp sites and bank-side scenery would be gone forever. Bat House Bluff, the Narrows, John Eddings Cave—all would disappear under tons of water. Untold numbers of other caves, archeological sites and historic features would be totally destroyed.

In their place would be a fluctuating impoundment, an eyesore to remind all the future of one generation's terrible mistake in letting it be built. Most of the year, the reservoir would be drawn down 28 vertical feet below its maximum level to provide storage for floods. In times of drouth it would sink even lower, for inflow would dwindle and the turbines, the trout stream and surface evaporation would all demand their share. Water level could then drop another 25 feet, to expose 53 vertical feet of ugly shoreline—dead and burned timber, rotting vegetation, great expanses of cracked mud and bleached rock.

The Newton County arm of the reservoir, nearly half the impoundment's total length, would be a long, narrow sliver of water seldom more than three-eighths of a mile wide even when full. At 'normal pool' to allow flood storage, the arm would usually be less than one-fourth mile wide, a dreary corridor of flat water flanked close on each side by the bare and ruined slopes of the flooding strip.

While the Searcy County portion of the impoundment would be wider, the ugly flooding strip would run around it all. Here would be a broad dirty yellow band of water stain across cliffs—White Bluff, Red Bluff, the palisades at Peter Cave. Here would be an even wider area of devastation on gentler slopes near the dam.

Drawdown of the reservoir would reveal up to three miles of once fertile and picturesque farm lands along the valleys of Richland and Calf Creeks. And there would be the most forlorn scenes of all—blackened tree stumps, foundations of vanished buildings, fields of sprouting weeds, vast open flats of mud stinking in the sun.

The re-regulation or pump-back reservoir below Gilbert Dam would be filled with chilled water and subject to daily drawdown by pumping, and to sudden sweeping surges from the turbines. The pool would remain sterile and lifeless, too cold for swimming, too cold for native fish, too unstable for stocking with trout, too turbulent for safety in boating.

The downstream fishery for hatchery-raised trout would also be too cold for native fish including the famous smallmouth bass. And the river would be too cold for

swimming. And the river's gravel bars, which are now washed clean and replenished with gravel and driftwood by occasional high water, would inevitably become less attractive as campsites.

Even the river upstream from the reservoir would suffer damage. Fisheries biologists say that low-grade or 'rough' fish would migrate upriver from the impoundment and usurp the habitat of the native game fish. Another likelihood is that this last remaining section of the natural warm-water stream would be so heavily used in its floating season that it too would lose much of its attractiveness.

The Corps of Engineers called Gilbert Dam a 'compromise.' Though the reservoir would inundate the middle third of the proposed National River, the Corps maintained that the Park Service could accept the remainder in two widely separated pieces. And if the Park Service would, said the Corps, the whole thing, a reservoir and a fragmented National River, would "afford to the people of the area and of the entire United States a veritable Utopia-in-existence . . . it would provide for the practical, preserve the splendrous beauty, and perpetuate the whole."

To that, the Park Service could only reply ". . . the Corps' announced plan is *not* compatible with the Buffalo National River . . . the proposed reservoir would destroy the river's national significance as a free-flowing stream . . . The river's integrity . . . its completeness, would be lost forever."

Every one of the benefits claimed for Gilbert Dam is of questionable value. The dam would prevent flooding of some of the overflow lands along the lower White River, but that would destroy scarce wetland habitat for wildlife and waterfowl, and the best farm lands on the Buffalo would be flooded permanently. The dam would produce hydroelectric power, but that could fail in competition with atomic energy long before the hydro generators pay out their own cost. The reservoir would provide a recreation area—but that, too, would be in competition, with the attractions of many larger lakes in the surrounding area, all of which lie closer to centers of population.

Nonetheless, the dam has had vocal support from people in portions of Newton and Searcy Counties. This is understandable when we remember that many of these people are—to use the word again—desperate. They have seen a short-term gain, a few years of prosperity while the dam is being built. They have overlooked the long term loss, the river being ruined forever. And they have imagined prosperity in having a recreation lake, for the surrounding reservoirs have brought good times in some measure to counties nearby. But to them a National River

Neil Compton

Thirty-foot drawdown of Table Rock Reservoir, Missouri, 1964

has been a new and unknown concept.

However, as part of the original Park Service study, economists at the University of Arkansas estimated the local economic impact of acquiring land along the river and developing it as a park. They predicted that within only six years after establishment of a National River, 'outside money' from visitor spending would add about seven million dollars a year to personal income of residents in the five counties nearest the Buffalo. In these five counties, some 1,500 jobs in non-farm occupations would be created in serving the needs of the visitors.

Gilbert Dam would cost about 60 million dollars. The

National River project, including acquisition of land and easements plus all development, would cost about ten million dollars.

It is wrong, though, to say that the best conservation of natural resources is merely a matter of getting the largest dollar returns from developing them.

If we think of it only in that way, we are apt to cheat ourselves and all who will come after us. 'Conservation' guided by economic gain alone can cause us to destroy every 'valueless' thing that stands in the way of making a dollar . . . things in the world of nature that seem to

Dad's day off

serve only as ornament, delighting the eye and the ear but not filling the pocketbook. If we are to keep our land a fit place to live in, we must develop more love of it, more understanding of it than we now possess.

In his *Sand County Almanac,* the late Aldo Leopold wrote about conservation based on a 'land ethic':

> Land is not a commodity belonging to us, but a community to which we belong . . .
>
> Quit thinking about decent land-use as solely an economic problem. Examine each question in terms of what is ethically and esthetically right, as well as what is economically expedient. A thing is right when it tends to preserve the integrity, stability, and beauty of the . . . community of all living things. It is wrong when it tends otherwise.

Saving the free-flowing Buffalo is more, then, than a matter of good economics, or of superficial enjoyment of the scenery. Aldo Leopold would cite deeper reasons for preserving the river, explaining that there are cultural values in the sports, customs, and experiences that renew contact with wild things. These values are of three kinds:

1. *The value in anything stimulating our awareness of history. Such awareness is 'nationalism' in its best sense.* Floating down the Buffalo or hiking its trails, we are experiencing—actually re-living—a mode of travel from our nation's past. The Buffalo River wildlands would be first of all a sanctuary for the primitive arts of wilderness travel.

2. *Value in any experience that reminds us of our basic dependency on the soil-plant-animal-man food chain, and of the fundamental organization of the living community.* In our processed-and-packaged civilization, we have largely forgotten the elemental ties between man and the land. But land, in a larger sense, is not just 'dirt' or 'earth' but a marvelous stream of energy moving from its sources in the sun and soil through plants to animals that eat plants, and to the meat-eating animals, and to the omniverous animals (including man) which eat both plants and other animals. That is the way of this world, and there is no better place than the wilderness for us to observe and learn about those relationships.

3. *Value in any experience that exercises those ethical restraints collectively called 'sportsmanship.'* Here the value might be in lessons for our children. We tell them it is not only wiser, but also fairer to other fishermen to release the undersize fish they catch. Or that a wildflower once picked is usually wasted and destroyed; it is fairer to leave them for others to enjoy. Or that any act which destroys the soil or any other part of a food chain will bring harm to living things—maybe human beings—dependent on what has been lost.

There are other important values in preserving the river. Hiking and canoeing provide wholesome exercise and physical training—things that simply don't exist in motorized recreation. And especially for young people, wilderness travel is an exercise in self-reliance. Shooting the rapids and adventuring over new ground provide both novelty and challenge in otherwise regimented and protected lives.

Aldo Leopold realized this need for adventure when he wrote

> The value of recreation is not a matter of ciphers. Recreation is valuable in proportion to the intensity of its experiences, and to the degree to which it *differs from* and *contrasts with* workaday life. By these criteria, mechanized outings are at best a milk-and-water affair.

In his writings, the wildlife biologist Harold Alexander further develops that idea:

> ...sport and recreation are primarily esthetic in nature. If this is not true, then all the efforts we give to perfecting fine tackle for fishing, skill in wing shooting, and our efforts to hunt in wilderness and seek out beauty in nature are wasted. We had best fish with seines and poisons, and kill our game by the most effective and lethal means.
>
> We have...largely ignored the factor of quality in sport, in recreation... Certainly, casting a fly in a fine swift clear-water stream is superior in quality to...casting a bobber among floating beer cans and other bobbers in a man-made reservoir. We may acknowledge the necessity of the beer cans...because of factors beyond our control, but we need to develop standards of quality, and preserve in our environment natural areas to which we can escape from the complexities and confusion of civilized living.
>
> ...we have two essential considerations: the perpetuation of both quality and diversity in the world of the future.

And the conservation teacher Paul Sears has observed that

> ...once existence is assured, its quality...is the chief preoccupation of the majority of mankind.

Any consideration of the future of the Buffalo River should also include a look at the problems of the river's watershed, the country that surrounds and sustains the main stream, country that is tied to the river in ways both geographic and economic.

We have already reviewed its sad history of resource depletion, land abuse, population loss and human impoverishment. And we have sampled its only natural resource left in abundance, the scenery. From all this we might conclude that the country's scenic places, now largely unknown and often difficult of access, offer the best opportunity for local economic uplift through their development for recreation and tourism.

But here, too, there is danger that the resource may be wasted and lost at the outset. Development of scenic attractions must be more than mass advertising, more than building new roads into lovely country. Remember Aldo Leopold: Good land-use is that which is "ethically and esthetically right, as well as . . . economically expedient."

Now, without time to analyze the more complex problems of land-use, we can only touch on a few of the needs for protecting the scenic resource—

Any development in this country must begin with building better roads. Beyond serving local travelers, paved roads would be a prime lure for vacationing 'outsiders' bringing their tourist dollars. But will new roads be built with respect for the scenery, or will they be laid out simply to increase travel speed, bulldozing scenery right off the map? One kind of road will entice people to stay. The other will hurry them on to far destinations.

Another need is to reduce the Buffalo's flash floods where they originate, on the thousands of acres of upland slopes laid bare by overgrazing, land clearing and fire. Part of the solution here might be in just waiting; those who persist in bad practices will eventually reach the end of their natural (and financial) resources and abandon their land to let the trees grow. The leaves will fall and eventually will build up a ground layer to catch and hold the rain.

Natural reforestation happens only by chance, though, and it can be extremely slow. It would be better to be

Boy Scout canoeists
approaching the State Park

159

Loss of a heritage: Cave formations stripped by vandals and (below) a settler's cabin abandoned to decay.

planting trees, covering the denuded lands *now,* to hasten the recovery of the watershed (and hasten the time when local forest products firms could depend on a sustained supply of good timber).

Another need is to recognize and protect the areas of exceptional beauty, for too often they aren't given any protection until they are already at least partly spoiled. The Forest Service, for example, has a scenic gem in the waterfalls area on upper Richland Creek. Will it be protected from logging and other uses which are adverse to people's enjoyment of the scenery?

Scenic protection often involves development—properly placed roads, trails and other facilities—but in some cases it is wiser to *not* develop. The area may be too small or too fragile for roads; this is so at the falls on upper Richland. And there should be a few large tracts left completely untouched, so that anyone wanting solitude, wanting wilderness, can find it.

Another need is to protect Indian archeological sites, for they are being vandalized and ruined at such a rate that there may be none left within ten years. Curio-hunters talked one Searcy County landowner into letting them go into his bluff shelter for whatever they could find. They hogged through the fill of the cave and paid him a few hundred dollars for artifacts; he'd collected a short-term gain. Archeologists had considered the shelter worthy of development as a state park, with a museum to house the artifacts, exhibits at the cave—and a paved road into the community having this rare but now-ruined attraction. Digging at Indian sites is best left to the experts who take care not to destroy anything.

Another need is to protect wild caves from the vandals who have been making a business of stripping them of their formations. These jackals give the cave owners practically nothing ("He paid me fifty cents a hundred pounds for those stalactites he took.") and sell their loot to unprincipled curio dealers. The long term loss is to anyone who would ever want to see a pristine, unspoiled cave . . . and to any owner who might later want to develop his cave for the public.

Another need is to recognize and protect the best of the pioneer relics; we have already seen that the log buildings and other remains will be nearly gone before many years have passed. Here again, whatever is saved as part of the cultural heritage of this country will depend on people's taking the initiative now.

Those are problems to be faced and dealt with if the watershed's scenic resource is to remain unspoiled. But by far the most important and overriding issue is that of saving the river itself.

Even without damming, the Buffalo is in real danger of being spoiled because of today's increasing pressures

Cottages stand shoulder-to-shoulder along Michigan's Huron River—is this also in store for the Buffalo?

of population and haphazard development. Already, parcels of river frontage have been subdivided and sold as house lots. In ten or fifteen years, long stretches of the Buffalo could easily be cluttered with cottages and resorts, and polluted by dozens of substandard sewage systems—and the most precious qualities of the river will then have been lost.

Moreover, various federal and state government agencies are now studying, planning and proposing land management and development schemes that will affect every portion of the Buffalo's watershed. This is inevitable; it has been brought on by the region's poverty and inability for self-help. And on the whole the government programs may bring good results. However, some of the agency projects could bring great damage to the Buffalo River.

For example, in July 1966 the Federal Power Commission issued a report which echoed the Army Engineers' assertion that Gilbert Dam was "needed" for power, flood control and recreation. Further, the FPC suggested two additional projects for the Buffalo, both pumped-storage developments for generating power. One, at Point Peter, would operate in conjunction with Gilbert Reservoir. The other, on the upper Buffalo near Compton, would include a dam just downstream from Hemmed-in Hollow—and that would destroy the most spectacular portion of the river. Both projects "appeared to be feasible" solely from estimated output of power. The single-purpose calculations of the FPC did not include the values to be lost.

In 1968 the Corps of Engineers will complete a massive study of the White River basin, and at that time the Engineers may again voice their desire to dam the Buffalo, at either the Gilbert or the Lone Rock site, or at both. Or there may be proposals for smaller dams at the river's headwaters and on several of the tributaries. The tributary dams have already been suggested as devices for multiple-purpose water storage while preserving the main stream. Any dam on a tributary, though, should be judged on its own effects, including those on scenic values and on water quality in the Buffalo itself.

It appears, then, that the threat of Gilbert Dam has faded for at least the present, but threats to the river from other interests, both public and private, are becoming ever more serious. Because of that, we who love the Buffalo see only one effective way to protect it—a federal law to establish the Buffalo National River.

At this writing (March 1967), two National River bills have just been introduced in Congress, one by Arkansas' Senators J. W. Fulbright and John McClellan, the other by Arkansas Congressman John Paul Hammerschmidt. Both bills embody the general recommendations made by the National Park Service in 1963.

During this year and those immediately following, the future of the Buffalo River will be decided. The decisions will be made by Congress, and by the President of the United States. Those decisions will be influenced by you, the readers of this book, to the extent that you tell your Congressmen and Senators, and your President, what future you personally desire for the Buffalo.

(next two pages) The Buffalo at Big Bluff, site of a proposed pumped-storage reservoir

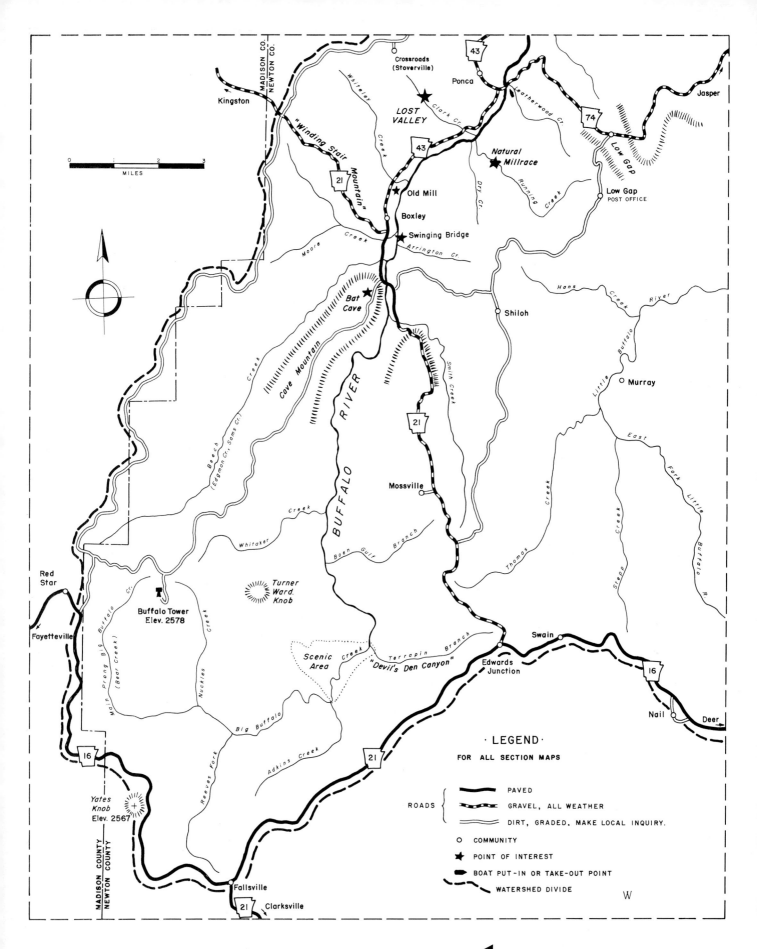

MADISON CO.
NEWTON CO.

Kingston

"Winding Stair Mountain"

21

MILES
0 1 2 3

Red Star

Fayetteville

Buffalo Tower
Elev. 2578

Main Prong Big Buffalo
(Bear Creek)

Nuckles Creek

Reeves Fork

MADISON COUNTY
NEWTON COUNTY

Yates
Knob
Elev. 2567

16

Fallsville

21

Clarksville

Moore Creek

Beech Creek
(Edgmon Cr. Sams Cr.)

Whitaker Creek

Cave Mountain

Bat Cave

Turner Ward. Knob

Scenic Area

Big Buffalo

Adkins Creek

Crossroads
(Stoverville)

Whiteley Creek

Clark Cr.

LOST VALLEY

Old Mill

Boxley

Swinging Bridge

Arrington Cr.

BUFFALO RIVER

Boen Creek

Gulf Branch

"Devil's Den Canyon"

Terrapin Branch

Creek

21

Edwards Junction

43

Ponca

43

Natural Millrace

Dry Cr.

Running Creek

Shiloh

Smith Creek

Mossville

21

Thomas Creek

Steep Creek

Swain

Leatherwood Cr.

74

Low Gap

Low Gap
POST OFFICE

Jasper

Hans Creek River

Little Buffalo River

Murray

East Fork Little Buffalo R.

16

Nail

Deer

· LEGEND ·

FOR ALL SECTION MAPS

ROADS {
PAVED
GRAVEL, ALL WEATHER
DIRT, GRADED. MAKE LOCAL INQUIRY.
}

○ COMMUNITY

★ POINT OF INTEREST

◼ BOAT PUT-IN OR TAKE-OUT POINT

--- WATERSHED DIVIDE

W

SECTION MAPS

1

HEADWATERS
COUNTRY, page 76

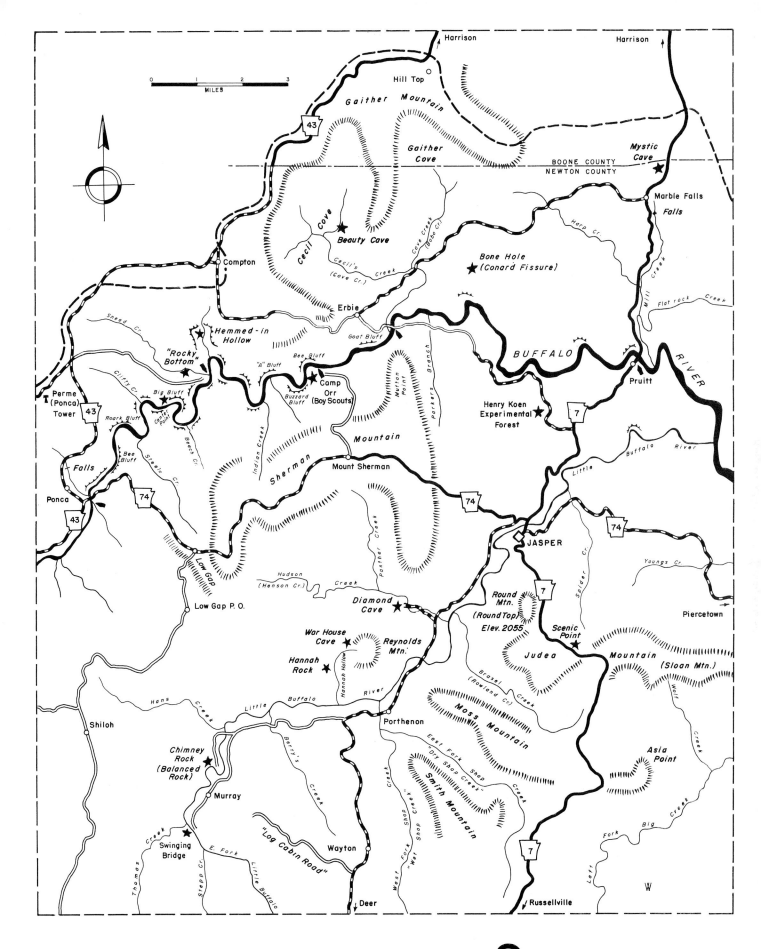

Harrison

Harrison

Hill Top

Gaither Mountain

Gaither Cove

43

Cecil Cove

Beauty Cave

Mystic Cave

BOONE COUNTY
NEWTON COUNTY

Marble Falls
Falls

Compton

Cecil's (Cove Cr.) Creek

Cove Creek (Bobo Cr.)

Harp Cr.

Mill Creek

Flat rock Creek

Erbie

Bone Hole
(Conard Fissure)

Sneed Cr.

Hemmed-in Hollow

Goat Bluff

BUFFALO

RIVER

"Rocky Bottom"

Bee Bluff

"A" Bluff

Mutton Point

Parkers Branch

Pruitt

Perme (Ponca) Tower

43

Cliffy Cr.

Big Bluff

Buzzard Bluff

Camp Orr (Boy Scouts)

Henry Koen Experimental Forest

7

Roark Bluff

Center Point

Sherman

Mountain

Buffalo River

Falls

Bee Bluff

Steele Cr.

Beech Cr.

Indian Creek

Mount Sherman

74

Little

Ponca

74

43

Low Gap

74

JASPER

74

Low Gap P.O.

Hudson (Henson Cr.)

Creek

Panther Creek

7

Round Mtn. (Round Top) Elev. 2055

Spider Cr.

Youngs Cr.

Piercetown

Diamond Cave

War House Cave

Reynolds Mtn.

Scenic Point

Mountain (Sloan Mtn.)

Hannah Rock

Hannah Hollow

River

Judea

Brasel Creek (Rowland Cr.)

Wolf Creek

Shiloh

Hans

Creek

Little

Buffalo

River

Porthenon

Moss Mountain

East Fork Shop Creek

Asia Point

Chimney Rock (Balanced Rock)

Barry's Creek

"Dry Shop Creek"

Smith Mountain

Murray

Creek

West Fork Shop Creek

"Wet Shop Shop Creek"

Left Fork

Big Fork

Creek

Swinging Bridge

Thomas Creek

E. Fork

Stepp Cr.

"Log Cabin Road"

Wayton

Deer

7

Russellville

W

0 1 2 3
MILES

PONCA TO PRUITT, page 15
CANYONS, CAVES AND CABINS, page 92

2

165

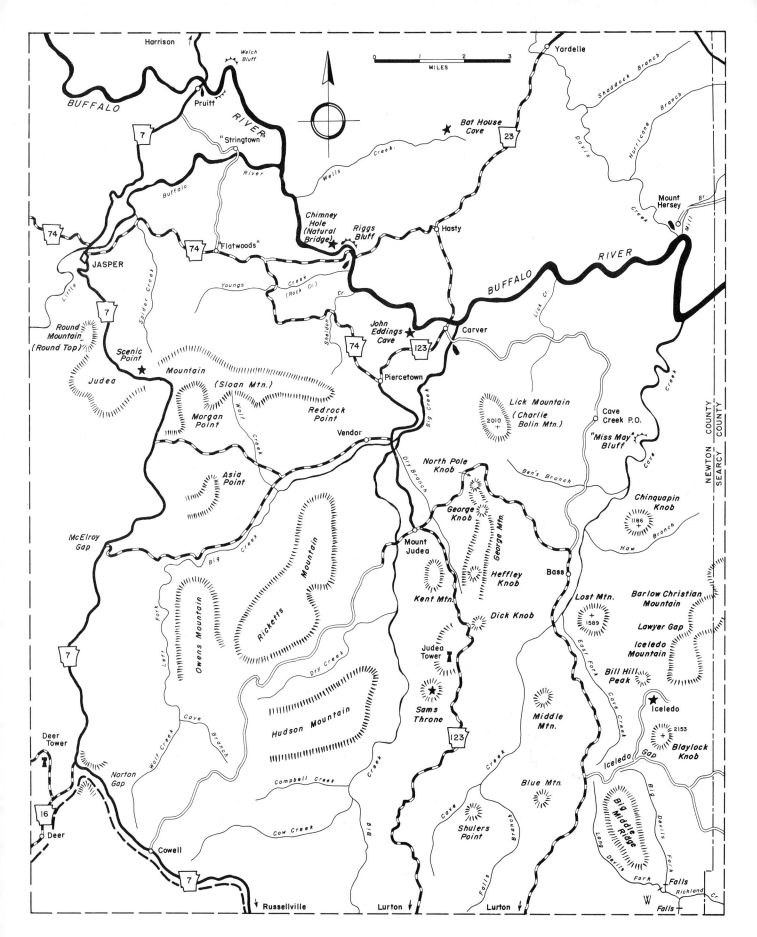

3

PRUITT TO MOUNT HERSEY, page 27
A SAMPLING OF THE PAST, page 104

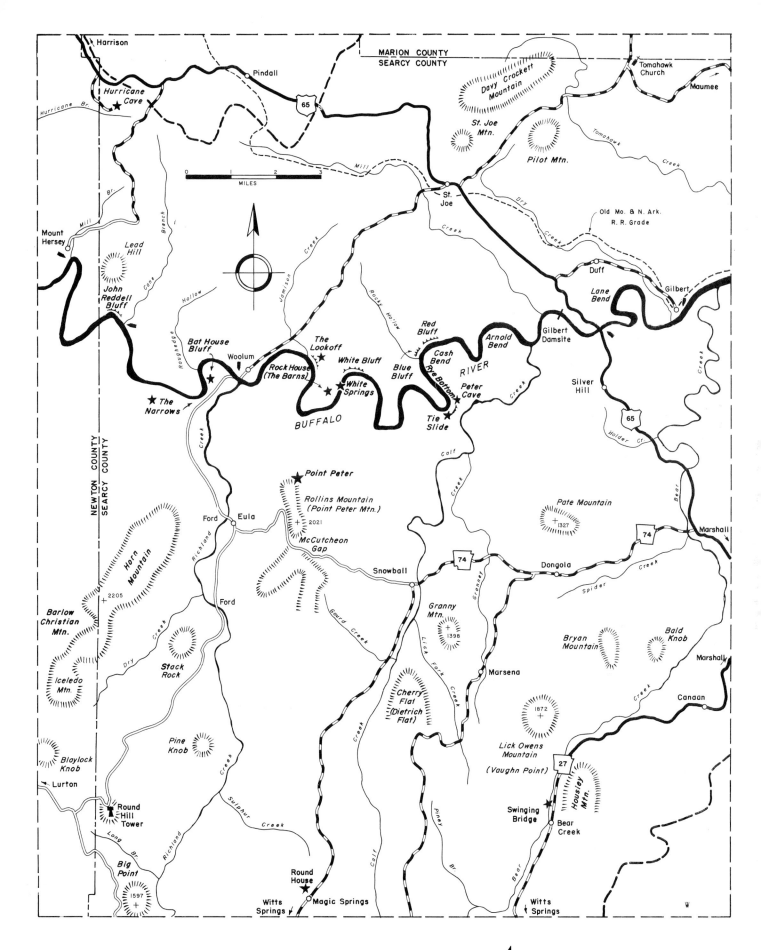

MOUNT HERSEY TO GILBERT, page 35
LONG LONELY RICHLAND, page 120

4

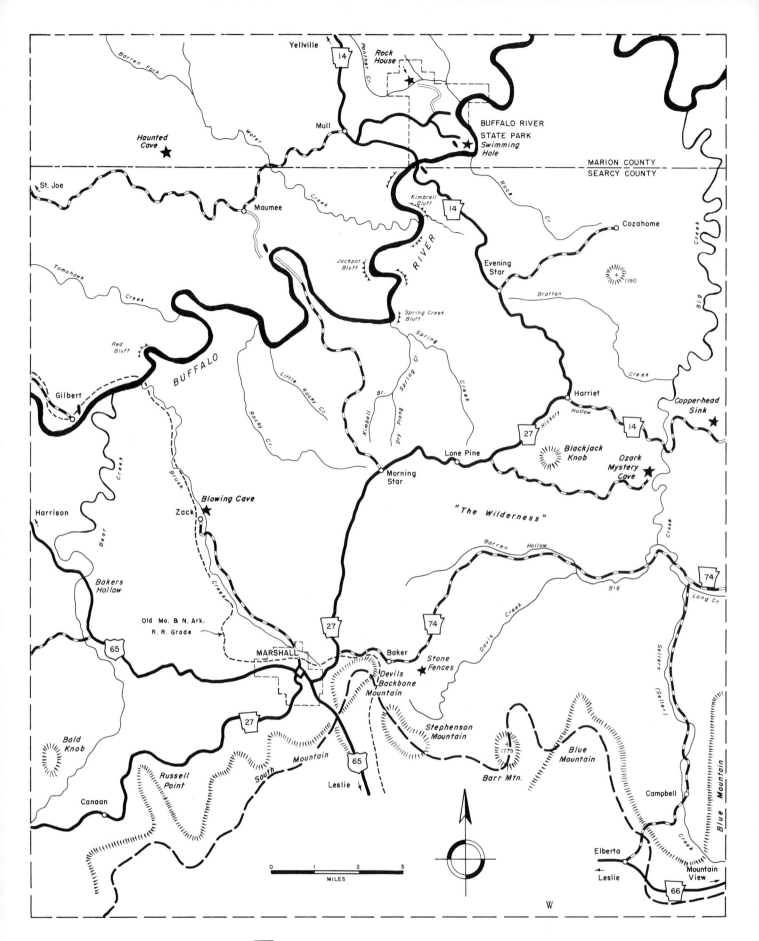

5

GILBERT TO STATE PARK, page 46
LAND OF ROCKS, page 133

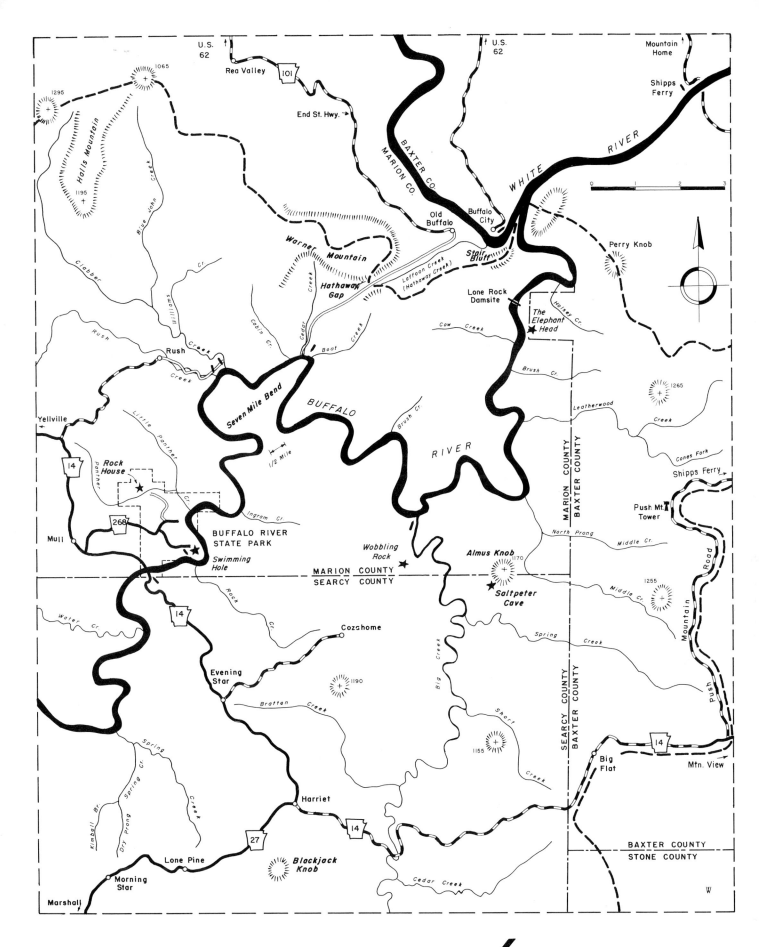

STATE PARK TO WHITE RIVER, page 63
LOST CORNER, page 144

6

Notes on the Maps

THE WATERSHED (End sheets of book)

Geographic names in the Buffalo River watershed are often repeated from one place to another. Among the Buffalo's tributaries, for example, there are two Big Creeks, two Mill Creeks and a Mill Branch, plus two Bear Creeks, two Beech Creeks and three Brush Creeks!

Also, single features often bear two or more differing names, the result of map makers' mistakes and local custom or preference (In Newton County, the peak that Cave Creek people call Lick Mountain is called Charlie Bolin Mountain by folks along Big Creek.). Some of these 'preference' names are given here on the maps, but obviously not all of them.

Of the eight *fire lookout towers* over the watershed, Ponca, Boat Mountain and Judea have perhaps the best views; the others too often look across even-layered ridges. Round Hill Tower above upper Richland valley is the most isolated; the tower man's son rides for two hours on the bus to school at Mount Judea.

Alum Cove Natural Bridge north of Deer in Newton County is a massive (12 feet wide, 25 high, 130 long) span of Atoka sandstone in a 200-acre scenic preserve of the Ozark National Forest. The Forest Service has developed an access road, parking and picnic areas, a short trail to the bridge, and a nature trail going on through the woods and past large rooms weathered out of the bluffs across the hollow from the bridge.

At the *Van Cleave Azalea Farm* northeast of Raspberry Mountain in Pope County, acres of wild azaleas cover an open hillside; in May there is a lush floral display, ranging in color from white to deep rose pink. To better care for the azaleas and the crowds who come to see them, Arkansas in 1966 purchased the area for inclusion in the state park system.

SECTION 1 (Page 164)

The *swinging bridge* at Boxley is the only one (in 1966) still in use on the Buffalo. Several others along the river have been torn down or have fallen into ruin.

Running Creek near Ponca flows for about half a mile over bare limestone, and for several hundred feet it streams through a *natural millrace,* a narrow groove which curves across the bedrock and finally opens into a tiny canyon where the creek pours down in a waterfall.

SECTION 2 (Page 165)

Half a mile above the mouth of Sneed Creek, the stream sprawls along *Rocky Bottom,* an expanse of bedrock 100 feet wide and 400 long—"big enough for football and flat enough for billiards" so one writer exclaimed.

Marble Falls on Highway 7 is the site of the 19th-century village of Willcockson which had a grist mill on Mill Creek

above the falls. A block of 'marble' (St. Joe limestone) which became Arkansas' commemorative stone in the Washington Monument was quarried here in 1836.

The 754-acre *Henry Koen Experimental Forest* north of Jasper is crossed by geological faults which bring together different types of soils normally widely separated in elevation. A Forest Service research team based in Harrison uses the area for experiments to improve forest productivity on soils and sites typical of the Ozarks.

Part of their work is to find the best native and foreign tree species for Ozark forest lands. Plantations of short-leaf-loblolly pine hybrids, Virginia pine and Chinese chestnuts, for example, have been set out and their growth is being closely watched. The larger task, though, is to learn better methods of managing Ozark timber lands for maximum economic return from trees and least damage to watersheds and other resources. Among the continuing experiments are ones to find the effects of tree spacing on growth; effectiveness of chemicals and drastic hardwood control on natural reseeding by shortleaf pine; and better means of timber stand improvement. In seven gaged watersheds over the area, the researchers measure runoff and sedimentation from 90 acres of typical Ozark cherty slopes.

SECTION 3 (Page 166)

Bat House Cave north of Hasty is the site of a legally licensed whisky still which operated before Prohibition came in 1919. All that remains now is a section of stone wall standing in the cave's broad entrance.

Sams Throne south of Mount Judea is a knob mountain rising 1000 feet above Big Creek valley. The mountain was named for Sam Davis, an early settler. Davis was considered bright, but egotism over this bordered on insanity. On Sundays he climbed to his 'throne', the half acre summit made nearly inaccessible by a ring of cliffs, and shouted sermons to the world below.

SECTION 4 (Page 167)

The *Rock House* (or the Barns), a quarter mile west of White Springs on the Buffalo, is a 30-foot overhang of a limestone bluff. Farmers since pioneer days have stored hay and farm equipment in this natural shelter.

Point Peter, the cliff summit at the north end of Rollins Mountain, lies two miles overland and 1300 feet above the Buffalo. A landmark widely seen from many parts of the watershed, Point Peter has a view equally broad, from Gaither Mountain on the west to Devils Backbone near Marshall, a span of more than 40 miles.

Snowball is on Calf Creek west of Marshall. In his lively history of Searcy County, Orville McInturff writes that in 1886 the villagers applied to the Post Office Department to change their post office name from Calf Creek to Snow Hall, for their new community building had just been given that name. But whoever wrote the application must have written Snow Hall as one word, Snowhall, and the *h* was taken as a *b,* for the application was approved as Snowball, and so it remains . . . .

The *Round House* north of Witts Springs is a three room circular dwelling of wood frame construction, now abandoned and going to pieces.

The Missouri and North Arkansas Railroad through St. Joe, Gilbert and Marshall was extended to Leslie in 1903, and later completed from Seligman, Mo., to Helena, Ark., on the Mississippi River. Buffalo River timber and produce were shipped out on the M & NA until depletion of forests and soil, along with labor troubles the railroad was having, led to the tracks being taken up after World War II. The old roadbed, now used in places for auto travel, can easily be traced across Searcy County.

SECTION 5 (Page 168)

The village of *Gilbert* on the Buffalo was founded about 1900 when the railroad came. In 1917 new people moved in from Illinois to found a religious colony and a newspaper called *The Kingdom Harbinger*. The paper soon shut down, and now the railroad is gone and there is no industry. But the colonizers, or their descendants, remain, and Gilbert's well-kept homes and church are the pride of those who live there.

Not far east of Marshall there is a large farm encircled and crisscrossed by miles of *stone fences*. For the past hundred years this land has belonged to the Treece family, and since 1900 or before, generations of the clan have been clearing fields and building walls. Today the rock fences lend a picturesque look to the whole countryside. Moreover, they stand as a long-lasting monument to hard work and persistence, to one family's commitment to the land.

SECTION 6 (Page 169)

Wobbling Rock lies precisely where people step out to enjoy the view alongside the road into lower Big Creek. Many sightseers have been startled as their footing has suddenly shifted under their weight, but there's little to fear. The rock's movement is only an inch or so, and it rests on a broad firm pedestal. Wobbling Rock is 8 feet square by 3 high and weighs about 14 tons.

Developed Caves

Exploring wild caves takes time, know-how and proper equipment, endurance and courage. It is much easier, however, to 'explore' a developed cave.

These in the Buffalo watershed have electrically lighted paths which can be walked in street clothes. Guided tours (one half to one hour) cost around $1 for grownups or 50¢ for children. The caves are usually open only in the warm months, April or May to September. Temperatures inside stay in the 50's or 60's the year round, so light wraps are advisable.

BIG HURRICANE CAVE

lies near U. S. 65 west of Pindall. The tour route follows a narrow stream passage where the walk is built above the water. Some beautiful white calcite formations decorate the walls. The tour's climax is a large room lavishly decorated with stalactites, stalagmites and flowstone. Stairs lead up to a 'balcony' with other interesting features. This is a very photogenic area . . . . . Indians once lived in the cave's entrance; they left many artifacts. Big Hurricane was named about 1895 after a windstorm toppled large oaks near the cave.

DIAMOND CAVE

four miles southwest of Jasper offers the longest tour of any of these caves. The trip is also the most strenuous; one short stretch is a 'duck-walk' below a 3-foot ceiling. But the cave abounds in formations of many kinds. Thousands of little soda-straw stalactites are still actively growing from the ceilings. Farther back on the tour there are remarkably thin rope-like columns, three or four inches in diameter and up to 18 feet high . . . . An 1832 log house and log barn stand near the cave's entrance.

MYSTIC CAVE

near Highway 7 north of Marble Falls has the shortest and easiest tour of any. Mystic is a fault cavern, essentially one big room, first opened when the hill split apart ages ago. Solution of limestone enlarged the space, now adorned with hundreds of formations ranging from tiny helictites to great columns. One massive 35-foot column is named the Pipe Organ; its flutes sound musical notes when struck with a mallet.

OZARK MYSTERY CAVE

lies four miles southeast of Harriet in Searcy County. Though the most isolated from main highways, this cave is worth a side trip to see. Beyond the entrance stairway down a sinkhole, the trail follows one large passage having an assortment of formations. The path ends among gigantic stalagmites and columns, probably the largest in any of these caves. A few yards farther on, dirt fill blocks the passage; you may wonder what lies beyond . . . . From the hilltop at the cave entrance, there is a fine view of Big Creek valley.

SHAWNEE CAVE

lies eight miles south and west of Yellville. Its sheltered entrance is said to have been the home of an Indian chief. When enlarging the opening the owners found many artifacts, some of types dating back several thousand years. Along the cave's easy tour route are a good number and variety of formations, including small travertine dams. One large stalagmite with unusual branched fluting is aptly named the Jungle Tree . . . . A log cabin museum houses the Indian artifacts, plus a collection of fossils from the surrounding hills.

GUIDEPOSTS
Sources of Information

All book prices include postage for mail orders. Bookstore prices would usually be slightly lower.

MAPS

County General Highway Maps of the Arkansas Highway Department show roads, bridges and many other man-made features. They are often revised, but watch for a few errors in location of back roads. Except for streams, these maps do not show topography. Write the Arkansas Highway Dept., Division of Planning & Research, Box 2261, Little Rock 72203, for further description and prices.

Topographic Maps of the U. S. Geological Survey show streams, hills, bluffs and other land features. Roads on older maps are often out-of-date. Area coverage and prices for maps are given in the current "Index to Topographic Mapping in Arkansas", free from the Geological Survey, Federal Center, Denver, Colo. 80225.

CANOEING

Canoeing is a good textbook on canoe handling, canoe repair and safety, with chapters on canoe trips, canoe racing and canoeing on swift rivers. 1956. Paperback; $1.25 through local Red Cross chapters, or American Red Cross, 4050 Lindell Blvd., St. Louis, Mo. 63108.

A White Water Handbook for Canoe and Kayak by John T. Urban is for those who deliberately seek the rapids. Paddling technique and white water problems are explained and illustrated, and there are chapters on equipment and safety. 1965. Paperback; $1.50 from Appalachian Mtn. Club Mail Order, 5 Joy St., Boston, Mass. 02108.

The New Way of the Wilderness by Calvin Rutstrum is an up-to-date guide to wilderness travel and camping. The chapter on canoeing discusses equipment and techniques and illustrates paddle strokes. Macmillan Co., New York, 1958. Clothbound; $5.10 plus $1 for life membership from Recreational Equipment Co-op, 1525—11th Ave., Seattle, Wash. 98122.

FLOAT FISHING

The Arkansas Game & Fish Commission, State Capitol, Little Rock 72201, distributes a handy pocket map of the Buffalo; also brochures furnished them by guide services. Ask the Commission for their current Fishing Regulations. A fishing license costs $3.50 for state residents, and non-residents in Arkansas less than 14 days; or $6 for the non-resident annual permit.

BUFFALO RIVER STATE PARK

The Park's attractive housekeeping cottages are available all year, but advance reservations are advised. The dining room is open only in the warm months, April through September. For information and reservations, contact the Superintendent, Buffalo River State Park, Yellville, Ark. 72687. His phone number is 501-449-6323.

ARCHEOLOGY

Archeological Field Methods by Robert F. Heizer is a valuable guide to site surveying and mapping, methods of excavation, data recording and care of specimens. National Press, Palo Alto, Calif., 1964. Clothbound, $5 through the N.W. Ark. Archaeological Society.

American Indian Projectile Points by Robert E. Bell consists of 2 volumes, each having actual-size drawings of 50 named types of arrow, dart, or spear points, plus descriptions and notes on distribution, age, and cultural affiliation of each type. Oklahoma Anthropological Society: No. 1, 1958; and No. 2, 1960. Paperback; available through the NWAAS for $4 each volume. Also available thru the NWAAS: *Ancient Man in North America* by Wormington, paper $3.65, cloth $5.20; and *The Ozark Bluff-Dwellers* by Harrington, cloth $4.50.

In Diamond Cave

CAVES

Speleology, the Study of Caves by Moore and Nicholas explains the origin of caves and growth of formations, and describes life in caves and man's uses of caves. D. C. Heath & Co., Boston, 1964. Paperback; $1.32 from National Speleological Society, 609 Meadow Lane, Vienna, Va. 22180. Allow at least one month for delivery.

Exploring American Caves by Franklin Folsom discusses the history and lore of spelunking; caving equipment, techniques and safety. Collier Books, N.Y., 1962. Paperback; 95¢ from the Natl. Speleological Society.

Bat/Saltpeter Cave, Newton County, Arkansas by David S. Taylor consists of a detailed map of the cave and 5 pages of description. Ark. Speleological Survey, 1964. 50¢ to Survey members; non-members $1.

Depths of the Earth, stories of caves and cavers in the United States by William R. Halliday, contains a vivid 7-page description of Beauty Cave. 1966. Cloth; $7.65 from Harper & Row, 307 Ash St., Scranton, Pa. 18509.

HISTORY

Bits and pieces here and there. See especially the county histories: *Newton County* by Walter F. Lackey; *Searcy County* by Orville J. McInturff; *Baxter County* by Frances Shiras. Several useful collections are in Little Rock, at the Arkansas Historical Commission, *Arkansas Gazette,* and Arkansas Library Commission.

NATURAL HISTORY

Either of these books is good for identifying birds: *A Field Guide to the Birds* (Eastern species) by Peterson. 1947. Cloth; $5.10 from Houghton Mifflin Co., 2 Park St., Boston, Mass. 02107. *Birds of North America* by Robbins, Bruun, Zim and Singer. 1966. Softbound; $3.10 from Golden Press, 150 Parish Drive, Wayne, N.J. 07470.

A pamphlet "The Seasonal Occurrences of Arkansas Birds" and bird check-list cards for field trips are available through the Arkansas Audubon Society. These are a big help to anyone wanting to identify birds in Arkansas.

The New Field Book of American Wild Flowers by H. W. Rickett illustrates and describes nearly all species in the Buffalo River area (Only the largest manuals show them all.). 1963. Cloth; $5.10 from G. P. Putnam's Sons, 200 Madison Ave., New York, N.Y. 10016.

Trees of Arkansas by Dwight M. Moore contains drawings of leaves, fruit and twigs; written descriptions; notes on uses, distribution and largest specimens; and a key for identifying species. 1961. Paperback; 75¢ from Arkansas Forestry Commission, Box 1940, Little Rock 72203.

Geological information on the Buffalo is scattered and incomplete. The Arkansas Geological Commission, State Capitol, Little Rock 72201, has a library with a number of useful items, mostly out-of-print. These, and others for sale by the Commission, are named in their "List of Publications" sent on request.... The *Geologic Map of the Snowball Quadrangle* by Glick and Frezon (USGS, 1965) shows rock formations of the middle Buffalo.

Neil Compton

Blundering through

CONSERVATION

A Sand County Almanac by Aldo Leopold has been called "the most vital statement to date on conservation in America." The enlarged 1966 edition contains all of Leopold's best essays on nature, together with his philosophy of conservation based on love of the land. Cloth; $6.65 from Oxford University Press, 16-00 Pollitt Drive, Fair Lawn, N. J. 07410.

The Quiet Crisis by Stewart Udall is a readable history of the relationship between Americans and their land since Indian times. And in discussing conservation needs for the future, Udall recommends that "the Buffalo of Arkansas . . . should be kept as a clean, wild river—a part of a rich outdoor heritage." Holt, Rinehart & Winston, N. Y., 1963. Now in paperback; $1.05 from Avon Books, 959 8th Ave., New York, N. Y. 10019.

Stars Upstream by Leonard Hall is the story of another Ozark river, the Current in Missouri. Its natural setting, history and conservation problems much resemble the Buffalo's. 1958. Cloth; $4.65 from the University of Chicago Press, 5750 Ellis Ave., Chicago, Ill. 60637.

Conservation of Water and Related Land Resources, Buffalo River Basin, Arkansas, in three volumes, contains data and justification for building the Gilbert Dam. U. S. Army, Corps of Engineers, Little Rock, December 1964. May be found in the larger libraries of Arkansas.

Field Investigation Report, Suggested Buffalo National River, Arkansas. U. S. Dept. of the Interior, National Park Service, Southeast Region, Richmond, Va., April 1963.

Economic Study of the Proposed Buffalo National River. Bureau of Business and Economic Research, and Industrial Research and Extension Center, University of Arkansas, May 1963. The National River report and economic study may both be found in Arkansas libraries.

Floaters' Check List

For canoeists and other floaters too, comfort and safety equals common sense. But reminders do help—

GETTING READY

1 Each canoe should have an extra paddle; bow and stern lines 10 to 15 feet long for walking the canoe down rapids; a repair kit; a bailing sponge; a first aid kit (and snakebite kit); a 50-foot rope for helping someone in trouble; matches and fire starter in waterproof case; an Army surplus folding shovel.

2 Have waterproof containers (Army surplus black rubber packs, heavy plastic or coated cloth bags, or gasketed metal boxes) for clothing, food and bedding. Use an Army ammo box for camera, billfold and watch.

3 Have life jackets (not life belts) for everyone. Jackets which protect the back of the head are best. Jackets are essential for non-swimmers and children, and for everybody in rough or extremely cold weather. A dunking in cold water can reduce a good swimmer to helpless numbness in minutes.

4 Have adequate clothing: A complete extra set in a waterproof bag (absolutely essential in cold weather). A hooded rain parka or poncho. A long sleeve shirt, hat with brim, and sun lotion to avoid sunburn. Warm clothes for cool evenings on the river. Canvas shoes for wading in warm weather, knee boots for spring and fall, or insulated hip boots for winter.

ON THE HIGHWAY

1 Be sure your top rack is secure to your car, *after* the canoe is on top. Tie the canoe to both the rack and the car's front and rear bumpers, to prevent it from sliding forward during a fast stop. Tie ropes seem to slip less than belts with buckles. Watch sharp bumper edges—they can cut rope. C-clamps can be used for clamping canoe gunwales to a top rack.

2 Stay within the speed limit. Don't drive if you are sleepy. Give yourself plenty of time. Don't follow too close behind the car ahead.

ON THE RIVER

1 Stow baggage low—not over a few inches above the gunwales. Balance the load from side to side, and so that the center of gravity is at the center of the canoe or just behind it. A bow-heavy canoe is very hard to manage. Have duffel units in waterproof bags, but not tied into the canoe, so that they can float free and not hinder recovery of a swamped canoe. Floating duffel can be grabbed as it goes by, or picked up downstream. *Put the extra paddle where you can reach it easily* (paddles break in rapids). Leave room in the canoe so you can duck when being carried into an overhanging hazard.

2 Practice in calm water with your paddling partner before heading downstream. Get signals straight.

3 Moving downstream, keep the canoe parallel to the current in swift water. Keep to the inside of blind bends to avoid being swept against hazards along the outside bank. Duck straight forward, not sidewise, when being carried into an overhanging hazard. Don't grab overhead limbs as you pass under.

4 When approaching major hazards—rapids, fallen trees, log jams, paved fords and low-water bridges—pull over, get out, and take a look. Know your limitations. There's nothing wrong with walking a rapids.

5 Pass through hazards one canoe at a time, to avoid pile-ups. Don't crowd the canoe ahead down a rapids. Don't try to float through fallen trees or log jams in deep water. Usually there is shallow water to one side where the canoe can be pulled past.

6 If swept broadside into an obstacle in the current, *lean downstream,* to prevent the upstream side from tipping down, catching water, and capsizing the canoe. Then work loose of the obstacle. If you do capsize, hang onto the boat and get to the upstream side to avoid being crushed against underwater rocks or snags . . . . People are more important than boats or duffel. Make sure that the upset paddlers are safe before you go after their equipment.

7 In large parties, designate one canoe with experienced paddlers to lead; another to come last. Nobody should pass the lead boat nor drop behind the last boat . . . . In rough water, stay with another canoe. You may need help . . . . On any trip, you're taking a risk going by yourself. Two canoes are safety twice.

8 Don't float when the river is in flood. Tricky currents and submerged hazards can be very dangerous.

IN CAMP

1 Take ample water for drinking. Spring water is usually (but not always) safe if picked up where not accessible to livestock. River water should be boiled. Do not use glass containers for water or gasoline. Paint gasoline cans red to better identify them.

2 Put your tent as high above river level as circumstances dictate. Check for an escape route in case the river rises unexpectedly during the night. Put in a stake at river level to check for rising water.

3 Don't mar the campsite and antagonize landowners by cutting or injuring trees. There is plenty of dead, downed firewood in drift piles. And when leaving, always douse campfires with water—put them dead out.

4 About the 'call of nature': Girls upstream, boys downstream. Take the shovel along, dig a hole, and cover it up.

5 Don't carry firearms. They aren't safe over water. The noise of guns ruins the peace of the river for many people. Most of the wildlife is protected or harmless. Most of the snakes you'll see are harmless water snakes. Don't kill them. If you do take firearms

for hunting, be sure you have the proper permit . . . .
And liquor: It just doesn't go with swift-water canoeing. Nor is it appropriate or permitted on the family-
type outings of canoe clubs.

6 *And don't litter the river and gravel bars!* We don't
scatter trash around our front yards at home—why do
it here in God's own front yard? It's just as easy to
carry out trash as it is to bring it in. Here's how—

Burnable trash can go into the campfire. Paper can
be saved for starting a fire at the next stop. Garbage
can be burned or buried. That leaves only metal and
glass; it can be put in a burlap sack carried in the
bottom of the boat. Have a piece of wire to tie the
neck of the sack.

Burlap sacks are durable and cheap (feed stores have
them for as little as 10¢ each). One alone is big enough
for refuse from several campsites on your trip—maybe
including those of some nitwits who littered before
you arrived. Take a few minutes and pick up their
junk. Then you'll be expressing real reverence and
tangible thanks for the beauty you have enjoyed.

7 Just before you leave, walk around your campsite.
You may have forgotten something of value. Is the
place tidy, even a little nicer than when you found
it? The next camper should appreciate it, and it may
inspire *him* to leave a clean camp, too.

Put-in and Take-out Points

Access points given are the principal ones that can be
reached by automobile. 'Private access road' means that
the road to the river bank is privately owned and maintained. The owner may charge a modest fee for access
across his land; also, he has the right to prohibit trespass
at any time.

The left-hand column shows river miles downstream
from the State Highway 74 bridge near Ponca, Newton
County. To find the length of your float, subtract the
mileage at the put-in point from that at the take-out.

MILES	POINTS OF ACCESS TO RIVER
0.0	Low-water bridge, Highway 74, the normal 'head of navigation' for floating. In high water, a few floaters have come from Boxley, 5 miles upstream. The 74 bridge is 25 miles downstream from the Buffalo's highest source.
6.3	Sneed Creek on left. Best access is where farm road crosses river about 250 yards above mouth of creek. Sneed Creek Road up long hill to State 43 is steep, rough; make local inquiry.
10.6	Camp Orr (Boy Scouts) on right. Take right-hand channel to concrete ramp installed by Arkansas Game & Fish Commission at lower end

MILES	POINTS OF ACCESS TO RIVER
	of camp property. Road up long hill to State 74 is steep; also slick in wet weather.
12.7	Erbie Ford. Paved low-water ford across river. County roads to Marble Falls and Pruitt.
20.8	Pruitt and State Highway 7 bridge. Private access roads to south bank.
27.8	Low-water bridge, road at Stillhouse Hollow.
31.7	State Highway 123 bridge. Access down high, steep bank at north end of bridge. Better access 0.1 mile up Big Creek, flowing in from right 0.3 mile below bridge.
39.0	Mount Hersey and Davis Creek on left. Last eighth mile of access road is muddy in wet weather.
43.0	Cane Branch on left. Steep, rough roads up hills, both sides of creek, and out to U. S. 65.
47.6	Woolum Ford. Wide gravel bar on left. Good county roads to St. Joe.
64.6	U. S. Highway 65 bridge. Private access road to right bank 200 yards downstream from bridge.
68.8	Gilbert on left. Village begins 200 yards up hill from long, wide gravel bar.
81.0	Maumee landing. Private access roads to both sides of river. North bank has a steep slick 30-foot 'boat slide' and a rough, narrow approach road. Gravel bar access area on south bank was posted against trespass in 1965.
90.4	State Highway 14 bridge. Roads to both banks at bridge. Road on north side is steep and narrow, but generally preferred. Road on south side may have deep ruts and chuck-holes.
91.8	Buffalo River State Park on left. Good public boat landing at upstream end of gravel bar.
99.2	Rush Creek on left. Private access road.
99.5	Clabber Creek on left. County road access to creek about 200 feet above mouth.
102.1	Cedar Creek on left. County-built road to river is rough and narrow, with some deep mudholes and steep grades. Make local inquiry.
109.6	Big Creek on right. Private access road is rough and steep, with creek ford and mud near the river. Make local inquiry.
122.8	Mouth of Buffalo River. Here there are three choices for taking out, as follows:

Buffalo City. Go up White River ½ mile,
keeping to left bank to avoid main current, then
cross to landing. Fortunately this upstream pull
isn't hard, and the landing has a paved ramp,
ample parking, and good roads out.

Shipps Ferry. This first landing down the
White is 5½ miles (about 2 hours' paddling)
from the mouth of the Buffalo. From the left
bank, the road leads out to Mountain Home.

Norfork. On the left about 11½ miles (or
half a day's float) below the Buffalo. You might
want to try the White River trout-fishing.

Organizations

Six young and growing conservation groups are described here because of their field programs, the opportunities they offer for all to enjoy and learn about the outdoors.

The ARKANSAS ARCHEOLOGICAL SOCIETY
was organized in 1960 "to study and preserve Indian prehistory and to foster and encourage a constructive public attitude toward the archeology of the state."

Each summer somewhere in Arkansas, the Society conducts a 9-day 'dig' where professional archeologists teach sound procedures to all comers. In the evenings, experts give lectures, adding to the knowledge participants gain during excavation. And in September the AAS holds its annual meeting, a weekend of exhibits and programs. The Society has several local chapters over the state, and members receive a quarterly bulletin, *The Arkansas Archeologist,* plus a monthly newsletter.

Inquiries: AAS Central Office, University of Arkansas Museum, Fayetteville, Arkansas 72701

The ARKANSAS AUDUBON SOCIETY
was founded in 1955 to foster a greater knowledge of the natural history and to be a force in conservation of the natural resources of Arkansas.

On two weekends a year, at the height of the spring and fall bird migrations, the Society meets for a series of outings, talks, films and discussions. In the field, members see and identify a great many species of migrating and resident birds, more than would be present at any other time of year. Under experts' guidance, newcomers learn much in a few short hours.

The Society also keeps state-wide records of bird sightings; annually awards a scholarship to an outstanding Arkansas teacher of natural science; and publishes a quarterly bulletin, *Arkansas Birds,* for members.

Inquiries: Dr. Douglas James, A.A.S. Curator, Dept. of Zoology, U. of Arkansas, Fayetteville

The ARKANSAS SPELEOLOGICAL SURVEY
was begun in 1963 to locate and classify all caves in the state, and to promote cave conservation and safety.

Survey members have set up a central file of cave information covering the entire state, and they are at work adding to it, surveying and mapping and reporting new caves. Some of them have also organized a cave rescue squad, available to help persons lost or trapped in caves, mines or wells, or on cliffs. Through the Survey, members can buy certain items of caving equipment at a discount. The Survey conducts an annual meeting with field trips, programs and discussion, and for members publishes the quarterly *Arkansas Caver.*

Inquiries: J. H. Schermerhorn, Director, Box 62, Harrison, Ark. 72601 (Phone 501-365-5925)

The NORTHWEST ARKANSAS ARCHAEOLOGICAL SOCIETY, organized in 1958, brings together people interested in the Indian archeology of northwest Arkansas and adjoining areas. The Society assists members and the public in understanding Indian culture and conserving its remains.

The NWAAS holds monthly program meetings in towns over northwest Arkansas; conducts field trips to archeological sites and museums; and enables its members to take part in surveys and excavations under the guidance of experienced amateurs or the staff of the University of Arkansas Museum. The Society has a loan library of books and periodicals on archeology for members' use. Members receive the monthly *Arkansas Amateur;* also the quarterly *Central States Archaeological Journal.*

Inquiries: Secretary, NWAAS, Box 1154, Fayetteville, Arkansas 72701

The OZARK SOCIETY
was incorporated in 1962 as a nonprofit organization under the laws of Arkansas, to promote the knowledge and enjoyment of the scenic and scientific resources of the Ozark-Ouachita mountain region, and to help protect those resources for our generation and those to come.

In addition to taking a well-known part in the battle to preserve the Buffalo River, the Ozark Society is engaged in a broad effort to let people see some of nature's beauty that they need to save. The Society sponsors hikes and float trips on the Buffalo and in other outstanding natural areas; and bus tours to spring's best displays of dogwood and azaleas, and through woodlands aglow with fall color. The Society cooperates with other organizations having similar objectives; provides scenic movies and slide programs for use by members and civic groups; and conducts an annual meeting having a timely selection of conservation talks and films. Members receive outing schedules and periodic reports on current conservation issues.

Inquiries: The Ozark Society, Box 38, Fayetteville, Arkansas 72701

The OZARK WILDERNESS WATERWAYS CLUB
was founded in 1956 for the enjoyment and preservation of Ozark streams in their natural, free-flowing state.

Centered in Kansas City but having members in several states, the OWWC is probably the largest family canoe club in America. Each month, members have a program meeting in Kansas City, and all year they float the streams of the Arkansas-Missouri Ozarks. Trips on Missouri streams are run on July Fourth and New Years, while Memorial Day and Thanksgiving weekends are reserved for the Buffalo. On Labor Day the OWWC runs a 'can clean up' on Missouri's Current River; in 1966 they gathered more than 4 tons of trash from 26 miles of that stream. The OWWC has of course taken a leading role in the effort to preserve the Buffalo.

Members receive trip schedules and a newsletter.

Inquiries: Carol Walters, Treasurer, 604 East 4th Terrace, Lee's Summit, Missouri 64129